Portland Cooks for the Performing Arts

A Collection of Favorite Recipes

From the Volunteers and Staff of the

Portland Center for the Performing Arts
and
Some of the City's Finest Restaurants

Portland, Oregon, USA

Portland Center for the Performing Arts (PCPA)
Attention Ms. Margie Humphreys
1111 SW Broadway, Portland, OR 97205-2999, USA

The Cookbook Committee

Rachel Baus	Susan Robblee
Roz Collins	Carl Selin
Jane Henderson	Camille Stark
Margie Humphreys	Barbara Utz
Jan Loewen	Sue Vonderheit

Photography by Carl Selin and PCPA

Index created by Indexplorations, Portland, OR

Printed by The Irwin-Hodson Company, Portland, OR

ISBN 0-9762455-0-7

The net proceeds from the sale of this book will be used to fund restoration and/or capital improvements to the PCPA facilities.

Cover photo by Carl Selin

Foreword

You have in your hands the first ever cookbook for the Portland Center for the Performing Arts - produced by our own fabulous volunteer corps. Like the wonderful art that takes place on our stages at Keller Auditorium, Arlene Schnitzer Concert Hall, the Newmark and Winningstad Theatres, this too is a work of art.

Through use of this cookbook you will not only experience the "art of cooking", the "art of good food" and - my personal favorite - "the art of eating", but the added bonus of seeing photographs of some of the spectacular art that abounds in the PCPA facilities - photographed by, who else? - a PCPA volunteer!

Thanks to the hundreds of volunteers who made this possible. You are the artists who continually add color to the canvas that is PCPA.

Thanks to the Portland chefs and restaurants who contributed recipes and continually give and give to support the arts in Portland.

Most importantly, thanks to you for purchasing this cookbook. Whether you are a visitor to our wonderful city or regular theater goer, may this long serve as a "tasteful treat" of your visit to our facilities.

Bon appétit!

Robyn Williams
Executive Director, PCPA

The Arlene Schnitzer Concert Hall reflects on the glass wall of the New Theatre Building on the corner of Broadway and Main Streets.

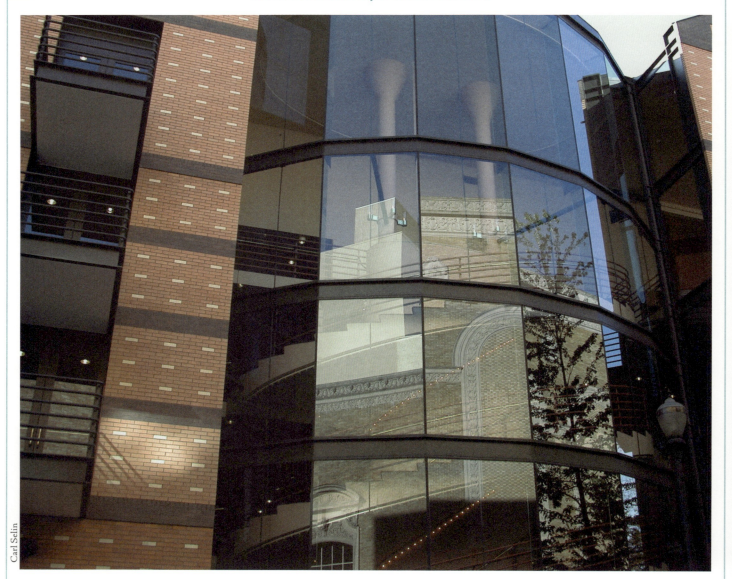

Carl Selin

Welcome to the Portland Center for the Performing Arts. (PCPA)

Table of Contents

A Brief History of the Portland Center for the Performing Arts

The history of what we now recognize as the Portland Center for the Performing Arts (PCPA) began back in 1917 when the citizens of Portland opened their first public assembly building. This municipal facility, later named the Portland Civic Auditorium, went through reconstruction in 1967 and acquired an international modernist design. Devotees flocked to the hall to be treated to ballet, opera, the symphony and many other cultural events. So successful was the facility in attracting tenants and patrons that many had to be turned away. Something had to be done.

In 1976, the Portland City Council appointed a citizen task force to study the need, use, location, and financing for additional performing arts space. Local theater, dance, and music groups pressed for an additional large hall to alleviate congestion at Civic Auditorium, plus a medium size, advanced staging theater, and a small, flexible performance space. In March 1977, the Council launched a massive project involving millions of dollars and thousands of people. Within a decade, this project went from dream to reality.

The Council reorganized the Performing Arts Center Committee in April 1980, and charged it not to study, but to build. In April 1981, voters supported a $19 million bond measure, stipulating that these bonds could not be issued until the Committee had raised $6 million in private seed money. It was difficult, but the private money was raised just in time, thanks in part to Arlene and Harold Schnitzer, who saved the day by funding the final $1 million needed from private means.

Next came the architects. After an international competition, the team of BOOR/A, Barton Myers & Associates, and ELS Design Group was selected. Together, these three firms possessed the needed ability to work with historic buildings, small spaces, and theatrical designs.

The search for a site led to the old Portland Publix Theatre, originally opened in March 1928 at Broadway and Main and renamed the Paramount Theatre in 1930. It served as a movie and vaudeville house until 1971, was placed on the National Historic Register in 1974, and housed rock concerts and closed circuit TV broadcasts from 1975 until the City brought condemnation proceedings in 1983. As acousticians, contractors, and builders restored the building, fund raising efforts continued. In September 1984, the elegant old theater reopened as the Arlene Schnitzer Concert Hall and the home for the Oregon Symphony Orchestra.

Meanwhile, the First Congregational Church, owner of three-quarters of the adjacent property across Main Street, agreed to lease half of their block to the City, who then purchased the other quarter block from PacWest Bancorp. The community broke ground for the New Theatre Building in April 1985, and in August 1987, opened its doors to a soaring, glass-domed rotunda and two new theaters - the intimate Dolores Winningstad Theatre, which is patterned after London's Globe Theatre and the Intermediate Theatre, now called the Newmark Theatre.

Two milestones were reached in 2000. Brunish Hall was completed in the New Theatre Building, and the Civic Auditorium, still the largest of the three PCPA facilities, was renamed the Keller Auditorium.

The citizens of Portland continue to support their public venues. Each year, approximately 1 million visitors pass through our doors. The City continues to own the PCPA facilities and the Metropolitan Exposition and Recreation Commission (MERC) manages the day to day operation of the halls.

Today, more than seven hundred PCPA volunteers serve the local arts community as ushers, greeters, tour guides, working in the gift shop and in the office. Their recipes intermingle in these pages with those of popular Portland chefs. We hope these dishes delight your family and guests.

Betty Burke, PCPA Tour Guide Volunteer

Twenty-one resident companies call the Portland Center for the Performing Arts (PCPA) home. Currently, the main tenants are The Portland Opera, Oregon Ballet Theatre, Portland Center Stage, The Portland Youth Philharmonic, Tears of Joy Theatre, Oregon's Children's Theatre, The Oregon Symphony Orchestra and the "Broadway in Portland" Series. These performance companies along with outside promoters help to bring over 900 shows into our four theaters each year, drawing over 1 million patrons.

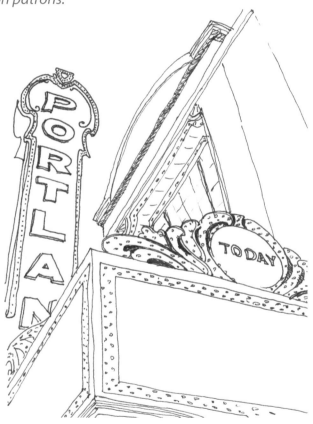

An artist's rendering of the famous **Portland** Sign
The sign lights the way to the
Portland Center for the Performing Arts (PCPA)

Appetizers

Carl Selin

Harmony in the Park Blocks
The design of the New Theatre Building blends with the architecture of the First Congregational
Church, our next-door neighbor.

Cervelle de Canuts

Pascal Sauton - CARAFE RESTAURANT - Portland, OR

1 cup fromage blanc
    white goat cheese is ideal
½ cup crème fraîche
1 medium lemon, both juice and
    grated zest
2 tablespoons extra virgin olive oil
1 tablespoon chopped parsley
1 tablespoon minced chives
1 shallot, finely minced
fine sea salt, to taste
fresh ground black pepper
4 slices toasted walnut levain bread

Whip fromage blanc and crème fraîche with juice and the grated zest of the lemon. Add olive oil, herbs and salt and pepper to taste.

Spread on toasted walnut bread.

See page 197 for crème fraîche recipe

Makes 4 servings

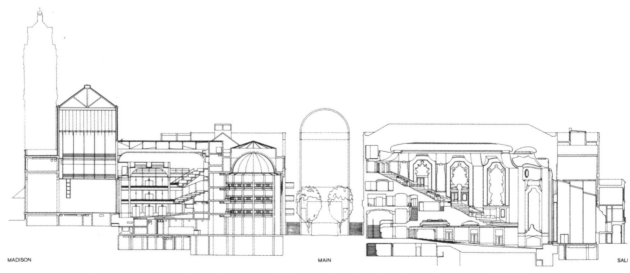

Cross section of the Portland Center for the Performing Arts (PCPA)

Artichoke Pesto Spread

1 (15-ounce) can artichoke hearts
    packed in water, rinsed and
    drained
1 cup basil pesto
Parmesan cheese, grated (to taste)
pepper (optional)

Place artichoke hearts in a food processor and chop coarsley.

Add pesto to artichoke hearts and combine. Add Parmesan cheese and pepper, and combine.

Serve with crackers.

Makes 1½ cups

Brandied Cheddar Cheese Ball

½ pound mild Cheddar cheese,
    grated
1 (8-ounce) package cream cheese,
    softened
¼ cup brandy
¼ cup parsley, minced
¾ cup roasted almonds, chopped

In a mixing bowl, combine Cheddar cheese, cream cheese, brandy, parsley and about half of the almonds until well blended. Chill mixture in the refrigerator until it is firm enough to form into a ball.

Form the cheese ball and coat it with the remaining almonds by either rolling the ball in the nuts or placing the almonds by hand. Wrap completed ball in plastic wrap and chill until ready to serve.

This cheese ball goes well with both raw vegetables and crackers.

Makes 1 ball

Brie Torte

1 (8-ounce) wedge Brie cheese
¼ cup butter, softened
¼ cup dried tart cherries, chopped
3 tablespoons pecans, finely
    chopped
½ teaspoon dried thyme

Makes 1 torte

Refrigerate Brie until chilled and firm. Cut wedge in half horizontally.

In a small bowl, combine butter, cherries, pecans and thyme; mix well. Evenly spread mixture on cut-side of one of the Brie wedges. Top with other half, cut-side down. Lightly press together. Wrap in plastic wrap; refrigerate 1 to 2 hours. Bring cheese to room temperature before serving.

Well wrapped, this appetizer will keep in the refrigerator for at least two weeks.

Cheese Torte

2 (8-ounce) packages cream cheese
1 ½ cups Feta cheese
4 bulbs roasted garlic
fresh basil, to taste
fresh parsley, to taste
¼ cup extra virgin olive oil
salt
pesto, to be used as a filling
1 package sun-dried tomatoes
¼ cup pine nuts, toasted
¼ cup shelled pistachios, toasted
1 small (8 ounce) jar Kalamata
    Olive Spread

Makes 1 torte

In a food processor, blend cream cheese, Feta, garlic, olive oil, and basil, parsley, and salt (to taste).

Line bottom of an 8 or 9-inch spring form pan with wax paper.

Spread half of cheese mixture in pan. Follow with a layer of pesto and a layer of sundried tomatoes. Finish with second half of cheese mixture. Put into refrigerator to cool overnight.

Before serving, toast pine nuts and pistachios. Take torte out of refrigerator and remove from pan. Place plate on top of torte and flip it so that bottom has now become top. Remove wax paper. Spread Kalamata Olive Spread on top and sprinkle with toasted nuts.

Cherry Crab Spread

1 (8-ounce) package cream cheese,
 softened
2 tablespoons milk
1 (7-ounce) can crabmeat, drained
 and flaked
1 tablespoon green onion, chopped
¼ teaspoon seasoned salt
⅛ teaspoon garlic powder
½ cup dried tart cherries, chopped
fresh parsley, chopped, as garnish
green onions, sliced, as garnish

In small bowl, beat cream cheese and milk until fluffy. Add crabmeat, green onions, seasoned salt and garlic powder; mix well. Stir in cherries.

Place mixture in a serving dish and chill for 20 minutes, or until the cheese begins to firm.

Garnish and serve with crackers.

Crabmeat impresses guests and cherries provide pizzazz.

Makes 2 cups

Chutney Cheese Ball

1 (8-ounce) package cream cheese,
 softened
¼ cup chutney
⅛ cup onions, diced
1 clove garlic, minced
½ cup Colby cheese, shredded
½ cup Monterey Jack cheese,
 shredded
½ cup pecans, chopped

In medium mixing bowl, combine cream cheese, chutney and onions together.

Fold in garlic, Colby and Monterey Jack cheeses. Form into a ball.

Roll cheese ball in pecans until coated. Refrigerate until cheese ball is firm enough to serve.

May substitute onions with scallions, or Colby cheese with sharp Cheddar cheese, if desired.

Yield: 1 ball

Cowboy Caviar

1 (15-ounce) can black eyed peas, drained
1 (11-ounce) can shoepeg corn, drained
2 medium avocados, peeled and diced
⅔ cup fresh tomatoes, chopped
½ cup onion, chopped
⅔ cup fresh cilantro, chopped
¼ cup olive oil
½ cup red wine vinegar
2 cloves garlic, minced
1 teaspoon ground cumin
salt
pepper

In large bowl, combine black eyed peas, corn, avocado, tomatoes, onion, cilantro, olive oil, red wine vinegar, garlic and cumin.

Add salt and pepper, to taste, and mix well. Can be chilled until serving time.

Serve with "scooper-style" chips.

If you want this to be "spicy", as a variation add 1 (4-ounce) can jalapenos and and some pimientos.

Makes 3 cups

Crabmeat Mold

1 (10¾-ounce) can cream of shrimp condensed soup
2 (3-ounce) packages cream cheese
¼ cup onions, finely chopped
1 cup mayonnaise
2 envelopes unflavored gelatin
1 cup cold water
2 (7½-ounce) cans crabmeat, drained and flaked
1 cup celery, finely chopped
salad greens
lemon wedges

Makes 15-20 servings

In saucepan, combine soup, cream cheese and onion. Heat until cream cheese is melted, stirring as needed. Blend in mayonnaise and remove from heat.

In another saucepan, sprinkle gelatin into water over a low heat. Stir until all gelatin is dissolved. Stir gelatin mixture into soup mixture. Add crabmeat and celery.

Pour mixture into a 6-cup mold. Refrigerate until serving. Remove from mold and garnish with greens and lemons.

Serve on rye or pumpernickel bread, toasted bread or crackers.

Easy Roll Ups

1 (8-ounce) package cream cheese
¼ cup dill pickle, chopped
¼ cup green onion, chopped
⅛ cup red pepper, chopped
3 tablespoons mayonnaise
6 large flour tortillas
2 packages ham luncheon meat,
　　thinly sliced

In a mixing bowl, combine cream cheese, dill pickle, green onions, red pepper and mayonnaise, and mix well.

Spread mixture over each tortilla. Top with a layer of meat. Roll and refrigerate overnight.

To serve, slice into 1-inch pieces.

May substitute ham with any preferred meat, as desired.

Makes 48 appetizers

Easy Tomato Aspic

1 (3.4-ounce) package lemon Jello
¾ cup boiling water
1 cup tomato juice
dash Worcestershire sauce
2 teaspoons wine vinegar

Makes 6-8 servings

In a small saucepan, bring water to boil. Dissolve gelatin until completely smooth.

Add tomato juice, Worcestershire and vinegar to the Jello mixture and blend well.

Pour into flat baking dish or mold. Chill until set.

Cut into squares to serve.

Serve on a lettuce leaf and add a dollop of mayonnaise for added interest.

You can substitute 1 cup of canned tomato sauce, spaghetti sauce, V-8 juice or Bloody Mary mix for the tomato juice. As gelatin sets, consider adding any of the following: cooked shrimp, diced celery, sliced ripe olives or sliced water chestnuts.

Eggplant Caviar

1 small eggplant, unpeeled and
    finely chopped
1 medium onion, coarsely chopped
⅓ cup green pepper, chopped
1 (4-ounce) can mushrooms,
    drained and chopped
2 cloves garlic, crushed
⅓ cup salad oil
1 teaspoon salt
½ teaspoon pepper
½ teaspoon oregano
1½ teaspoons sugar
1 (6-ounce) can tomato paste
¼ cup water
2 tablespoons wine vinegar
½ cup stuffed olives, chopped
3 tablespoons pine nuts
¼ cup capers

In a large skillet, combine eggplant, onion, green pepper, mushrooms, garlic and oil.

Cover skillet and simmer for 10 minutes.

Add salt, pepper, oregano, sugar, tomato paste, water, vinegar, olives, pine nuts and capers. Mix and simmer, covered, for 25 minutes or until eggplant is cooked but not mushy.

Chill overnight. Prior to serving, bring caviar to room temperature. Serve with corn chips.

Makes approximately 4 cups

Guacamole for the Whole Gang

12 avocados, peeled, pitted and
    diced
½ cup lime juice, freshly squeezed
1 cup plain yogurt
1 teaspoon ground cumin
1 teaspoon hot pepper sauce
½ teaspoon salt
½ teaspoon ground black pepper
2 pounds plum tomatoes, seeded
    and diced to ¼-inch
6 ounces red onion, diced
1 ounce fresh cilantro, chopped

Place avocados in a large bowl. Sprinkle with lime juice and stir lightly to mix.

Mix yogurt, cumin, hot pepper sauce, salt and pepper into avocado until well mixed.

Stir tomatoes, onion, and cilantro into avocado mixture.

Serve with tortilla chips or as a condiment.

This recipe is perfect for a large gathering.

Hoisin Chicken Canapés

⅔ cup cooked chicken, finely chopped
⅔ cup packaged cole slaw mix (shredded cabbage)
1 tablespoon chopped peanuts
2 tablespoons bottled Hoisin sauce
hot pepper sauce, to taste
12 leaves Belgian endive

In a bowl, combine chicken, cole slaw, peanuts, Hoisin sauce and pepper sauce. Mix well.

Spoon a generous portion onto individual endive leaves.

Serve immediately.

You can use two red or yellow sweet peppers or two cucumbers for serving. Cut each pepper into 6 wedge-shaped pieces. Cut the cucumbers lengthwise, remove seeds and cut into thirds. This recipe can be doubled.

Makes 12 canapes

Northwest Salmon Dip

1 pound smoked salmon
1 (8-ounce) package cream cheese, softened
2 tablespoons sour cream
2 tablespoons mayonnaise
2 teaspoons horseradish
3 green onions, chopped
½ teaspoon soy sauce
½ teaspoon lemon juice

In a medium bowl, combine softened cream cheese, sour cream, mayonnaise, horseradish, green onions, soy sauce and lemon juice. Gently flake the salmon and fold into the cheese mixture. Be certain to mix well.

Chill in the refrigerator until ready to serve.

Always serve well chilled. Serve with crackers or raw vegetables.

Makes about 2 cups

Party Cheese Ball

1 (8-ounce) package cream cheese,
    softened
1 jar Old English sharp Cheddar
    cheese, softened
2 ounces Bleu cheese, softened
½ clove garlic, minced
¼ medium onion, minced
½ cup walnuts or pecans, chopped

Combine cream cheese, Cheddar cheese and Bleu cheese. Add minced garlic and minced onion. Mix well. Form mixture into a ball and roll in the chopped nuts until the cheese ball is well covered.

Wrap in plastic wrap. Refrigerate until ready to serve. (Allow at least 60 minutes for best results.)

Makes 1 ball

Pineapple Cheese Ball

2 (8-ounce) packages cream cheese,
    softened to room temperature
1 (8½-ounce) can crushed
    pineapple, drained
¼ cup green pepper, finely chopped
2 tablespoons onion, finely chopped
seasoned salt
2 cups pecans, finely chopped

Mix cream cheese, pineapple, green pepper, onion and seasoned salt. Shape into a ball and refrigerate.

When ball is firm (but not hard), roll in pecans to cover. Store in the refrigerator but let it warm to room temperature before serving.

Serve with crackers.

Makes 1 ball

Salmon Paté

1 (6-ounce) can salmon
1 envelope Good Seasons Italian
   salad dressing
1 (8-ounce) package cream cheese
⅓ of a cucumber, peeled and
   chopped
2 drops liquid smoke flavoring
   (optional)

Combine all ingredients in a bowl and mix well.

Line a 2 cup bowl (or other mold) with plastic kitchen wrap. Pour salmon mixture into lined bowl and refrigerate for at least an hour.

Invert chilled pate onto serving platter and remove wrap very carefully. Serve with crackers.

Makes 8 servings

Secret Triscuit Spread

1 (8-ounce) package cream cheese,
   softened
½ cup butter (1 cube), softened
1½ teaspoons anchovy paste
1 small onion, grated
1 teaspoon salad mustard
½ cup stuffed green olives, chopped

In a medium bowl, combine cream cheese, butter, anchovy paste, onion, mustard and olives. Mix by hand, making sure the olive bits are evenly distributed. Cover and refrigerate for at least 24 hours before serving.

Serve with Triscuits. Caution! Once served, this one disappears before your eyes!

Works best if all ingredients are at room temperature when you begin.

Sandwich Loaf

1 whole loaf sandwich bread, crusts
  removed
3 favorite sandwich spreads/fillings
butter (as needed), softened
1 (8-ounce) package cream cheese,
  softened
mayonnaise or sour cream
fresh parsley leaves, minced

Prepare 3 favorite sandwich spreads ahead of time.

Slice loaf horizontally, making four uniform slices (layers).

Butter 3 layers of bread. Spread each layer with a separate filling. Restack the loaf, one layer at a time, finishing with the top slice.

Soften the cream cheese. Add small amounts of mayonnaise or sour cream to form a "frosting-like" texture. Frost the entire loaf with the cream cheese.

Sprinkle the frosted loaf with fresh parsley. Chill at least an hour before serving. Slice and serve.

This was always a Sunday Night Supper favorite, served with assorted fruit.

Suggested fillings: Chicken salad, tuna salad, egg salad, pimiento cheese spread, thinly sliced cucumbers and sour cream, thinly sliced Roma tomatoes and sour cream, grated carrots with pickle juice.

Makes 12 servings

*The New Theatre Building opened on August 29, 1987. **Sunday in the Park with George** was the opening show in the Intermediate Theatre (now named the Newmark Theatre). The Dolores Winningstad Theatre hosted **14 Karat Soul** that same week.*

Smoked Salmon Bean Dip

1 (15-ounce) can white beans,
    rinsed and drained
½ medium sweet onion, coarsely
    chopped
¼ cup olive oil
salt and pepper
hot sauce, to taste
6-8 ounces smoked salmon, broken
    up
parsley or chives for garnish

In blender or food processor, puree white beans, onion, smoked salmon and olive oil. (If desired, saute onions first to tame the onion flavor.) Add salt and pepper to taste. Add hot sauce to taste. Chill several hours or overnight.

Garnish with parsley or chives prior to serving.

Serve with sliced raw vegetables (carrots, cucumbers, bell peppers, etc.)

Makes enough for 6-8

Walla Walla - Green Pea Guacamole

2 (10-ounce)packages frozen peas,
    thawed
1 cup chopped Walla Walla onion
    (approximately 4 ½ ounces)
2 cloves garlic, minced (2
    teaspoons)
2 teaspoons lemon juice
¼ cup fresh cilantro leaves
½ teaspoon salt
¼ teaspoon freshly ground pepper
a dash of hot pepper sauce

Place peas, onion, garlic, salt, pepper, lemon juice and dash of hot pepper sauce in the bowl of a food processor fitted with a steel chopping blade. Process until smooth. Stir in the cilantro, pulse gently and season to taste with additional salt and pepper and hot pepper sauce. Scrape into a bowl and chill until needed.

Serve with baked tortilla chips, bread sticks or pita chips.

Makes 8 servings

Oregon Hazelnut Crunch

6 cups Kix cereal
1½ cups coarsely chopped or whole,
　　roasted Oregon hazelnuts
1 cup golden raisins
1 cup banana chips
1 small package non-instant vanilla
　　pudding
½ cup honey
½ cup peanut butter

Mix cereal, nuts, raisins and banana chips together.

In saucepan, combine vanilla pudding and honey; bring to a boil and boil 30 seconds. Remove from heat. Stir in peanut butter; mix well. Pour over cereal mix and toss until coated. Put on cookie sheet to cool.

Watch this one disappear! Kids love it.

Makes 12 servings

Olive-Nut Spread

2 (3-ounce) packages cream cheese,
　　softened
½ cup mayonnaise
1 cup chopped olives
2 tablespoons juice from olive jar
½ cup pecans, chopped
black pepper

Mix cream cheese, mayonnaise, chopped olives, olive juice, pecans, and pepper. Store in sealed container in the refrigerator until ready to serve.

Serve with assorted crackers.

Makes 8-10 servings

Roquefort Cheese Puffs

¼ cup butter
¾ cup water
¾ cup flour
3 large eggs
⅔ cup Roquefort cheese, crumbled

Preheat oven to 400 degrees. In a 2 to 3-quart saucepan over high heat, bring water and butter to a full boil. Remove from heat. Add flour all at once, and stir until mixture is a smooth, thick paste with no lumps.

Add eggs one at a time to the mixture, stirring vigorously after each addition until the dough is no longer slippery. Stir in the cheese and let the mixture stand for 15 minutes. Evenly space 24 rounded tablespoons of dough on a buttered 12 x 15-inch baking sheet.

Bake at 400 degrees for 25 to 30 minutes, or until puffs are dry and golden brown. If making ahead of time, let puffs cool on a rack. Wrap airtight and keep up to 1 day, or freeze up to 2 weeks. Reheat thawed puffs on a baking sheet at 350 degrees until warm (about 3 minutes).

May substitute Roquefort cheese with Stilton or Maytag Blue, if desired. Serve warm.

Makes 24 pieces

An international competition was held to choose the architects for the restoration of what is now the Arlene Schnitzer Concert Hall and the construction of the New Theatre Building. A team of three firms won the assignment: Broome, Oringdulph, O'Toole, Rudolph, Boles & Associates (BOOR/A) of Portland, OR, Barton Myers & Associates, Toronto, Canada and ELS Design Group, Berkeley, CA.

Buffalo Pierogi (Piroghi)

4½ teaspoons hot pepper sauce
1 tablespoon vegetable oil
½ teaspoon chili powder
1 (16-ounce) package frozen potato
    & Cheddar cheese pierogies

Makes 4-6 servings

Preheat oven to 400 degrees. Spray a baking sheet with nonstick cooking spray.

In a medium bowl, combine hot sauce, oil and chili powder. Add frozen pierogies; toss until well coated. Arrange on prepared baking sheet. Bake for 20 minutes, or until golden and crisp, turning after 10 minutes.

Serve with Bleu cheese dressing as a dip. Celery and carrot strips make a nice addition, too. Best when served warm.

Buffet Stuffed Mushrooms

20 whole large fresh mushrooms
¼ cup butter, melted
6 slices bacon, cooked and crumbled
½ cup low-carb bread crumbs
¼ cup fresh parsley, chopped
¼ cup green onions, chopped
¼ teaspoon thyme
1 (3-ounce) package cream cheese,
    softened
1 cup reduced fat Cheddar cheese,
    shredded

Makes 26 appetizers

Wash mushrooms and pat dry. Remove stems. If needed, use a spoon to hollow out a larger space in the cap for the filling. Save all the mushroom bits.

Chop mushroom stems. Melt butter in a pan. Sauté mushroom stems and leftover bits, bread crumbs, parsley, thyme and green onions in the butter. Remove from heat.

In a bowl, combine softened cream cheese with Cheddar cheese. Mix until smooth. Stir in bread crumb mixture. Add bacon.

Fill each mushroom cap with a generous amount of stuffing. Spray a cookie sheet with non-stick spray and arrange mushroom caps. Broil 4-inches from heat for 3 to 5 minutes. The cheese will be bubbly.

Can be assembled earlier in the day and refrigerated until time to serve. Serve warm.

Cheese Filled Triangles

½ pound fresh Phyllo dough
1 cup butter (2 cubes), melted
5 ounces cream cheese, softened
½ pound Feta cheese, room
    temperature and crumbled
1 egg, beaten

Makes 100 triangles

Preheat oven to 350 degrees. In a bowl, combine egg, cream cheese and Feta cheese. Mix well with beater. Place cheese mixture in refrigerator for one hour. When ready to put together, melt butter and keep it warm as you work. If butter cools, it may tear the thin Phyllo.

Cut Phyllo into 2-inch wide strips. Keep pastry covered as you work so it does not dry out. On wax paper, lay out 3 strips of pastry at a time. Place a small teaspoon of filling on one end of each strip of Phyllo and fold corner over to make a triangle shape.

Continue to fold from side to side until you reach end of strip. (It is like folding a flag.) Brush triangles with butter and place on a cookie sheet and cover. When sheet is filled, freeze. Bake 12 to 18 minutes at 350, or until golden brown.

Dining in the Round (New Theatre Building)

*The official name for the rotunda in the New Theatre Building is **Heather Hall.** The versatile space is used for many types of gatherings, including receptions and dinners. **Heather Hall** is the heart of PCPA.*

Cheesy Spinach Pinwheels

1 (8-ounce) can refrigerator
    crescent dinner rolls
6 tablespoons garlic & herb
    spreadable cheese
6 slices cooked deli ham
24 pieces fresh spinach leaves

Preheat oven to 350 degrees.

Separate dough into four equal rectangular pieces. Press perforations to seal the individual rolls together.

Spread each piece of dough with the cheese to within ¼-inch of the edge on all four sides.

Cover the cheese with ham and spinach.

Roll up each rectangle, starting at the shortest side. Cut each roll into six pieces.

Place the pieces on an ungreased cookie sheet. Bake 12 to 18 minutes or until golden brown. Serve warm.

Makes 20-24 appetizers

Crab Dip

1 cup plus 2 tablespoons
    mayonnaise
1⅓ teaspoons garlic, minced
½ teaspoon Old Bay Seafood
    seasoning
6 drops hot sauce
6 ounces crab meat
6 ounces Parmesan cheese, grated
1 (12-ounce) can artichoke hearts
    packed in water, rinsed, drained
    and finely chopped

Preheat oven to 400 degrees.

In a medium mixing bowl, combine mayonnaise, garlic, Old Bay seasoning, hot sauce, crab, Parmesan cheese and artichokes and mix well.

Place in ovenproof dish and bake at 400 degrees for 15 minutes, or until mixture begins to bubble.

Serve warm on thinly sliced baguettes.

Makes about 3 cups

Crab Won Tons with Blackberry Szechuan Sauce

Sauce:
½ cup blackberry purée
½ cup sake
1 tablespoon cornstarch
½ teaspoon salt
½ teaspoon red pepper flakes
½ teaspoon grated ginger
1 teaspoon lime juice
2 cloves garlic, minced
1 ½ tablespoons honey

Filling:
2 ounces fresh spinach, trimmed
    and washed
1 tablespoon butter
4 tablespoons onion, finely chopped
3 ounces cream cheese, cut into
    small chunks
2 tablespoons lemon juice
2 tablespoons dry bread crumbs
½ pound flaked, cooked crabmeat
dash salt
dash pepper
dash Tabasco sauce, (optional)

Won Tons:
3 dozen won ton wrappers
Vegetable oil to cover bottom of
    wok to ¼-inch

Sauce:
In saucepan, mix blackberries, sake, cornstarch, salt, red pepper, ginger, lime juice, garlic and honey. Bring to a boil over medium-high heat and cook until clear and thickened. Set aside.

Filling:
Wash spinach. With water still clinging to leaves, place in large pan over medium-high heat. Cook until spinach just begins to wilt and most of water has evaporated. Empty onto cutting board and chop finely. Set aside.

Melt butter in sauté pan. Add onion and sauté until transparent. Reduce heat to low; add cream cheese. When the cheese begins to soften, add lemon juice to blend. Remove from heat and stir in crab, bread crumbs, spinach, salt, pepper and Tabasco.

Won Tons:
Place 1 to 2 teaspoons of filling in each wrapper and seal according to package directions. Place a single layer of won tons in hot oil and fry 2 to 3 minutes until golden brown. Drain on paper towels, and serve immediately with Blackberry Szechuan Sauce.

Consider making the sauce ahead of time. The flavor improves if allowed to stand in the refrigerator overnight. May substitute sake with dry sherry, if desired.

Makes 36 appetizers

Cranberry Chutney Stuffed Brie

1 pound fresh or frozen cranberries
1 cup sugar
1 cup water
¼ cup onion, finely chopped
1 tablespoon Grand Marnier,
    (optional)
2 pounds Brie cheese, softened
½ cup slivered almonds, toasted
3 tablespoons butter - softened

Preheat oven to 350 degrees. In medium sauce pan, simmer cranberries in water and sugar for 10 minutes, or until skins pop. Remove from heat and add onion and Grand Marnier. Set aside and allow to cool. Cut a cardboard circle the size of the Brie and cover cardboard with aluminum foil. Using a sharp knife, slice cheese horizontally into 2 equal round pieces. Place one half of cheese on cardboard circle, cut side up and spread with chutney. Cover with top half of cheese, with cut side down. Spread softened butter around sides of cheese and roll in toasted almonds. Refrigerate for 1 hour. Place filled Brie cheese in a baking dish and bake at 350 degrees for 10 minutes, or until slightly softened.

After chutney is done, add in optional dry cranberries for more texture. The knife blade may be sprayed with oil or cooking spray for easier slicing.

Hot Shrimp Dip

2 (4½-ounce) cans shrimp, rinsed
    and drained
1 (8-ounce) package cream cheese
6 tablespoons butter, softened
8 green onions, chopped

Makes about 2 cups

Dry shrimp with a paper towel and chop into smaller pieces.

In a mixing bowl, combine cream cheese and butter, blending thoroughly. Add the green onions and shrimp. Mix well.

Transfer mixture to a medium saucepan and heat until the cream cheese and butter begin to melt. Transfer dip to a chafing dish to keep warm.

Serve with toasted bread rounds or crackers. Stir occasionally.

Marvelous Mushrooms

1 pound fresh mushrooms
10 cloves garlic, finely chopped
2 tablespoons vegetable oil
2 tablespoons soy sauce
1 tablespoon fresh parsley, finely
    chopped

Wipe mushrooms to clean them. Cut a thin slice off stem ends. Cut mushrooms in half. If mushroom are large, cut into quarters.

Heat oil in a large frying pan. Add garlic and cook over medium-low heat until golden brown, stirring occasionally. Don't allow garlic to burn. Increase heat to high. Add mushrooms and cook 2 to 3 minutes, stirring continuously. Sprinkle on soy sauce. Garnish with parsley and serve immediately over thin slices of lightly toasted French bread.

Makes 4 servings

Mock Rumaki

¾ cup brown sugar
½ cup water
⅓ cup lemon juice
¼ cup cider vinegar
1 teaspoon orange rind, grated
¼ teaspoon nutmeg
½ teaspoon cinnamon
⅛ teaspoon salt
1 (8-ounce) package pitted dates
¾ pound sliced bacon, each piece
    cut in half

Makes about 24 appetizers

Blanch bacon before using to reduce fat. In a small saucepan, combine sugar, water, lemon juice, vinegar, orange rind, spices and salt. Bring to boil. Reduce heat and simmer for 5 minutes.

Place dates in a glass bowl and cover with marinade mixture. Allow to cool. Cover and refrigerate for 24 hours.

Just before serving, drain dates. Wrap each date in a ½ slice of bacon. Secure with a toothpick. Broil until bacon is crisp. Serve immediately.

For variety, stuff dates with water chestnuts or almonds before wrapping with bacon.

Mushroom Tarts

Mushroom Filling:
2 tablespoons oil
3 tablespoons butter
¾ pound mushrooms, diced
½ cup parsley, diced
5 small green onions, diced
¼ cup grated Parmesan cheese
½ cup bread crumbs

Tartlet Shells:
3 ounces cream cheese, softened
½ cup softened butter
1 cup flour

Makes 26 tartlets

Preheat oven to 350 degrees.

Filling:
Melt 3 tablespoons butter in a heavy skillet, add oil and sauté mushrooms until they are mushy. Add parsley, green onions, Parmesan and bread crumbs. Mix well. Remove from heat.

Tartlet Shells:
Cream remaining butter and cream cheese together. Add flour and mix well. Texture should be somewhat elastic but not sticky. Use a large melon ball scoop (about ¾ inch diameter) and place one scoop of mixture in each tartlet cup. Spread out with fingers to fill cups. The crust should be thin. Scrap off any excess on the tops if you desire. Fill tartlet shells with filling and bake at 350 degrees for 30 minutes.

May be prepared ahead, covered and put in refrigerator. Reheat on a cookie sheet for 10 minutes at 350 degrees.

Olive Cheese Nuggets

1 cup Cheddar cheese, shredded
¼ cup butter, softened
¾ cup sifted flour
⅛ teaspoon salt
½ teaspoon paprika
1 (5-ounce) jar small-sized green Spanish olives stuffed with pimientos, drained

Makes 6 servings

Preheat oven to 400 degrees. In a bowl, blend cheese and butter. Sift flour, salt and paprika into the cheese mixture. Continue mixing until dough is formed. Using a teaspoon, shape dough around each individual green olive, covering completely. Place on ungreased cookie sheet.

Bake at 400 degrees for 12 to 15 minutes, or until golden brown. Serve warm. May be made ahead of time and refrigerated. Reheat at 325 degrees for 5 to 10 minutes before serving.

Philippine Egg Roll (Lumpia)

½ pound lean ground pork
½ pound shrimp, finely chopped
¼ pound onions, finely chopped
¼ cup soy sauce
½ tablespoon salt (optional)
50 Lumpia wrappers
oil for deep-fat frying

Lumpia wrappers are available in most large grocery stores and all Asian markets.

In a frying pan, saute pork, shrimp, onions, soy sauce and salt until pork and shrimp are thoroughly cooked.

Fill an individual wrapper with a heaping tablespoon of the mixture. Make a long roll about ¾ of an inch in diameter. Repeat until all wrappers are filled.

Using a sharp knife, cut each roll into 2-inch pieces.

Deep fry pieces until wrappers are a light golden brown. Remove and drain excess oil on paper towel. Serve warm.

Serve with soy sauce with lemon or sweet and sour sauce.

Makes 100 pieces

Piggy Hot Wings

1 pound pork ribs (with or without bones), cut into 1-rib portions
2 tablespoons butter, melted
1 tablespoon hot pepper sauce
2 tablespoons Cajun seasoning
2 tablespoons cracker crumbs or cornflake crumbs

Preheat oven to 350 degress. In small bowl, mix together butter and hot pepper sauce. In shallow plate, mix together Cajun seasoning and crumbs. Dip ribs into butter mixture and then roll in the seasoning mixture. Place ribs an inch apart on an ungreased cookie sheet or other shallow pan. Bake at 350 degrees for 45 minutes, until golden. Serve warm.

Serve with Bleu cheese dressing for dipping.

Makes 4 servings

The Ultimate Hot Artichoke Dip

1 pint sour cream
½ cup mayonnaise
2 (6-ounce) jars marinated artichoke hearts, drained and chopped
½ cup Parmesan cheese, grated
½ cup green onions, white part only, finely chopped, reserve green portions for garnish.
1 baguette French bread, thinly sliced

Preheat oven to 375 degrees. In a medium bowl, combine sour cream, mayonnaise, artichoke hearts, cheese and green onions. Spoon mixture into a shallow 1-quart oven-proof casserole dish.

Bake at 375 degrees until dip is hot and bubbly, about 25 minutes. Serve warm, garnished with reserved onions and surrounded by sliced French bread and assorted vegetables.

Makes 3 ½ cups

Spinach Cheese Strata

½ cup chopped onion
¼ cup chopped sweet red pepper
¼ cup chopped green bell pepper
2 tablespoons butter
1 (10½-ounce) package frozen chopped spinach, thawed and well drained
2 cups Wheat Chex
½ cup shredded Cheddar cheese
½ cup shredded Swiss cheese
6 eggs
2 cups milk
⅓ cup crumbled cooked bacon
1 teaspoon Dijon mustard
1 teaspoon salt
¼ teaspoon white pepper

Preheat oven to 325 degrees. In a skillet, sauté onions and peppers in butter until crisp tender. Remove from heat. Add spinach and cereal; mix well. Spoon into a greased 11 x 17 x 2-inch baking dish. Sprinkle with cheeses.

In a bowl, combine eggs, milk, bacon, mustard, salt, and pepper. Pour over cheeses. Bake at 325 degrees for 45 to 50 minutes or until a knife inserted near the center comes out clean. Let stand for 10 minutes before cutting.

Can be an appetizer or a side dish. It's just a matter of how you slice it!

Makes 6-8 servings

Rumaki

1 pound fresh chicken livers
1 (4-ounce) can sliced water
   chestnuts, drained
½ pound bacon, sliced
toothpicks
½ cup marinade of your choice

Makes about 24 pieces

Rinse chicken livers and remove any gristle or fat. Place chicken livers in a container that can be sealed tight. Add marinade. Cover and refrigerate for a minimum of 4 hours , or overnight.

Just before serving, drain chicken livers. Pat dry with a paper towel for easier handling. Wrap 1 piece of liver around 1 water chestnut slice. Quickly wrap ½ slice of bacon around the liver and water chestnut. Secure with a tooth pick. Place on broiler pan. Proceed until all the livers are used. Broil for 5 minutes, keeping Rumaki about 4 inches from the heat, until bacon is crisp. Serve hot.

Worcestershire sauce, lemon juice and favorite seasonings is always a winner as a marinade.

Sally's Hot Artichoke Dip

1 (14-ounce) can artichoke hearts,
   packed in water, drained
1 cup Mozzarella cheese, shredded
1 cup Parmesan cheese, grated
1 cup mayonnaise
1 teaspoon basil
2 cloves garlic, crushed
1 teaspoon lemon juice

Preheat oven to 350 degrees. Cut artichokes into smaller pieces. Mix artichokes, Mozzarella, Parmesan, mayonnaise, basil, garlic and lemon juice together. Blend well.

Bake at 350 degrees in an oven-proof dish for 20 to 25 minutes or until hot and bubbly. Serve warm with crackers.

Salmon Won Tons

1 (8-ounce) package cream cheese, softened
1 cup flaked salmon (canned or cooked)
1 tablespoon onion, minced
1 clove garlic, crushed and minced
1 package Won Ton wrappers

Sauce:
1 cup chili sauce or seafood cocktail sauce
2 tablespoons horseradish
1 teaspoon Worcestershire sauce

Preheat deep fat fryer to 375 degrees. Mix cream cheese, salmon, onion, and garlic together.

Lay out won ton wrappers, and place 1 teaspoon of mixture in center of each. Moisten edges of each with water. Fold over and pinch edges well to seal.

Deep fat fry the won tons at 375 degrees until golden brown. Drain well on absorbent paper.

Mix sauce ingredients in a small bowl and serve with hot won tons.

Makes 12 servings

Salmon-Stuffed Mushrooms

1 pound mushrooms, medium sized
¼ cup butter, divided
½ cup onion, minced
1 pound canned salmon, well drained and flaked
½ cup dry bread crumbs
¼ teaspoon pepper
¼ teaspoon paprika

Preheat oven to 450 degrees. Wash mushrooms well, remove stems and place caps aside. Chop stems and onions.

Melt half of the butter in a frying pan over medium heat, add chopped stems and onions and cook until tender stirring (about 10 minutes). Remove pan from heat, stir in flaked salmon, bread crumbs, pepper, and paprika. Fill mushroom caps with salmon mixture and place in a large baking dish.

Melt remaining butter and brush over stuffed mushrooms. Sprinkle lightly with paprika. Bake at 450 degrees for 20 minutes and serve warm.

Makes 12 servings

Sausage Stuffed Mushrooms

1 pound hot pork sausage
1 (8-ounce) package cream cheese
1 package Hidden Valley Ranch
    salad dressing, dry mix only
1 medium onion, finely chopped
1 pound large, fresh mushrooms
    (15-18 pieces)
Parmesan cheese (optional), grated

Brown sausage and onion. Drain excess fat from pan.

Add cream cheese and dry dressing mix to the meat mixture. Stir until thoroughly heated and well mixed. Set aside. If meat/cheese mixture seems runny, place in refrigerator to firm until needed.

Clean mushrooms with a damp paper towel or mushroom brush. Remove stems from caps. Enlarge opening in cap if need be. Stuff each mushroom with meat/cheese mixture until well rounded, but take care not to break sides of cap. Place mushrooms on baking sheet, spacing them so none of them touch.

Broil until brown (about 5 minutes). Remove and sprinkle with Parmesan cheese. Serve hot.

Makes 8 servings

Spicy Cocktail Franks

1 cup currant jelly
½ cup spicy mustard
1 pound miniature franks

Makes about 10 -12 appetizers

Preheat oven to 350 degrees. In a small bowl, combine the jelly and mustard. Mix well. Place the franks in a casserole dish. Cover with the jelly-mustard mixture.

Bake at 350 degrees for 30 minutes. Serve hot, using individual toothpicks for easy pick-up.

You may substitute hot dogs, cut in 1-inch pieces.

Spinach Artichoke Dip

¾ cup mayonnaise
½ cup Parmesan cheese
2 tablespoons lemon juice
½ of a (14- ounce) can artichoke
    hearts, chopped
1 (10½-ounce) package frozen
    chopped spinach (thawed),
    drained and pressed to remove
    excess water.
¼ teaspoon garlic powder
dash of Tabasco sauce

Preheat oven to 350 degrees. In a medium bowl, combine mayonnaise, Parmesan cheese, lemon juice, artichoke hearts, spinach, garlic powder and Tabasco sauce. Mix well.

Bake in greased casserole dish at 350 degrees for 20 to 30 minutes. Serve hot.

Serve with tortilla chips designed for dipping.

Makes enough for 10 -12

Carl Selin

Lights dance in circles on the stairwell.
(New Theatre Building)

The New Theatre Building is a thin-skinned building, architecturally speaking, because 80% of the exterior walls are made of glass, allowing light to penetrate into the rotunda. Columns support the building, and this makes for interesting spaces and curving lines.

Puff Surprise

20 ounces frozen spinach,
    defrosted, rinsed and drained
1 cup ham (or chicken), chopped
1 teaspoon lemon juice
1 pinch salt
1 pinch pepper
¼ teaspoon thyme (or Italian
    seasoning)
⅓ cup sour cream
¾ cup Swiss cheese, grated
1½ teaspoons olive oil
⅓ cup water
2 frozen puff pastry sheets,
    defrosted
1 egg yolk, beaten
2 pinches thyme for garnish

Defrost puff pastry sheets by setting out at least 30 minutes before use. Preheat oven to 350 degrees.

In a skillet, brown meat in olive oil over medium heat. Reduce heat to low. Add spinach, salt, pepper, thyme, lemon juice and water. Cook for 15 minutes. Add sour cream. Remove from heat and let stand up to 10 minutes to cool. Place puff pastry sheets on a lightly oiled cookie sheet.

Arrange sheets side by side. Fill center third of each sheet, dividing spinach mixture equally. Top with Swiss cheese. Fold left side of each sheet over filling. Fold right side of each sheet over left side and filling. Gently press edges of pastry with a fork to pinch the 3 layers of pastry together to prevent filling from coming out. Brush dough with beaten egg yolk, and garnish with a pinch of thyme.

Bake at 350 degrees for 20 to 25 minutes or until dough is golden brown and flaky. Cool for 10 minutes before serving.

Makes 8 servings

The PCPA Gift Shop is located on the street level of the New Theatre Building at 1111 SW Broadway. The shop carries a wide assortment of jewelry, gifts and toys - all with a performing arts theme.

Turkey Tartlets with Cranberry Salsa

1 pound ground turkey
¼ cup onion, chopped
1 teaspoon dried thyme
½ teaspoon ground pepper
¼ teaspoon salt
1 egg
⅓ cup light sour cream
24 frozen mini tart shells

Cranberry Salsa:
1 cup fresh or frozen cranberries
⅓ cup sugar
2 green onions
¼ cup fresh coriander leaves
1 lime, grated and juiced
2 teaspoons chopped ginger root
1 jalapeño pepper, sliced

Preheat oven to 375 degrees. Place frozen tart shells on a cookie sheet. Bake at 375 degrees for 10 minutes or until slightly golden around edges. Remove. Turn oven up to 400 degrees.

While tart shells bake, combine turkey, onion, thyme, salt and pepper in a non-stick skillet heated to medium-high. Sauté until meat is no longer pink, about 10 minutes. Remove from heat. Mix egg and sour cream together, stir into meat mixture. Fill tart shells; bake at 400 degrees for 12 to 15 minutes. Serve warm topped with salsa.

Cranberry Salsa:
Combine cranberries, sugar, onion, coriander, lime juice, rind, ginger root and jalapeño pepper in food processor bowl. Pulse until mixture is chopped (not puréed). Cover and chill at least 2 hours or up to 1 week.

Makes 24 mini tarts

Theatre	Stage Width	Stage Depth
Keller	*107 feet*	*41 feet*
Schnitzer	*94*	*32*
Newmark	*79*	*44*
Winningstad	*45*	*25*

Masala Chai Tea

1 cup water
4 teaspoons Assam or other black
    tea
½ teaspoon ground cinnamon
1 slice of fresh ginger, ¼-inch slice
½ teaspoon ground cardamom
10 whole cloves
3 cups milk
2 tablespoons sugar or to taste

In a saucepan, bring water, tea, cinnamon, ginger, cardamon and cloves to a full boil. Simmer until a deep amber color.

Add milk and sugar. Heat until the milk barely boils. Strain and serve. If fresh ginger is not available, try ½ teaspoon ground ginger.

This tea is served all over India. It is especially soothing on cold days.

Makes 4 servings

Russian Tea

1 cup sugar
1 cup water
2 sticks cinnamon
1 cup orange juice
6 tablespoons lemon juice
1½ quarts water
1 cup brewed tea

In a large saucepan, bring the sugar, one cup of water and the cinnamon sticks to a boil. Reduce the heat and simmer for 5 minutes.

Add orange juice, lemon juice and remaining water. Remove the cinnamon sticks. Keep simmering.

Brew a strong cup of tea and let it steep for at least 3 minutes. Use at least 3 tea bags to one cup of boiling water. Add the tea to the sugar water-juice base. Pour into serving pot and serve hot.

The sugar water and juice base can be stored in the refrigerator until needed.

Makes 10 servings

Keller Auditorium Martini Bar Menu

CREATED BY CRAIG HEDSTROM

Symphony Martini
- 4½ oz. Bombay Sapphire Gin
- a hint of vermouth
- shake well
- add two cocktail olives

Broadway Cosmopolitan
- muddle three fresh lime wedges
- 3 oz. Absolut Vodka
- ½ oz. Cointreau
- 1 oz. cranberry juice
- shake
- garnish with a fresh lime wedge

Mozart Manhattan
- 4 oz. Makers Mark Bourbon
- a splash of sweet vermouth
- a dash of bitters
- shake well
- top with a maraschino cherry

Higher Level Martini
- 4½ oz. freezer chilled Absolut Level Vodka
- shake well
- finish with a lemon twist

Melange (French) Martini
- 3 oz. Absolut Kurant Vodka
- 1 oz. pineapple juice
- ½ oz. Chambord
- shake
- finish with a lemon twist

Chocolat & Vanilla Martini
- 3 oz. Absolut Vanilla Vodka
- 1½ oz. Godiva Chocolat Liqueur
- shake
- serve with a sugared rim
- garnish with a vanilla bean

Lemonade Drop
- muddle four fresh lemon wedges
- 3 oz. Absolut Citron Vodka
- 1 oz. Odwalla Lemonade
- ½ oz. Cointreau
- shake
- serve with a sugared rim
- garnish with a fresh lemon wedge

Big Apple Martini
- muddle two fresh lime wedges
- 3 oz. Absolut Vodka
- 1 oz. Rose's Apple Infusion
- shake
- garnish with a fresh apple wedge

Margarita Martini
- muddle or juice one half of a fresh lime
- 1 oz. Odwalla limeade
- 2½ oz. Jose Cuervo Tequila
- 1 oz. Cointreau
- shake
- serve with a salted rim
- garnish with a fresh lime wedge

Mississippi Mudslide Martini
- 1½ oz. Absolut Vanilla Vodka
- 1½ oz. Kahlua Coffee liqueur
- 1 oz. Baileys Irish Cream
- 1 oz. fresh cream
- shake
- garnish with a vanilla bean

Mojito Martini
- muddle three lime wedges
- 3 oz. Bacardi Silver Rum
- ½ oz. simple syrup (sugar & water)
- shake
- stir in a teaspoon of chopped fresh mint
- serve with a sugared rim
- garnish with a lime wedge

Citrus Bloody Mary Martini
- muddle three lemon & two lime wedges
- 2 oz. Absolute Citron Vodka
- 3 oz. custom made or Ocean Spray Bloody Mary Mix
- shake well
- serve with a salted rim
- garnish with a lemon & lime wedge & two cocktail olives

Mandarin Lemonade Martini
- muddle two lemon wedges
- 3 oz. Absolut Mandarin Vodka
- 2½ oz. Odwalla Lemonade
- shake
- garnish with a fresh mandarin and/or lemon wedge

Single serving drinks portioned for 7 to 9-ounce martini glasses

The Martini Bar at the Keller Auditorium is open prior to the performance and closes well after the final curtain. Drink orders may be preordered for the intermission. The Keller also has a café on the 1st balcony level. Light dinners are served just prior to the performance.

Carl Selin

*The Ira **Keller Fountain** is located across the street from Keller Auditorium.*

The Keller Auditorium has a very unusual claim to fame. It sits on the largest square block in downtown Portland. Most city blocks are 200 feet from one end to the other. Not true for the Keller block. During the reconstruction in 1968, additional land was annexed to the site so the theater could finally have a stage large enough for the grandest productions, and room enough to accommodate larger audiences.

Bread & Rolls

Carl Selin

The Keller Auditorium (originally known as the Civic Auditorium)
The Keller was built in 1917 and was completely renovated in 1968. Throughout the years, it has been the 'workhorse' theater for the City of Portland, hosting innumerable performing arts events each year, including ballet, operas, touring companies of Broadway shows and family events.

Banana Bread

1 cup sugar
½ cup margarine
3 small ripe bananas, mashed
2 eggs, beaten
1¼ cups flour
½ teaspoon salt
1 teaspoon baking soda

Preheat oven to 325 degrees. Grease standard loaf pan.

In a mixing bowl, cream together the sugar and margarine. Add the mashed bananas and eggs, and blend. Add flour, salt and baking soda, and blend, making sure not to over mix.

Pour batter into pan and bake at 325 degrees for 1 hour or until toothpick in the center comes out clean.

Makes 1 loaf

Banana Cake Bread

½ cup shortening
1½ cups sugar
2 large eggs
2 cups flour
¼ teaspoon baking powder
¾ teaspoon baking soda
½ teaspoon salt
¼ cup sour milk
1 teaspoon vanilla
1 cup banana, mashed

Preheat oven to 350 degrees. Grease two standard loaf pans.

In a mixing bowl, cream shortening and sugar. Add eggs and beat until fluffy. In a separate mixing bowl, sift flour, baking powder, baking soda, and salt. Add dry ingredients to egg mixture and mix for 2 minutes. Add bananas, sour milk, and vanilla, and mix until well blended.

Pour batter into pans and bake at 350 degrees for 35 minutes.

Makes 2 loaves

Banana-Orange Bran Muffins

1 cup orange juice
3 cups unprocessed wheat bran
2 eggs, beaten
3 medium ripe bananas, mashed
½ cup honey
1 cup plain yogurt
2 cups whole wheat flour
½ cup flour
1 teaspoon salt
2½ teaspoons baking soda

Makes 24 muffins

Preheat oven to 375 degrees.

In a small saucepan, heat orange juice to simmer; add bran and let cool.

In a large bowl, mix together eggs, bananas, honey, and yogurt. Add bran mixture and blend. In a separate mixing bowl, sift together wheat flour, flour, salt, and baking soda and then add all at once to bran mixture. Stir just enough to incorporate wet and dry, being careful not to over mix.

Spoon mixture into greased muffin tins or use paper liners. Bake at 375 degrees for 20 minutes.

Blueberry Muffins

Topping:
1 tablespoon sugar
1 teaspoon lemon rind, grated

Batter:
1 cup blueberries
2 cups flour, sifted
⅓ cup sugar
3 teaspoons baking powder
1 teaspoon salt
1 egg, well beaten
1 cup milk
4 tablespoons butter, melted

Makes 8-10 muffins

Preheat oven to 425 degrees.

Topping:
In medium mixing bowl, combine 1 tablespoon of sugar with the lemon rind and set aside.

Batter:
In medium mixing bowl, combine flour, sugar, baking powder, and salt. In a separate small bowl, combine egg, milk, and melted butter. Add liquid ingredients to dry ingredients and stir lightly (batter will be lumpy). Fold in blueberries.

Spoon the mixture into greased muffin tins, filling 2/3 full. Sprinkle with topping.

Bake at 425 degrees for 20 to 25 minutes.

Sweet Potato Biscuits

3 cups flour
2 tablespoons sugar
2 teaspoons baking powder
½ teaspoon baking soda
dash salt
¼ cup shortening
¾ cup mashed, cooked sweet
  potatoes (or yams)
1 cup buttermilk

Preheat oven to 450 degrees. Combine flour, sugar, baking powder, baking soda and salt. Cut in shortening with pastry blender. Stir in mashed sweet potatoes. Add buttermilk. Stir with fork until dry ingredients are moist.

Knead lightly. Roll to ½-inch thick. Cut with 2-inch diameter biscuit cutter. Bake for 8 to 10 minutes.

Makes about 2 dozen biscuits

Chocolate Chip Coffee Cake

1 cup sugar
¾ cup butter, separated
2½ cups flour, separated
1 cup sour cream
2 eggs
1 teaspoon baking powder
1 teaspoon baking soda
1 teaspoon vanilla extract
6 ounces chocolate chips, separated
½ cup light brown sugar, packed
1½ teaspoons cocoa powder
½ cup walnuts, chopped

Makes 8-10 servings

Preheat oven to 350 degrees. Grease a 9-inch tube pan.

In a large bowl, beat sugar with ½ cup butter at medium speed until fluffy. Add 2 cups flour, sour cream, eggs, baking powder, baking soda and vanilla extract. Beat at low speed until blended. Increase speed to medium and beat for three minutes, scraping bowl occasionally. Stir in ½ cup chocolate chips. Spread evenly in the pan.

In a medium bowl, combine ½ cup flour, brown sugar and cocoa. With a pastry blender, cut in ¼ cup butter until mixture resembles coarse crumbs and is well blended. Stir in walnuts and remaining chocolate chips. Spread crumble mixture evenly over the batter in the pan.

Bake at 350 degrees for 60 to 65 minutes or until cake pulls from the sides of the pan. Cool cake completely in the pan on a wire rack.

Corn Bread

½ cup butter (1 cube)
1 cup sour cream
1 (15½-ounce) can creamed corn
2 eggs
2 teaspoons sugar
2 (8½-ounce) boxes Jiffy Corn
    Muffin mix

Makes 12 servings

Preheat oven to 350 degrees.

Melt butter in a 9 x 13-inch pan. In a medium bowl, mix sour cream, creamed corn, eggs, sugar and muffin mix. Pour mixture into the pan.

Bake at 350 degrees for 30 to 45 minutes.

A very moist taste treat!

Cracker Bread

4 cups flour
½ teaspoon salt
½ teaspoon baking soda
½ teaspoon sugar
½ cup margarine
1½ cups plain yogurt

Makes 12 servings

Preheat oven to 325 degrees. Lightly grease a cookie sheet.

In a large mixing bowl, combine flour, salt, baking soda, sugar, margarine and yogurt, and mix well. Let the mixture rest for at least five minutes.

Roll out on a flat surface and aerate the dough with a fork.

With a butter knife, cut the dough into 1½-inch squares. Place the squares on the cookie sheet and bake for 10 to 12 minutes.

Good accompaniment to Mount Vernon Colonial Peanut and Chestnut Soup (see page 87)

Check out the PCPA website at www.pcpa.com

Cranberry Bread

1 cup walnuts, chopped
½ package fresh cranberries
¾ cup boiling water
2 tablespoons butter
1 medium orange; juiced and rind
    finely chopped
2 cups plus 2 tablespoons flour
1 cup sugar
1½ teaspoons baking powder
1½ teaspoons baking soda
1 egg, beaten

Makes 1 loaf

Preheat oven to 325 degrees. Grease standard loaf pan. Wash cranberries and place in a plastic bag; set aside.

Pour boiling water over butter in a mixing bowl. Add orange juice and rind. Allow mixture to partially cool while sifting 2 cups of flour, sugar, baking powder and baking soda together. Add lukewarm liquids to dry ingredients and stir. Add beaten egg, followed by nuts. Dredge the cranberries really well with the 2 tablespoons of flour and fold into batter. Pour into prepared loaf pan.

Bake at 325 degrees for 90 minutes.

Keep in the refrigerator or freezer. This is tasty when toasted!

Pear Bread

½ cup butter (1 cube)
1 cup sugar
2 eggs
2 cups flour
½ teaspoon salt
½ teaspoon baking soda
1 teaspoon baking powder
⅛ teaspoon nutmeg
¼ cup yogurt or buttermilk
1 cup cored pears, coarsely chopped
1 teaspoon vanilla

Makes 1 loaf

Preheat oven to 350 degrees. Grease a standard loaf pan.

Cream butter and gradually beat in sugar. Beat in eggs one at a time. Combine flour, salt, baking soda, baking powder, and nutmeg. Add to egg mixture alternately with yogurt or buttermilk. Add pears and vanilla. Pour into prepared loaf pan. Bake at 350 degrees for 1 hour or until toothpick comes out clean. Cool on wire racks for 15 minutes, then remove from pan and continue cooling.

This recipe may be increased 4 fold, which makes about 9 small loaves.

Pumpkin Bread

6 eggs
1½ cups vegetable oil
1 cup water
4½ cups sugar
5¼ cups flour
1 (20-ounce) can pumpkin
1½ teaspoons ground cloves
1½ teaspoons ground nutmeg
1½ teaspoons ground cinnamon
1½ teaspoons ground allspice
2 tablespoons baking powder
3 teaspoons baking soda
3 teaspoons salt
2 cups raisins
1 cup nuts

Preheat oven to 350 degrees. Grease and flour 4 standard loaf pans. Combine flour, sugar, baking soda, salt, cloves, cinnamon, nutmeg and allspice. Mix well. Blend in pumpkin, eggs, oil and water. Add raisins and nuts. Mix well.

Divide batter into 4 standard loaf pans. Bake at 350 degrees for 1 hour and 15 minutes.

Makes 4 loaves

Pumpkin-Orange Bread

1 cup vegetable oil
3 cups sugar
4 whole eggs
1½ teaspoons salt
½ teaspoon ground cloves
½ teaspoon ground nutmeg
1 teaspoon ground cinnamon
⅔ cup orange juice, heated
2 teaspoons baking soda
2 cups pureed pumpkin (canned)
3½ cups flour
1 cup nuts, chopped

Preheat oven to 350 degrees. In a large bowl, combine oil and sugar. Add eggs, one at a time, beating well after each addition. Beat in salt, cloves, nutmeg and cinnamon.

Heat orange juice, being careful not to boil. Blend baking soda into hot orange juice. Stir orange juice into sugar and egg mixture. Add pumpkin and flour. Mix well. Fold in nuts. Pour into 3 greased and floured standard loaf pans. (9 x 5 x 2-inches).

Bake at 350 degrees for 1 hour or until an inserted toothpick comes out clean.

Makes 3 loaves

Raspberry Streusel Muffins

⅓ cup nuts, chopped
1¼ cups sugar, divided
2 cups plus 3 tablespoons flour, divided
⅓ cup plus 2 tablespoons butter, divided
¼ teaspoon nutmeg
2 teaspoons baking powder
½ teaspoon baking soda
¼ teaspoon salt
1 egg
½ cup milk
½ cup sour cream
1½ cups Oregon raspberries

Makes 16 muffins

Preheat oven to 400 degrees. Grease standard muffin tin. In small bowl, mix ¼ cup sugar, 3 tablespoons flour, 2 tablespoons butter, nutmeg and nuts to make streusel. When mixture forms crumbles, set aside.

In medium bowl, mix 2 cups flour, 1 cup sugar, baking powder, baking soda, and salt. Set aside.

Melt remaining butter. In a second medium bowl, blend eggs, milk, sour cream, and butter. Fold egg mixture into dry ingredients. Add raspberries. Fold gently. Pour into prepared muffin tin and top each muffin with streusel mix. Bake at 400 degrees for 25 minutes. Streusel should be golden brown. Use toothpick test on muffins.

Skillet Cornbread

2 cups cornmeal
1 teaspoon baking soda
1 teaspoon salt
2 eggs
2 cups buttermilk
¼ cup vegetable oil

Makes 10-12 servings

Place well-greased cast iron skillet in oven. Heat oven to 450 degrees.

Combine cornmeal, baking soda and salt. Mix together eggs, buttermilk and oil. Add to dry ingredients and mix well.

Remove skillet from oven. (Oven temperature should be up to 450 degrees.) Pour batter into hot skillet and return to the oven.

Bake 40 minutes, or until golden brown. The bread will have pulled away from the side of the skillet.

Sesame Swiss Cheese Quick Bread

2 cups flour, sifted
3 tablespoons sugar
4 teaspoons baking powder
1 ½ teaspoons salt
1 cup Swiss cheese, shredded
⅓ cup plus ½ teaspoon sesame
    seeds, toasted and divided
2 eggs, beaten
1 ¼ cups milk
¼ cup oil

Makes 1 loaf

Preheat oven to 375 degrees. Grease standard 8½ x 4½-inch loaf pan. Sift together flour, sugar, baking powder, and salt into a mixing bowl. Stir in cheese and 1/3 cup sesame seeds. In separate bowl, blend together eggs, milk and oil. Add liquid all at once to flour mixture, stirring just until flour is moistened.

Pour into loaf pan. Sprinkle with ½ teaspoon sesame seeds. Bake at 375 degrees for 65 to 70 minutes. Use toothpick test to check loaf.

Cool in pan on a wire rack for 15 minutes then remove from pan and cool completely. Serve warm or cool. Store in refrigerator.

Carl Selin

Crowning the rotunda of the New Theatre Building is the Spectral Light Dome, designed by New York artist, James Carpenter. The dome is constructed of chemically treated glass suspended below its steel support frame in curved strips, layered as many as three deep. The treated glass refracts light passing through it in colors ranging from pink to turquoise. Because the colors are determined by the angle of the light, the display differs from hour to hour and day to day.

The **Spectral Light Dome** (at dusk) -
James Carpenter, Artist, (New Theatre Building)

Soft Baked Pretzels

4-4½ cups flour, divided
1 package Fleischmann's Rapid Rise
  Yeast
2 tablespoons sugar
1½ teaspoons salt
1 cup milk
½ cup water
2 tablespoons vegetable oil
1 egg, lightly beaten with 1
  tablespoon of water

Makes 24 pretzels

The **Walk of Stars** outside the Main Street entrance to the New Theatre Building honors individuals who have contributed to Portland's arts, urban design and environment. Artist Tad Savinar donated his design services for the granite stars. The sidewalk was dedicated on September 13, 1998.

Set aside 1 cup flour. In large bowl, mix remaining flour, undissolved yeast and salt.

Heat milk, water and oil until hot to touch (125 to 130 degrees); stir into dry ingredients. Mix in enough additional flour to make soft dough. Knead dough on lightly floured surface until smooth and elastic, about 5 minutes. Cover; let rest 10 minutes.

Preheat oven to 350 degrees. Divide dough into 24 pieces. Roll each piece to 16-inch rope. To make pretzels, curve ends of each rope to make circle; cross ends at top. Twist ends once and lay down over bottom of circle. Place pretzels on greased baking sheets. Cover; let rest in warm, draft-free place for 5 to 10 minutes, until risen slightly.

Brush pretzels with beaten egg mixture and sprinkle with selected topping. Bake at 350 degrees for 35 minutes or until done. Cool pretzels on wire rack.

Variation for Herb Pretzels: Follow recipe adding ¾ teaspoon each - thyme, marjoram and oregano (leaves).

Toppings: Select one of the following - flavored salt (hickory smoked salt, celery salt, onion salt or garlic salt) or seeds (sesame seeds, poppy or whole celery seeds).

Caramel Rolls

1 package active dry yeast
¾ cup warm water (110 to 115 degrees)
¾ cup warm milk (110 to 115 degrees)
¼ cup sugar
3 tablespoons vegetable oil
2 teaspoons salt
4 cups flour

Filling:
¼ cup butter
¼ cup sugar
3 teaspoons cinnamon

Topping:
¾ cup brown sugar, packed
½ cup whipping cream
1 cup pecans, coarsely chopped

Preheat oven to 350 degrees.

In large mixing bowl, dissolve yeast in warm water. Add milk, sugar, oil, salt, and 1 ¼ cups flour. Mix at medium speed for 2 to 3 minutes. Stir in enough flour to make a soft dough. Turn out onto a floured surface and knead in remaining flour (6-8 minutes). Cover, and let rise for 1 hour. Punch dough down and roll into an 18 x 12-inch rectangle.

Filling:
Spread formed bread with butter and sprinkle with sugar and cinnamon. Roll it in a jelly roll fashion. Cut into 12 rounds.

Topping:
In a 13 x 9 x 2-inch pan, mix brown sugar, whipping cream and pecans. Place the 12 rounds on top of topping mixture, with cut end facing upwards. Let it rise until double in size.

Bake at 350 degrees for 30 to 35 minutes or until golden brown.

Makes 12 rolls

Cheese Bread

1 wide loaf Italian bread
¾ cup butter (1½ cubes)
2 tablespoons onion, grated
1 tablespoon poppy seeds
1 tablespoon mustard
Swiss cheese slices

Makes 1 loaf

Preheat oven to 350 degrees.

Carefully remove crusts off top and sides of the bread. Slice bread ¾ of the way through. Butter one side of each slice. Turn loaf around and butter the other side of each slice. Insert cheese between the slices. Butter the top and the sides.

Using two sheets of heavy-duty foil (one lengthwise and one crosswise), wrap the bread in the foil. Open the foil on the top to allow steam to escape.

Bake in 350 degree oven for 30 minutes, using the foil as the baking tray. Just before serving, slice the loaf all the way through.

Mary's Banana Bread

2 ripe bananas, mashed
2 eggs
1¾ cups flour
1½ cups sugar
1 cup walnuts, optional
½ cup oil
¼ cup buttermilk, optional
1 teaspoon baking soda
1 teaspoon vanilla
dash of salt

Preheat the oven to 325 degrees. Grease a standard loaf pan (8 ½ x 4 ½ x 2 ½-inches). Mix all the ingredients together in large mixing bowl.

Pour mixture into the prepared pan. Bake at 325 degrees for 80 minutes.

Makes 1 loaf

Best Quick Pancakes

1 cup flour
2 teaspoons baking powder
½ teaspoon salt
2 tablespoons sugar
1 large egg, lightly beaten
1 cup milk
2 tablespoons unsalted butter,
    melted
melted butter for griddle

Heat griddle to 375 degrees (or heat a griddle pan over medium-high heat).

In a medium bowl, whisk together flour, baking powder, salt and sugar. Add egg, milk and 2 tablespoons butter; whisk to combine. The batter should have small to medium lumps.

Using pastry brush, brush remaining butter onto griddle. Wipe off excess.

Using a 2-ounce ladle, pour batter onto griddle, forming pancakes about 2 inches apart. When pancakes have bubbles on top and are slightly dry around the edges, about 2 ½ minutes, flip them over. Cook until golden on bottom, about 1 minute. Repeat with remaining batter.

Serve with your favorite toppings.

The stages in Shakespeare's day were often raised in the back and angled down toward the audience, giving the patrons better visibility. But this meant that actors literally walked up an incline each time they went to the rear of the stage…thus moving "upstage". If someone is upstaged, it means a fellow actor deliberately moved upstage to force the other actor to turn his back to the audience.

Pumpkin Nut Waffles

2 cups flour
1 tablespoon baking powder
¾ teaspoon pumpkin pie spice
¼ teaspoon salt
3 eggs, separated
1¾ cups milk
½ cup vegetable oil
½ cup canned or thick mashed
   cooked pumpkin
½ cup pecans or walnuts, chopped

Makes 6 cups batter

Preheat waffle iron. Spray it with cooking spray. Thoroughly stir together flour, baking powder, pumpkin pie spice, and salt. Beat egg yolks and stir in milk, oil, and pumpkin. Stir this mixture into dry ingredients. Beat egg whites until they form stiff peaks. Fold this mixture into pumpkin mixture. Stir in nuts.

Pour appropriate amount of batter onto a hot waffle iron and bake until waffle is golden brown. Serve immediately. Repeat with remaining batter.

Serve hot waffles with butter or margarine and maple syrup.

Toffee Mix

1 cup butter (2 cubes)
2⅓ cups brown sugar, firmly packed
½ cup light corn syrup
1 teaspoon vanilla
5½ cups Crispix
5½ cups Rice Chex
7 cups Corn Chex
1 pound salted mixed nuts

Preheat the oven to 250 degrees. Mix butter, brown sugar, corn syrup, and vanilla in a saucepan over medium heat. Bring it to a boil and boil for 5 minutes.

Mix cereals and nuts together in a large bowl. Pour syrup over cereal mixture. Mix well. Pour into a large roasting pan. Bake at 250 degrees for 1 hour. Spread mixture on wax paper to cool. Break up into pieces. Store in an airtight container.

Aunt May's Light Rolls

1 package active dry yeast
1 cup very warm water
3 eggs, beaten
½ cup sugar
¾ cup shortening
5½ cups flour, sifted
1 teaspoon salt

Preheat oven to 350 degrees.

In a large bowl, combine warm water and yeast and set aside until all yeast is dissolved.

Add eggs to yeast mixture and blend. Add sugar and shortening, and blend. Sift flour and salt together, add to yeast mixture and blend well.

Cover dough with a damp cloth and let sit for 10 minutes. Turn dough out onto lightly floured surface and knead until the dough is smooth. Place dough into a large bowl and let raise until double in size.

Roll dough out onto lightly floured surface and either cut with a biscuit cutter and fold it over, or cut into strips and tie into knots. Let prepared rolls rise until double in size.

Bake at 350 degrees for 15 to 20 minutes, or until golden brown.

May refrigerate dough for up to one week in a plastic bowl with a tight lid.

The PCPA volunteers are trained to perform specialized duties. These jobs include working as an usher at the Newmark Theatre, as ticket-takers and ushers at the Winningstad Theatre, and as greeters at both the Arlene Schnitzer Concert Hall and Keller Auditorium. In addition they staff the PCPA Gift Shop, assist in the office, conduct free public tours af the PCPA facilities and give PCPA presentations to various groups and organizations.

Bread & Rolls

Cardamom Braided Bread

¼ cup warm water
1 package active dry yeast
2½ cups warm milk
¾ cup butter, melted and cooled
1 egg
½ teaspoon salt
1 cup sugar
1 tablespoon lemon peel, grated
1½ teaspoons ground cardamom
7 cups flour

Icing:
2 cups powdered sugar
¼ cup milk
1 teaspoon lemon extract

Makes 2 loaves

Theatre	Stage Size
Keller	60 x 30 feet
Schnitzer	54 x 32
Newmark	40-48 x 26
Winningstad	32 x 26

Preheat oven to 350 degrees.

In large mixing bowl, combine warm water and yeast. Let stand for 5 minutes or until yeast is dissolved. Stir in milk, butter, egg, salt, sugar, lemon peel and cardamom until blended. Gradually beat in flour to make stiff dough.

Turn out onto lightly floured surface and knead in enough additional flour to make moderately stiff dough that is smooth and elastic. Shape bread dough into a ball. Place dough in a lightly greased bowl, turning once to grease the surface. Cover and let bread dough rise in a warm place until doubled (about 2 hours).

Punch dough down; turn out onto lightly floured surface. Divide dough into six equal portions. Roll each portion by hand, into an evenly thick rope 22 to 24-inches long. Line up three of the ropes, 1-inch apart, on a greased baking sheet. Pinch the tops together and loosely braid - leaving room for bread to rise. Pinch the ends together. Repeat with remaining three ropes. Cover breads and let rise until almost doubled (about 45 to 60 minutes).

Bake at 350 degrees for 30 to 35 minutes or until lightly brown on top. Remove from baking sheets and cool on racks for 10 minutes.

Icing:
In medium mixing bowl, blend powdered sugar, milk and lemon extract until smooth. Drizzle icing over top of bread.

Lemon Bubble Ring

2 packages active dry yeast
1 teaspoon salt
5½ cups flour, divided
1 cup sugar, divided
½ cup water
1 cup milk
8 tablespoons butter, divided
2 large eggs
grated peel of 2 lemons
¼ teaspoon ground mace

Makes 16 servings

Theatre	Approximate Seating
Keller	3,000 seats
Schnitzer	2,700
Newmark	900
Winningstad	300

Preheat oven to 350 degrees. In a large mixing bowl, combine yeast, salt, 2 cups flour, and ½ cup sugar. In a small saucepan over low heat, heat milk, 4 tablespoons butter, and ½ cup water until very warm (120 to 130 degrees).

Gradually beat liquid into dry ingredients. Add eggs and beat 2 minutes, occasionally scraping bowl with rubber spatula. Beat in 1 cup flour to make a thick batter; continue beating 2 minutes, occasionally scraping bowl. With spoon, stir in 2 cups flour to make soft dough.

Turn dough onto lightly floured surface and knead, working in more flour (about ½ cup) while kneading (about 3 minutes). Shape dough into ball and place in greased large bowl. Cover with towel; leave until doubled in size, about 1 hour. Punch down dough and turn onto lightly floured surface; cut dough in half, cover with bowl and let rest 15 minutes for easier shaping. Meanwhile, in small bowl, combine lemon peel, mace, and ½ cup sugar. In small saucepan, melt 4 tablespoons butter. Grease a 10-inch angel food cake pan. Roll each half of dough into a log shape and cut each into 16 pieces.

Shape each piece into a ball. Dip each ball in melted butter and then lemon mixture to give a light coat. Place balls in greased pan. Cover with towel; let rise until doubled, about 45 minutes.

Bake bubble ring 35 minutes, or until golden and loaf sounds hollow when lightly tapped with fingers. Cool in pan for 10 minutes, then place onto a plate. Cool slightly to serve warm, or cool completely to serve later.

Multigrain Bread

8 cups warm water
4 packages active dry yeast
1 teaspoon sugar
3 teaspoons salt
8 cups dark rye flour
2 cups 10 grain cereal
8-10 cups unbleached white flour

Makes 4 loaves

In large bowl, blend water, yeast, sugar, salt, rye flour, and 10 grain cereal. Mix into a thick dough. Sprinkle about 1 cup of white flour over it, cover with a towel and let rest in a warm place for about 45 minutes or until dough almost doubles in size.

Mix remaining white flour into the dough, scraping sides of the bowl as you work, until firm (dough does not stick to hands or spoon). Remove from bowl when dough too firm to stir with spoon. Finish kneading flour into dough on floured board. Return dough to bowl, cover and let rise again (45 minutes to 1 hour). In the meantime, grease 4 loaf pans. When the dough has risen, remove from bowl and knead it on floured board to remove air. Divide into 4 equal loaves. Put into prepared pans and let rise until dough is up to the top of the pans.

Preheat oven to 425 degrees and bake loaves for 45 minutes or until they are nicely browned.

Bread freezes very well for later use. For a slightly shiny crust, splash about ½ cup of water inside hot oven when you load the loaves for baking and close the door quickly. The additional steam creates the shiny crust. (This tip works best with an electric oven.)

Potato Refrigerator Rolls

1 large potato, peeled, boiled and
    mashed (about 1 cup of mashed
    potato), lukewarm temperature
1½ cups warm water
1 package active dry yeast
⅔ cups sugar
1½ teaspoons salt
⅔ cup butter, softened
2 eggs
7-7½ cups sifted flour

Makes about 3 dozen rolls

Preheat oven to 400 degrees. Add sugar, salt, butter and eggs to lukewarm mashed potato. Set aside. In small bowl, add yeast to warm water and stir. Add yeast to potato mixture. Gradually add 7 to 7 ½ cups flour. Mix by hand until dough is easy to handle. Knead until smooth and elastic. Grease dough. Place greased side up in a greased bowl. Cover with a damp cloth. Place in refrigerator until needed. (Dough will stay fresh for 2-3 days!)

About 2 hours before baking, shape dough into rolls by making 6 inch long ropes, about ½-inch in diameter. Tie rope into a knot. Place rolls on a greased cookie sheet. Let rise for 2 hours.

Bake 12 to 15 minutes or until golden brown.

Super Delicious Refrigerator Rolls

1 package active dry yeast
¼ cup water
2 cups milk
½ cup shortening or margarine
½ cup sugar
1 egg, slightly beaten
5 cups flour (plus extra for
    kneading), sifted
½ teaspoon baking powder
½ teaspoon baking soda
½ teaspoon salt

Makes about 2 dozen rolls

Preheat oven to 400 degrees. In a small bowl, dissolve yeast in water. Set aside. In a small saucepan, combine milk, shortening, and sugar. Heat until shortening is melted. Allow to cool to lukewarm, then add egg and yeast mixture.

In large bowl, combine flour, baking powder, baking soda, and salt and gradually add milk mixture. Mix thoroughly. Set aside and allow dough to rise until doubled in size. Knead on floured board. Shape into rolls. Let rolls rise again. Bake for 10 to 15 minutes.

Form the risen dough into a rope and cut to appropriate size. Coil the dough into a round circle to make roll. Dough may be refrigerated after the first rising for 16 to 24 hours.

Whole Wheat Batter Bread

1½ cups lukewarm water
1 package dry yeast
2 tablespoons honey
2 cups whole wheat flour, divided
1 cup flour, divided
1 teaspoon salt
2 tablespoons unsalted butter,
    softened

Place water in large bowl of an electric mixer. Sprinkle with yeast and stir in the honey. Let stand until foamy, about 5 minutes.

On medium speed, beat in 1 cup whole wheat flour, ½ cup flour, salt and butter. Beat 2 minutes, scraping the sides of the bowl. On low speed, beat in the remaining flours. Cover and let rise in a warm place until doubled in volume, about 1 hour.

Stir the dough down by beating 25 strokes with a wooden spoon. Spread dough into a greased 9 x 5 x 3-inch loaf pan. Cover loosely with a flour-rubbed tea towel and let rise in a warm place until dough reaches the top of the pan, about 1 hour.

Preheat oven to 400 degrees. Bake bread until golden brown and the bread sounds hollow when tapped, about 30 minutes. Remove from pan; cool on rack.

Makes 1 loaf

*The original 1928 **Portland** sign stood over 65 feet tall and contained over 7,000 light bulbs and 1,000 feet of neon tubing. When the movie theater name was changed to the Paramount in 1930, the original sign was repainted and the lights were moved to outline the new name. The Ballard Sign Company of Salem, OR built the present day **Portland** sign. It is an exact replica of the 1928 original (but with fewer light bulbs!).*

Side Dishes

Carl Selin

*The **Portland** sign and the Main Street Towers are representative of the combined architecture that bridges the historic Arlene Schnitzer Concert Hall and the modern New Theatre Building.*

Italian Peppers

4 sweet red and/or yellow peppers,
    seeded and hollowed
4 ripe tomatoes, chopped
3 tablespoons capers
½ cup Kalamata olives, pitted and
    chopped
½ cup Parmesan cheese, grated
2 tablespoons fresh basil, chopped
2 tablespoons Italian parsley
salt
pepper
¼ cup olive oil
¼ cup bread crumbs
2 tablespoons olive oil

Cut peppers into bite-size pieces and arrange in an oiled baking dish.

Combine tomatoes, capers, olives, cheese, parsley, basil, salt and pepper; toss with ¼ cup olive oil. Pour over peppers then sprinkle with bread crumbs. Drizzle remaining olive oil over the top.

Bake at 350 degrees, covered with foil for 20 minutes. Remove foil and bake an additional 20 minutes.

Makes 6-8 servings

Black Bean Pasta

4 cups cooked bow tie pasta
⅓ cup red pepper, diced
½ cup zucchini, diced
1 (14½-ounce) can recipe ready
    tomatoes
1 teaspoon Italian seasoning
1 (15-ounce) can black beans,
    reserve liquid
freshly grated Parmesan cheese

Cook pasta according to package directions. Set aside.

In a medium fry pan, sauté pepper and zucchini until tender. Add tomatoes and drained black beans.

When heated thoroughly, toss together with the pasta. If too dry, add some of the bean liquid. Add Parmesan cheese to taste.

Makes 6-8 servings

Hazelnut Wild Rice Pilaf

½ cup wild rice
½ cup brown rice
5½ cups chicken stock
½ cup celery, diced
2 tablespoons butter
1 cup hazelnuts, diced and toasted
1 cup golden raisins
¼ cup olive oil
¼ cup fresh mint, chopped
4 green onions, thinly sliced
freshly ground pepper
1½ teaspoons salt
2 tablespoons orange rind, grated
⅓ cup fresh orange juice

Rinse rice thoroughly with cold water. Add brown rice, wild rice and chicken stock to a heavy saucepan. Bring to rapid boil. Reduce heat and simmer, uncovered, for approximately 35 to 45 minutes. Do not overcook the rice.

Meanwhile, sauté celery in butter until tender; set aside.

When rice is done, remove from heat and drain. Add sautéed celery, hazelnuts, raisins, olive oil, mint, onions, pepper, salt, orange rind, and orange juice. Toss gently. Adjust seasonings to taste.

Makes 6 servings

Rice Bake

¼ cup butter
1 cup onion, chopped
4 cups freshly cooked rice
2 cups sour cream
1 cup cottage cheese
1 large bay leaf, crumbled
½ teaspoon salt
⅛ teaspoon pepper
3 (4-ounce) cans green chiles
2 cups sharp Cheddar cheese, grated
parsley, chopped

Makes 8-10 servings

To make 4 cups rice: bring 2½ cups water to boil; add 1 cup rice and teaspoon salt; cover and cook on low for 25 minutes. Preheat oven to 375 degrees. Prepare 12 x 8 x 2-inch pan by lightly greasing or spray with Pam.

Sauté onion in butter about 5 minutes. Remove from heat and stir in cooked rice, sour cream, cottage cheese, bay leaf, salt and pepper. Mix well.

Layer half of rice mixture in dish. Top with half of chiles. Sprinkle with grated cheese. Repeat layering. Bake uncovered 25 minutes. Sprinkle with parsley.

Perfect accompaniment for barbeque or potluck.

Risotto Basilica

5 cups chicken broth
3 tablespoons olive oil
1 cup green onion, chopped, with
    some tops
1½ cups arborio rice
½ cup dry white wine
2 cups basil leaves, chopped, lightly
    packed
3 tablespoons green onion tops,
    chopped
3 tablespoons Italian parsley,
    chopped
⅓ cup Parmesan cheese, grated
¼ cup half and half, or cream
½ teaspoon thyme
salt
pepper

Bring broth to simmer over medium-high heat. Reduce heat and keep broth hot.

Heat olive oil in a large, heavy saucepan over medium heat. Add green onion and sauté until soft but not brown, about 5 minutes. Add arborio rice and stir for 2 minutes. Add wine and reduce heat to medium low. Simmer until wine is absorbed, stirring constantly, about 1 minute. Add 1 cup hot broth and simmer until broth is absorbed, stirring often, about 3 minutes. Continue adding broth ½ cup at a time and simmer until broth is absorbed before each addition, stirring often. After about 20 minutes the rice should be tender but still slightly firm in the center. The mixture should be creamy and the broth should all be used.

Mix 1½ cups basil, green onion tops, and Italian parsley and add into risotto. Simmer 3 minutes, stirring often.

Remove risotto from heat and mix Parmesan cheese, half and half (or cream) and thyme.

Season with salt, if needed, and freshly ground pepper.

Transfer risotto to a shallow serving bowl. Sprinkle with ½ cup finely chopped basil and grated Parmesan cheese. Pass additional grated Parmesan cheese if desired.

Makes 6 servings

PCPA Gift Certificates make nice presents! The recipients may redeem them for theater tickets. You may purchase Gift Certificates at the PCPA Box Office or online at www.pcpa.com.

Baked Beans

1 pound white beans, small
½ pound brown sugar
2 cups tomato sauce
1 teaspoon salt
1 teaspoon chili powder
1 teaspoon dry mustard
1 pinch powdered ginger
2 cloves garlic, minced
1 large onion, minced
2 tablespoons vinegar
1 pound bacon, chopped

Place beans in a large saucepan and add water until 2 inches above beans. Simmer for 2 hours. Drain, leaving just enough water to cover beans.

Mix beans with brown sugar, tomato sauce, salt, chili powder, mustard, ginger, garlic, onion, vinegar and bacon. Transfer to a 3-quart casserole.

Bake at 300 degrees, uncovered, for at least 4 hours.

Makes 12 servings

Beets with Walnuts and Gorgonzola

3 large beets
¼ cup walnuts
¼ cup Gorgonzola cheese, crumbled
1 shallot, chopped
butter
salt
pepper

Makes 4-6 servings

Preheat oven to 350 degrees. Butter a gratin dish.

Place walnuts on a cookie sheet and bake for 12 minutes. They will continue to cook some after removal from the oven. Parboil the beets for 10 to 12 minutes. Peel and cube into ¾-inch cubes. Sauté the shallots in 2 tablespoons butter for 2 minutes. Add ground black pepper to the shallot mixture.

Mix beets and shallot mixture in a small bowl to mix well. Add crumbled Gorgonzola into the mix and stir well. Add salt if necessary. Place mixture in the gratin dish. Bake at 350 degrees for 40 minutes. Top with walnuts and serve.

This side dish is exceptional with lamb. But would also be good with poultry and pork.

Cauliflower Gratin with Chilies and Cheese

1 large cauliflower
2 tablespoons butter
8 ounces Monterey Jack cheese,
    grated
1 cup sour cream
1 (4-ounce) can chopped green
    chilies, drained
½ cup onion, diced
½ teaspoon salt
½ teaspoon black pepper
½ teaspoon white pepper
2 tablespoons butter, melted
1 cup fine dry bread crumbs

Makes 6-8 servings

Preheat oven to 350 degrees. Grease a 2-quart baking dish.

Remove outer leaves and stem from cauliflower and break into florets. Steam for 10 to 12 minutes or until tender. Drain well.

In a large bowl, combine butter, cheese, sour cream, chilies, onion, salt and peppers, and blend well. Add cauliflower, tossing gently. Place in prepared baking dish.

Combine melted butter and bread crumbs; stirring well. Sprinkle over casserole. Bake at 350 degrees for 25 to 30 minutes, or until lightly brown.

Cauliflower Supreme

1 large cauliflower
½ cup mayonnaise
2 tablespoons Dijon mustard
¾ cup Cheddar cheese, grated

Wash cauliflower and remove outer leaves and stalk. Place in a microwave dish with a small amount of water. Cover with plastic wrap and microwave on high for 8 minutes. Drain water.

Combine mayonnaise and mustard in a small bowl. Spread mixture evenly over cauliflower, and sprinkle with cheese. Return to microwave and heat on high for 2 to 3 minutes or until cheese melts.

Cut and serve in wedges.

Makes 6-8 servings

Company Vegetable Casserole

2 (10-ounce) packages frozen cut
    green beans
1 (16-ounce) can bean sprouts,
    drained
1 (4-ounce) can water chestnuts,
    sliced and drained
1 (4-ounce) can mushroom pieces,
    drained
1 (10½-ounce) can cheese sauce
1 small onion, minced
1 (3½-ounce) can fried onion rings

Cook green beans until barely tender. Drain.

In a large colander, toss bean sprouts, water chestnuts and mushrooms so as much liquid as possible is drained out. Turn into a shallow, 2-quart casserole.

In a bowl, combine cheese sauce with minced onion and spoon over vegetables.

Bake, uncovered, at 350 degrees for 25 minutes. Top with fried onion rings and bake for 10 minutes more.

Makes 6-8 servings

Green Bean Casserole

2 (9-ounce) packages frozen
    French-style green beans
1 onion, chopped
2 tablespoons butter
2 tablespoons flour
salt
pepper
½ cup skim milk
1 cup non-fat, plain yogurt
1 cup reduced fat sharp Cheddar
    cheese, shredded

Cook green beans according to directions on package; drain well. In a medium skillet, sauté onion in butter until tender. Blend in flour, salt, and pepper. Gradually add milk, stirring and cooking until thickened and bubbly. Stir in yogurt and green beans; heat thoroughly.

Transfer to 1½-quart casserole. Sprinkle with cheese and broil in oven until cheese melts.

May substitute one (28-ounce) can of cut green beans, if desired.

Makes 4-6 servings

Fresh Carrot Ring with Peas and Cauliflower

1 tablespoon vegetable oil
½ cup fine bread crumbs
4 eggs, separated
1½ cups butter (3 cubes), softened
1 cup light brown sugar
3 cups fresh carrots, finely grated
2 tablespoons milk
2 tablespoons fresh lemon juice
1 teaspoon salt
2 teaspoons baking powder
1 teaspoon baking soda
2 cups flour
3 tablespoons butter
2 cups fresh or frozen peas
salt
freshly ground black pepper
1 head fresh cauliflower, cut into
    florets and cooked until tender
    in salted water

Preheat the oven to 350 degrees. Grease a 3-quart ring mold or bundt pan with the oil. Dust the pan with the bread crumbs.

In the bowl of an electric mixer, whip egg whites on medium-high until stiff. Remove and set aside.

In another bowl, cream butter and sugar together. Add egg yolks one at a time, beating until smooth. Add carrots, milk and lemon juice. Beat well. Add salt, baking powder, baking soda and flour. Beat well. Fold in whipped egg whites. Pour mixture into prepared pan and spread evenly.

Bake for 1 hour, or until center is set and cake springs back from pan. Remove from oven and cool for 5 minutes in pan. Remove from pan and turn onto a serving platter.

In a sauté pan, over medium heat, melt butter and cook for about 1 minute or until butter starts to turn brown. Add peas.

Season with salt and pepper. Sauté for 2 to 3 minutes. Remove from heat and spoon around the carrot ring. Spoon the cauliflower in the center of the ring. Serve warm.

Makes 8-10 servings

Green Beans Almondine

2 tablespoons butter
1 ounce sliced almonds
½ cup onion, chopped
2 cloves garlic, minced
1 teaspoon fresh parsley, minced
¼ teaspoon salt
dash fresh ground pepper
3 cups fresh green beans, trimmed
    and halved; cooked until tender

In a 10 or 12-inch nonstick skillet, heat butter over medium heat until bubbly and hot. Add almonds, onions, garlic, parsley, salt and pepper, and sauté until almonds are golden (2 to 3 minutes). Add green beans and cook, stirring occasionally, until vegetables are heated through (2 to 3 minutes).

Makes 4-6 servings

Green Beans with Tomato-Mushroom Sauce

2 tablespoons dried wild (boletus)
    mushrooms
½ cup hot water
3 tablespoons olive oil, light-bodied
1 medium onion, minced
2 large cloves garlic, minced
1 (16-ounce) can plum tomatoes,
    seeded, drained and crushed
¼ cup tomato paste
¼ cup chicken broth
2½ teaspoons dried basil
2 teaspoons sugar
salt
ground pepper
2 pounds fresh green beans,
    trimmed and halved diagonally

Makes 6-8 servings

Rinse mushrooms quickly under cold running water; drain well. Crumble into small bowl. Add hot water and let stand for 30 minutes.

Pour oil into medium non-aluminum skillet. Place over high heat until hot. Add onion and brown quickly. Add garlic and cook several seconds; do not burn. Add mushrooms and their liquid, tomatoes, tomato paste, broth and basil; blend well. Boil until thickened, about 5 minutes. Remove from heat and stir in sugar, salt and pepper.

Steam green beans until just crisp-tender, about 10 minutes. Rinse under cold running water to stop cooking process and retain color; drain well.

Transfer beans to medium skillet. Add sauce, tossing to coat and heat through.

Turn into heated shallow bowl and serve immediately.

Side Dishes

Green Corn Tamale Casserole

1 (15-ounce) can cream style corn
1 (4-ounce) can whole green chilies
½ cup Cheddar cheese, grated
⅔ cup yellow cornmeal
¾ cup milk
2 eggs, beaten
2 tablespoons vegetable oil
½ teaspoon salt

Preheat oven to 350 degrees. Grease a 2-quart casserole dish.

In a medium bowl, combine corn, chilies, cheese, cornmeal, milk, eggs, oil and salt. Place in prepared casserole. Bake at 350 degrees for 1 hour.

Makes 6-8 servings

Grilled Green Beans with Warm Gorgonzola Vinaigrette

6 cups boiling water, lightly salted
1 pound green beans (about 5 cups)
3 tablespoons olive oil, divided
¼ cup balsamic vinegar
¼ cup Gorgonzola cheese, crumbled
1 tablespoon brown sugar, firmly packed
1 teaspoon garlic, chopped
1 tablespoon shallots, chopped
½ teaspoon fresh thyme, chopped
½ teaspoon fresh basil, chopped
salt
pepper

In a medium saucepan, bring water to boil. Add the beans and blanch them for 4 minutes. Drain the beans in a colander and immediately immerse in an ice-water bath to stop from cooking; drain.

In a small saucepan, combine 1½ tablespoons of the olive oil, vinegar, Gorgonzola, brown sugar, garlic, shallots, thyme and basil. Warm over medium heat until the ingredients start to combine (about 7 minutes).

Toss the green beans in the remaining 1½ tablespoons olive oil and season lightly with salt and pepper. Quickly grill the beans on a hot grill (about 30 seconds on each side). Toss the beans in the warm vinaigrette and serve immediately.

Makes 4 servings

Hot Bean Casserole

8 slices bacon, cut into pieces
¾ cup brown sugar
½ teaspoon garlic powder
½ cup cider vinegar
1 teaspoon dry mustard
1 teaspoon salt
1 (15-ounce) can kidney beans,
  drained
1 (16-ounce) can green lima beans,
  drained
4 large onions, sliced
1 (15-ounce) can butter beans,
  drained
1 (21-ounce) can baked beans

Preheat oven to 350 degrees.

In a skillet, fry bacon and remove from pan. Sauté onions in bacon grease. Drain grease from pan. Return bacon to onions and add brown sugar, garlic powder, vinegar, mustard and salt. Cover and simmer for 20 minutes.

Place drained beans and the baked beans in a 3-quart casserole. Add the bacon mixture as a topping for the beans. Bake at 350 degrees for 1 hour covered and 30 minutes uncovered.

Makes 12 servings

Szechwan-Style Eggplant

1½ pounds peeled eggplant in
  ¾-inch cubes
1-2 slices peeled ginger, chopped
2 cloves garlic, chopped
2-4 large green onions, chopped
¼ cup peanut oil
1 tablespoon plus 1 teaspoon
  sesame oil
1 teaspoon cornstarch
1-2 teaspoons salt

Sauce:
2 tablespoons dry sherry
2 tablespoons wine vinegar
2 tablespoons sugar
1½ tablespoons soy sauce
½ teaspoon chili paste with garlic

Toss eggplant in colander with salt. Let stand ½ hour. Rinse to remove excess salt, pat dry. In a wok or heavy frying pan with cover, add the peanut oil and 1 tablespoon sesame oil. When hot, throw in ginger, garlic and green onions. After 1 minute add eggplant and toss to coat with oil. Reduce heat to medium, cover until eggplant softens - about 8 minutes. Meanwhile, mix 1 teaspoon sesame oil and the cornstarch together and set aside.

Add the mixed sauce to the softened eggplant and stir for 2 minutes. Then add the sesame oil - cornstarch mixture. Stir until glossy. Serve immediately.

Vary amount of chili paste according to your taste.

Makes 4 to 6 servings

Mushroom Quiche

3 eggs
1½ cups whipping cream
¼ cup grated Swiss cheese
3 tablespoons butter
1 tablespoon butter, cut into tiny
     pieces
2 tablespoons minced shallots
1 pound fresh mushrooms, sliced
1 teaspoon salt
1 teaspoon lemon juice
2 teaspoons Madeira (or port)
1 (9-inch) pie shell, partially baked
     (7 minutes at 400 degrees)

Makes 8 servings

Make certain your pastry shell has been partially baked before beginning. Preheat oven to 375 degrees.

In a heavy-bottomed saucepan, cook shallots in 3 tablespoons of butter for just a few moments. Stir in the mushrooms, salt, lemon juice and Madeira. Cover pan and cook over moderately low heat for 8 minutes. Uncover. Raise heat and boil for several minutes until liquid is completely evaporated and mushrooms are beginning to sauté in their butter.

Beat eggs and cream until smooth. Gradually add the mushrooms to the eggs and cream, stirring gradually. Pour mixture into prepared pastry shell, sprinkle with cheese, dot with butter, and bake for 25 to 30 minutes at 375 degrees.

The pre-cooked pastry shell and the mushroom-egg mixture can be prepared ahead. Keep the mixture cool and add to the pastry shell just before baking.

Pork & Bean Casserole

24 ounces canned pork and beans
1 pound ground beef, browned and
     drained
1 (1-ounce) package onion soup
½ cup water
1 cup ketchup
2 tablespoons prepared mustard
2 tablespoons vinegar
bacon strips, fried crisp for garnish

Mix all ingredients and bake 20 to 30 minutes at 400 degrees. Garnish with crisp fried bacon strips.

Good side dish for picnics, potlucks or barbeques.

Makes 4-6 servings

Parmesan Genoise

4 eggs
¾ cup flour
1 teaspoon sugar
⅛ teaspoon salt
5 turns pepper mill (black pepper)
⅓ cup Parmesan cheese, grated
½ cup chives (or green onions),
   minced
½ cup oliive oil

Makes 8 servings

Preheat oven to 350 degrees. Line 9-inch round cake pan with parchment paper or waxed paper.

Butter and flour pan and paper. Set aside. Beat eggs at high speed for 7 minutes.

While eggs are beating, sift flour, sugar, and salt together in a medium sized bowl. Grind the pepper over the flour. Add Parmesan cheese and chives to the flour, stir gently to mix.

After beating eggs, add olive oil and dry ingredients to eggs. Gently fold together. Pour batter into pan and bake for 25 minutes or until cake has pulled away from the side of the pan.

Cool on rack for 15 minutes. Unmold onto rack to finish cooling. To serve, place on platter and cut into wedges.

Potato Casserole

2 pounds frozen southern-style
   hash browns, thawed
1 (10½-ounce) can cream of
   chicken soup
1 cup sour cream
¼ cup butter, melted
⅓ cup green onion, chopped
2 cups Cheddar cheese, shredded
1 cup corn flakes, crushed
2 tablespoons butter, melted

Makes 10 servings

Preheat oven to 350 degrees. Melt ¼ cup butter in a glass casserole dish. In a large mixing bowl, combine soup, sour cream, onions and cheese. Add thawed potatoes and place in casserole.

Mix 2 tablespoons of melted butter with the corn flakes and spread over the potato mixture as a topping. Bake for 45 to 50 minutes.

For a variation, use shredded hashbrowns and increase soup to 2 cans and sour cream to 2 cups.

Simple Chili Relleno

1 dozen eggs, beaten
1 pound Monterey Jack cheese,
   grated
1 (4-ounce) can roasted chopped
   green chilies

Makes 6 servings

Preheat oven to 350 degrees. Combine ingredients in a greased casserole. Bake at 350 degrees for 30 minutes.

Serve with your favorite salsa.

Potato-Jerusalem Artichoke Gratin

1 garlic clove, peeled and split
1 teaspoon butter
3½ cups heavy cream
⅛ teaspoon nutmeg, freshly grated
2¼ teaspoons salt
⅛ teaspoon fresh white pepper
⅛ teaspoon cayenne pepper
1¾ pounds white potatoes (Russet
   or similar)
8 ounces Jerusalem artichokes (or
   leeks), scrubbed
2½ cups Gruyère cheese
   (8 ounces), grated

Makes 6 servings

Preheat oven to 350 degrees. (If using convection oven, 325 degrees.) Grease a gratin dish with the garlic and butter.

Combine cream, nutmeg, salt, pepper and cayenne in a large bowl. Slice peeled potatoes paper thin with a mandoline or blade of a hand grater. As you work, place slices in bowl with cream. Slice Jerusalem artichokes with mandoline. Pat dry, add to cream. Add cheese and stir gently.

Pour mixture into gratin dish, making sure vegetable slices are lying flat and level. Place gratin dish inside a roasting pan, fill pan ¾ up the sides with hot water to make a bain-marie.

Place in center of oven and bake, uncovered, 2½ hours until gratin is completely set and golden on top. If it begins to brown too soon, cover loosely with foil.

Let stand 15 minutes before serving.

Santos Corn Casserole

½ cup butter
1 green pepper, diced
1 onion, diced
1 (2-ounce) jar pimiento
3 eggs, beaten
1 (15¼-ounce) can corn kernels
    and juice
1 (15-ounce) can creamed corn
1 (8½-ounce) package Jiffy Corn
    Muffin mix
2 cups sour cream
2 cups medium Cheddar cheese,
    shredded

Preheat oven to 350 degrees. Sauté green pepper and onion in butter; add pimiento and put in 9 x 13-inch glass dish.

Mix in eggs. Add cans of corn. Add Jiffy Corn Muffin mix. Spread sour cream on top and sprinkle with cheese. Bake at 350 degrees for 35-40 minutes.

Most of the dish can be made ahead of time. Once the corn is added, refrigerate until ready to serve. When ready to bake, add the remaining items and bake.

Makes 12-15 servings

Potato Cauliflower Purée

1¼ pounds cauliflower (with 2
    inches of stem), broken into
    small pieces
2 medium boiling potatoes, peeled
    and cut into ½ to ¾-inch dice
½ cup whipping cream or more
½ cup Parmesan cheese, grated
3 tablespoons unsalted butter
½ teaspoon white pepper, freshly
    ground
1 large pinch of nutmeg

Steam cauliflower with potatoes until soft, about 12 to 15 minutes. Transfer to food processor. Add cream, cheese, butter, pepper and nutmeg and mix until completely smooth. Add additional cream, in small amounts, to make a thinner puree. Season with salt to taste.

Can be prepared ahead to this point and reheated.

Makes 8 servings

Rice and Noodle Pilaf

2 teaspoons canola oil
¾ cup fine egg noodles, broken into
   pieces
¾ cup long-grain white rice
2 cups defatted reduced-sodium
   chicken stock
2 tablespoons chopped fresh parsely
salt and freshly ground black
   pepper

Heat oil in a heavy saucepan over medium heat. Add noodles and cook, stirring constantly until the noodles are golden brown, 3 to 5 minutes. Add rice and cook, stirring for 1 minute.

Pour in stock and bring to a boil. Reduce heat to low and simmer, covered, until the liquid is absorbed and the rice and noodles are tender, about 20 minutes.

Remove from heat. Stir in parsley and season with salt and pepper.

Makes 4 servings

Zucchini à la Stove Top

1 (10½-ounce) can cream of
   mushroom soup
1 cup sour cream
6 cups sliced zucchini
½ cup chopped onion
1 package Stove Top Stuffing Mix
½ cup butter (1 cube)

Preheat oven to 350 degrees. Mix together soup, sour cream, zucchini and onion. Set aside.

In a separate bowl, melt butter and pour over stuffing mix with seasoning package added. Put one half of stuffing in the bottom of a 9 x 13-inch baking dish. Pour zucchini mixture over and top with the remaining dressing mixture. Bake at 350 degrees tfor 30 minutes.

Makes 10 servings

Spiced Pear and Shallot Relish

½ cup dry red wine
½ cup water
⅓ cup sugar
¼ cup fresh lemon juice
1 cinnamon stick
1 bay leaf
12 whole cloves
¼ teaspoon whole allspice or
    cardamom
3 firm-ripe Bosc pears, peeled,
    cored and cut into ¼-inch cubes
2 shallots, minced

In a saucepan bring wine, water, sugar and lemon juice to a boil, stirring to dissolve sugar. Tie spices in a cheesecloth bag and add to wine syrup. Simmer 5 minutes. Poach pears in syrup at a bare simmer, uncovered, stirring once or twice, 5 minutes, and discard spice bag.

Remove pan from heat and stir in shallots. Strain and reduce liquid if too juicy. Relish may be made 1 week ahead, chilled and covered.

Makes about 2/3 cup

Cranberry Chutney

1⅓ cups apple, peeled and diced
3 cups fresh cranberries
1 cup currants
½ cup walnuts, chopped
2 tablespoons crystallized ginger,
    minced
2 tablespoons lemon juice
2 tablespoons onion, minced
½ cup water
1⅓ cups brown sugar, firmly packed
4 sticks cinnamon

Combine all ingredients in medium saucepan and bring to a boil, uncovered. Reduce heat and simmer for 10 to 15 minutes.

Cool completely to room temperature in pan. Cover and refrigerate at least one day before serving.

Fuji or Gala apples work best. Will keep in the refrigerator for three weeks.

Makes 2-3 cups

Cranberry-Almond Chutney

2 pounds fresh cranberries, washed
1 pound dried apricots, quartered
6 medium red onions, peeled and
chopped
6 medium white onions, peeled and
chopped
3 medium green peppers, chopped
1 pound seedless raisins
2 whole lemons for juice and peel
6 cups white wine vinegar
4 cups sugar
1 teaspoon salt
2 teaspoons ground cloves
½ teaspoon white pepper
2 cups blanched almonds, chopped

Grate the peel of the two lemons and set aside. Squeeze lemons for juice and set aside.

In a large saucepan, combine the cranberries, apricots, red and white onions, green peppers, raisins, vinegar, sugar, salt, cloves and pepper. Add the lemon juice and grated peel.

Bring mixture to a boil, stirring often. Cover and simmer for 30 minutes, stirring often.

Add the almonds and simmer for another 20 minutes, or until the chutney has reached the desired consistency.

If desired, pack in hot, sterilized jars, seal, and process in boiling water bath for 5 minutes.

Suggested variations include: mixing gold raisins with the black variety; substituting white wine vinegar with rice wine vinegar; and substituting sugar with Splenda.

Makes 4 pints

Curried Fruit

2 (17-ounce) cans fruits for salad,
reserve juice
¼ cup brown sugar
2 teaspoons curry powder
2 tablespoons butter

Preheat oven to 350 degrees.

Arrange fruit in a casserole and cover with half of the juice. Sprinkle with brown sugar and curry powder. Dot with butter.

Bake at 350 degrees for 20 minutes.

Serve hot with steak or pork.

Makes 4 servings

Soups

Portland Town - *Henk Pander, Artist (New Theatre Building)*
This mural is done with an anamorphic perspective and is homage to the early days of the Storefront Theatre.

Carl Selin

Pumpkin Soup with Apple Cider

Cory Schreiver - WILDWOOD RESTAURANT - Portland, OR

4 pounds sugar pumpkin (two medium or one large pumpkin)
3 teaspoons salt, divided
1 teaspoon freshly ground black pepper
2 tablespoons unsalted butter
6 cloves garlic chopped
4 carrots, peeled and chopped
3 leeks, (white part only) washed and chopped
2 yellow onions, chopped
1 bulb fennel, trimmed and chopped into ½-inch pieces
4 cups chicken or vegetable stock
4 cups apple cider
¼ cup undiluted orange juice concentrate
2 teaspoons fennel seeds
¼ cup ground cloves
1 tablespoon sherry wine vinegar
1 tablespoon fresh lemon juice
½ teaspoon cayenne pepper
1 unpeeled red apple, cored and chopped into ¼-inch pieces for garnish
½ cup sour cream for garnish

Preheat oven to 375 degrees. Season pumpkin with 1 teaspoon of salt and black pepper. Lightly oil a jellyroll pan and place squash, cut-side down, on pan. Bake for about 45 minutes, or until tender. Let cool completely, scrape out flesh and set aside.

In a heavy 3-quart pan, melt butter over medium heat. Add garlic, carrots, leeks, onions, chopped fennel, and 1 teaspoon of salt. Cover, reduce heat to low and simmer, stirring occasionally, for 25 to 30 minutes, or until vegetables are soft. Mix in cooked pumpkin, stock, apple cider, orange juice concentrate, fennel seeds, and cloves. Simmer, covered, for 20 minutes. Add vinegar, lemon juice, cayenne, and remaining 1 teaspoon of salt. Let cool completely. In a food processor or blender, purée soup in batches if necessary, until smooth. Press through a fine-meshed sieve. Heat soup and add more stock if soup is too thick. To serve, ladle into soup bowls and garnish with chopped apple and a spoon of sour cream.

Makes 6 servings

African Avocado Soup

2 large avocados
4 tablespoons sweetened condensed
    milk, more to taste
cinnamon
1 large banana, sliced (optional)
shredded coconut meat (optional)
raisins, soaked until plump
    (optional)

Mash the avocados until smooth and creamy. Slowly whisk in the sweetened condensed milk, to taste. Sprinkle with cinnamon and stir.

Serve immediately at room temperature to avoid browning of the avocado, accompanied by side dishes of banana, coconut and raisins.

This soup will surprise you. Use your imagination with condiments, but soft textures work best. Enjoy!

Makes 4 servings

Ranch Seasoned Oyster Crackers

1 (14-ounce) bag oyster crackers
½ cup olive or vegetable oil
1 package Hidden Valley Ranch dry
    seasoning mix for salad dressing

Preheat oven to 325 degrees. In a large plastic bag, combine oyster crackers and dry Hidden Valley seasoning. Add oil and mix. Place seasoned oyster crackers on a cookie sheet and bake for 20 minutes at 325 degrees. May be served immediately in soup.

This will help any creamed soup come alive.

Makes 14 servings

Cold Beet Soup with Raspberries

8 beets, peeled and cut into ½-inch
    cubes
⅓ cup shallots, chopped
2 cups chicken stock
2 cups water
1½ cups juice of fresh oranges
    (about 3 large oranges)
grated zest of 2 oranges
2 tablespoons sugar
½ cup raspberries, fresh or frozen
2 tablespoons raspberry vinegar
1 cup crème fraîche
salt
freshly ground pepper
crème fraîche, as garnish

In a medium saucepan, place beets, shallots, chicken stock, and water, and heat to boiling. Reduce heat and simmer uncovered for 30 minutes, or until beets are very tender.

Remove from heat and stir in orange juice and zest. Let cool to room temperature. Add raspberries when beets are cool. Stir in sugar.

Purée soup in a blender or food processor until smooth. Pour into a bowl. Stir in vinegar, crème fraîche, salt and pepper (to taste). Refrigerate soup until cold.

Ladle soup into bowls and garnish each serving with a dollop of crème fraîche.

See page 197 for crème fraîche recipe

May substitute raspberry vinegar with red wine vinegar, or crème fraîche with heavy cream, as desired.

Makes 6 servings

Summer Gazpacho

3 large tomatoes, finely chopped
1 cucumber, finely chopped
1 green pepper, finely chopped
½ medium sweet Spanish onion, minced
3 cups vegetable cocktail juice
1 (10½-ounce) can beef bouillon (undiluted)
1 cup commercially prepared salsa
5 tablespoons white vinegar
¼ cup olive oil
2 teaspoons Worcestershire sauce
1 teaspoon dried basil
1 teaspoon dill weed
½ teaspoon salt
¼ teaspoon Tabasco sauce
1 clove garlic, finely minced or pressed
6 green onions, chopped

Garnishes:
sour cream, croutons, avocado chunks, tortilla chips

Combine all ingredients in a large bowl. Refrigerate at least 4 hours, but best after 24 hours.

Serve very cold with side bowls for the garnishes - sour cream, croutons, avocado chunks, tortilla chips.

If you plan to freeze the soup, do not add the green onions until after it has thawed and is ready to serve.

Makes 6-8 servings

Soups

Architectural Reproductions, a Portland area firm, restored and recreated all the ornamental cast plaster on the interior and all the cast stone on the exterior for the transformation from movie theater to the Arlene Schnitzer Concert Hall. Recreating the exterior stone was a very difficult task. It took over a year to find a way to produce the right texture and color for the stone. Samples were subjected to accelerated weathering tests to determine potential changes in color and other properties. Once the proper materials for the cast stone were chosen, the molds were hand packed and hand finished to produce the correct texture and look. During the renovation, approximately 3,500 square feet of the pink cast stone had to be recreated.

Gazpacho

1 (28-ounce) can whole tomatoes, juice and all
1 medium green pepper, chopped, divided
1 medium cucumber, peeled, seeded and chopped, divided
1 medium white onion, chopped, divided
½ cup garlic flavored croutons
2 tablespoons dry white wine (optional)
2 tablespoons Worcestershire sauce
½ cup chicken broth
2 tablespoons olive oil
2 tablespoons white vinegar
¼ tablespoon black pepper
salt
dash of hot sauce (optional)

Accompany with:
finely chopped onion
finely chopped cucumbers, peeled and seeded
finely chopped green pepper
crème fraîche
croutons

In a blender, place tomatoes with half the amounts of green pepper, cucumber and onion. Add croutons, wine, Worcestershire, olive oil, chicken broth, vinegar and spices. Cover and blend on medium until soup is well mixed, but vegetables are still in small pieces.

Do not overdo the blending as traditional Gazpacho is chunky.

Pour soup into glass bowl. Add remaining chopped vegetables. Cover and refrigerate at least overnight.

Serve cold with suggested garnishes. If the soup appears to be too thick, thin with canned V-8 or tomato juice.

See page 197 for crème fraîche recipe

Makes 6-8 servings

Soups

Chilled Cream of Walla Walla Onion Soup

5 slices lean bacon, cut crosswise in strips
½ cup unsalted butter (1 cube)
3 pounds Walla Walla onions, chopped
8 cloves garlic, minced
4 cups chicken stock
2 cups dry white wine
1 tablespoon fresh thyme
1 bay leaf, whole
1 cup heavy cream, well chilled
1 cup crème fraîche
3 tablespoons fresh lemon juice
⅛ teaspoon Tabasco sauce
⅛ teaspoon nutmeg, freshly grated
2 cups croutons
1 cup scallions, thinly sliced
salt
pepper

In a heavy kettle, cook the bacon over moderate heat, stir occasionally, until it is crisp. Transfer it with a slotted spoon to paper towels to drain.

Add the butter, onions and garlic to the kettle and cook, covered, over low heat, stirring occasionally, for 25 to 30 minutes, or until they are colored lightly and softened. Add chicken broth, wine, thyme, and bay leaf, and simmer the mixture, covered, for 20 minutes.

Discard the bay leaf and in a food processor purée the mixture in batches. Strain the mixture into a bowl, pressing hard on the solids, and chill it, covered, for 3 to 4 hours, or until it is cold.

Whisk in the heavy cream, crème fraîche, lemon juice, Tabasco, nutmeg, salt and pepper (to taste). Serve the soup in chilled bowls, sprinkled with the bacon, croutons, and scallions.

See page 197 for crème fraîche recipe

Makes 8-10 servings

Soups

Winter Vegetable Soup

3 (14-ounce) cans chicken broth
1 pound butternut squash, peeled,
    seeded and cubed
3 carrots, sliced
3 cups water, divided
½ teaspoon salt
¼ teaspoon pepper
½ pound Kielbasa sausage, sliced
1 medium onion, chopped
1 cup any style pasta (optional),
    uncooked
1 (16-ounce) can red kidney beans,
    rinsed
½ pound Swiss chard, chopped

Combine broth, squash, carrots, 2 cups water, salt and pepper in a pot. Cover and bring to a boil.

Cook onion and Kielbasa in a skillet on medium heat for 5 minutes. Transfer to soup pot. Add 1 cup water to skillet and bring to boil; transfer to pot. Cover pot and return to boiling; simmer 5 minutes. Stir in pasta and beans. Return to boil, cover and boil 6 minutes. Stir in Swiss chard; simmer, uncovered, 2 to 3 minutes until chard is tender.

Great tasting soup that even the kids will love!

Makes 6 servings

Carl Selin

Muse, Gaze, Mirror, Maze *- Linda Ethier, Artist (New Theatre Building)*
The fireplace is made of various forms of glass and reflects the ever-changing scene before it. Unlike other pieces of fine art, you are encouraged to touch this one.

Soups

Squash Chili

2 tablespoons olive oil
2 medium onions, diced
2 tablespoons garlic, chopped
2 medium red peppers, diced
3 tablespoons chili powder
2 tablespoons cumin
1½ tablespoons dried oregano
¼ teaspoon allspice
1 pinch red pepper flakes
2 (28-ounce) cans tomatoes,
    chopped with juices
½ cup dry red wine
2 butternut squash, diced in ½-inch
    pieces
zest of 1 orange, finely grated
2 (16-ounce) cans kidney beans,
    drained
salt
pepper
2 tablespoons cilantro, chopped
2 tablespoons parsley, chopped
3 green onions, chopped for garnish

Heat oil in large heavy pot over medium-low heat. Add onions, garlic and peppers. Cook for 10 minutes or until vegetables have wilted. Add chili powder, cumin, oregano, allspice, pepper flakes and cook 1 minute longer.

Stir in tomatoes, wine, squash, zest, salt and pepper. Bring to boil, reduce heat to medium-low and simmer uncovered for 20 minutes or until squash is tender. Adjust seasoning to taste. Fold in beans and simmer 10 minutes.

Just before serving, stir in cilantro and parsley. Serve garnished with green onions.

Makes 6-8 servings

Turkey Chili

2 (15½-ounce) cans black beans
2 (15½-ounce) cans white beans
2 (15½-ounce) cans small red beans
2 (15½-ounce) cans tomato sauce
2 (15½-ounce) cans stewed or
    Italian tomatoes
1 cup salsa (to taste)
1 tablespoon basil
1 tablespoon tarragon
½ tablespoon ground cumin
½ tablespoon chili powder
1 pinch crushed red pepper flakes
1 cup diced carrots
4 stalks celery, diced
1 large yellow or white onion, diced
2 green peppers, diced
4 cloves (or more) minced garlic
1 pound ground turkey

Open all cans and drain juice. Combine in a large pot. Add salsa and all seasonings. Heat over medium heat for 30 minutes so all seasonings get absorbed. Remove from heat.

In a large fry pan, sauté carrots, celery, onion, peppers and garlic to desired consistency. Add cooked vegetables to bean mixture. Cook ground turkey with a little oil in large fry pan, breaking meat into small pieces. Add cooked turkey to bean mixture. Cook over medium-low heat until desired consistency is reached.

Makes 6-8 servings

The Choir Loft of the Arlene Schnitzer Concert Hall has an interesting history. As a movie house, the original stage area was not large enough to have a large symphony orchestra and a full chorus perform at the same time. The problem was solved by cutting a hole in the backstage wall into the Studio Building next door on Salmon Street. The Choir Loft can comfortably accommodate 75 people.

Soups

Borscht with Basil and Sour Cream

1 tablespoon olive oil
1 small onion, chopped coarsely
1 teaspoon sugar
2 tablespoons red wine vinegar
1 carrot, peeled and chopped
    coarsely
1 medium potato, peeled and
    chopped coarsely
3 celery stalks, chopped coarsely
3 large beets, peeled and chopped
    (about 1¼ pounds)
5 cups chicken stock
⅓ cup fresh or frozen peas
salt
3 tablespoons basil, minced
½ cup sour cream

Heat oil in a large saucepan; add onion and sugar; sauté until onion softens. Add vinegar and cook until vinegar is evaporated. Add carrot, potato, celery, beets and chicken stock; bring to a boil.

Cover and simmer 20 to 30 minutes, or until vegetables are tender. Add peas and cook 2 minutes longer. Season with salt to taste. Purée with food processor. Refrigerate up to three days. Serve warm or chilled. Garnish with basil and a dollop of sour cream.

The soup improves by chilling and melding flavors for a day before serving.

May substitute basil with dill, as desired.

Makes 4-6 servings

Boston Clam Chowder

1½ pints shucked clams
2 (7-ounce) cans minced clams
3 cups water
¼ cup salt pork, diced
1 medium onion, chopped
3 medium potatoes, peeled and
    cubed
2 tablespoons butter
2 cups half and half
3 teaspoons salt
¼ teaspoon pepper

Drain and chop the clams, and set aside. Combine clam liquid with water, and set aside.

In saucepan, lightly brown salt pork and onion. Add clam liquid and potatoes, and cook until potatoes are tender, about 15 minutes.

Stir in butter, half and half, salt, pepper and clams. Heat, but do not boil.

May substitute salt pork with bacon, as desired.

Makes 6 servings

Broccoli Soup

4 cups broccoli, cooked and
    chopped
½ medium onion, chopped
2 cups vegetable broth
¾ cup half and half
⅓ cup white wine (optional)
Sprigs of cilantro or parsley for
    garnish (optional)
Sour cream or whipped tofu for
    garnish (optional)

In a saucepan, combine broccoli, onion, wine and broth. Heat to boiling. Remove from heat and stir in half and half.

Pour soup into food processor. Process until the broccoli is puréed. Reheat soup before serving.

Serve with Pumpkin Soup (see page 86) for a special presentation. When ladeling the soups into the soup plate, place the Broccoli soup on one side and the Pumpkin soup on the other. May substitute vegetable broth with chicken broth, half and half with Rice Dream, or white wine with brandy, as desired.

Makes 2-4 servings

Carl Selin

An Usher Call Box (Arlene Schnitzer Concert Hall)

The hall has two such boxes on display; one on the main floor and another on the mezzanine level. They are no longer used for their original purpose.

Originally, both call boxes were connected to wall units located at the entrances to the seating area. By using light panels, these boxes indicated the seating availability in the movie theater, enabling a head usher to direct late arriving patrons to sections where an usher could seat them. The call boxes were offered at the 1975 auction but were so blackened and in such poor condition that they went unsold. The opening bid was only $2.00, but no bidders.

Cheddar Cheese and Vegetable Soup

1 cup unsalted butter (2 cubes)
1 large onion, minced
1 cup celery, minced
1 cup carrots, minced
⅔ cup flour
6 cups chicken stock
1 cup whipping cream
½ pound sharp Cheddar cheese, grated
salt
ground white pepper
croutons, for garnish
chopped parsley, for garnish

In a large saucepan, melt butter over low heat. Add onion, celery and carrots and sauté for 15 minutes, or until tender but not brown. Add flour and cook roux, stirring constantly. Add chicken stock, whisking into roux until smooth. Cool slightly. Transfer to food processor and purée until creamy. Return to saucepan and gradually add cream and cheese. Stir over medium heat until cheese has melted. Season with salt and pepper to taste. Serve garnished with croutons and parsley.

Makes 6-8 servings

Chicken Peanut Soup

1 large onion, chopped
1 large sweet red bell pepper, chopped
2 cloves garlic, mashed
1 tablespoon salad oil
1 tablespoon sesame oil
4 cups chicken broth
1 (14-ounce) can diced tomatoes in juice
1 teaspoon curry powder
¼ teaspoon black pepper
⅛ teaspoon ground red pepper
½ teaspoon salt
¼ cup raw rice
1 cup cooked chicken, chopped
¼ cup peanut butter
chopped peanuts, for garnish

Sauté the onion, pepper and garlic in the salad and sesame oil, until the onion is tender and translucent, but not browned. Add the chicken broth, tomatoes and spices. Simmer uncovered for 30 to 45 minutes.

Add the rice and cook over low heat, covered, about 20 minutes, or until the rice is tender. Add chicken and heat through. Add peanut butter and whisk until the peanut butter is dissolved. Bring back to a simmer before serving. Serve hot with a sprinkling of peanuts as a garnish.

Use chunky or creamy peanut butter, as desired. Add additional chicken broth or water to thin, if needed.

Makes 4-6 servings

Soups

Savory Pumpkin Soup

3 cups fresh pumpkin or butternut
    squash
2 tablespoons olive oil
2 small leeks, sliced thinly
1 clove garlic, minced
2 carrots, sliced thinly
3 cups vegetable stock or chicken
    stock
1 cup Rice Dream or half and half
2 teaspoons curry powder
1 teaspoon cumin to taste
fresh grated nutmeg

Preheat oven to 350 degrees. Prepare squash for baking. Poke several holes in skin with a knife. Bake at 350 degrees for about 45 minutes or until tender when pierced with a knife. Allow to cool. Slice in half. Remove seeds and fiber and discard. Scrape flesh from skin.

In a saucepan, sauté leeks, garlic and carrots in olive oil. Sprinkle with curry powder and cumin. Add broth and pumpkin and stir. Simmer on low heat for about 15 or 20 minutes.

Purée soup mixture in a food processor. Return to saucepan and add Rice Dream (or half and half). Blend. Reheat soup before serving.

See Broccoli soup recipe on page 84.

Makes 4-6 servings

Easy Squash Soup

3 yellow zucchini, chopped (about
    ¾ pounds)
1 medium onion, chopped
butter (for browning onions)
1 small clove garlic, chopped
1 (14½-ounce) can chicken stock
pinch red pepper flakes (to taste)
pinch salt
milk
Cheddar cheese, grated

In large saucepan, brown onion in butter until it is softened. Add garlic, squash, and chicken stock, and simmer until squash is very tender. Add red pepper flakes and salt, to taste.

Remove from heat and mash mixture in pan. Add milk and cheese to thicken soup to desired consistency.

May substitute milk with cream for a richer flavor. May substitute zucchini with crooked neck squash, or Velveeta for Cheddar as desired.

Makes 2-4 servings

French Country Vegetable Soup

4 tablespoons butter
2 leeks, washed and sliced
2 celery stalks, sliced
1 clove garlic, minced
1 teaspoon fresh thyme, chopped
1 teaspoon summer savory
    (optional)
1 (48-ounce) can chicken stock
1 medium onion, chopped
2 medium Yukon Gold potatoes,
    chopped
1 medium turnip, chopped
1 parsnip, chopped
⅓ head cauliflower, chopped
4 carrots, sliced
salt
freshly ground white pepper
crème fraîche

In a medium stock pot, sauté leeks, celery, garlic and herbs in butter for 10 to 15 minutes, or until tender.

Add chicken stock and vegetables to sautéed vegetables. Simmer for 20 to 30 minutes or until all vegetables are very tender. Remove from heat and purée in a food processor. Return vegetable purée to pot and add a small amount of crème fraîche. If soup is too thick, thin with additional chicken stock or milk.

May substitute crème fraîche with sour cream or milk, as desired.

See page 197 for crème fraîche recipe.

Makes 6-8 servings

Mount Vernon Colonial Peanut and Chestnut Soup

1 medium onion, finely chopped
¼ cup margarine
1 tablespoon flour
2 quarts chicken broth
1 cup creamy peanut butter
½ cup unsalted peanuts, chopped
1 tablespoon Worcestershire sauce
½ cup water chestnuts, chopped

Sauté onion in margarine. Stir in flour to make a roux. Once all the flour is absorbed and texture is very smooth, add chicken broth and bring to a boil. Remove from heat and strain. Add peanut butter, Worcestershire sauce and stir. Garnish with chopped peanuts and water chestnuts.

For an accompaniment, see Cracker Bread recipe on page 39.

Makes 8-10 servings

Parsnip and Apple Soup

Soup:
1 large boiling potato, peeled and
    diced
2 parsnips (about ½ pound), peeled
    and chopped fine
3 shallots, chopped fine (about ¼
    cup)
1 leek (white and pale green
    part only), trimmed, halved
    lengthwise, washed well, and
    chopped fine
2 tablespoons chopped fresh parsley
¼ cup unsalted butter
2-2½ cups chicken broth
1 cup apple cider (or juice)
½ cup heavy cream
salt and pepper

Parsnip:
vegetable oil for deep-frying parsnip
1 parsnip, peeled and cut into thin
    strips

Soup:
In a heavy kettle cook potato, parsnips, shallots, leek and parsley in butter over moderate heat, stirring, until leek is softened, about 12 minutes. Add broth and simmer, covered, 20 minutes, or until vegetables are very soft. In a blender purée mixture in batches and transfer to a large saucepan. Stir in cider or juice, cream, and salt and pepper to taste. Cook over moderately high heat, stirring occasionally, until heated through. Keep soup warm.

Fried Parsnips:
In a heavy saucepan heat 1 inch oil to 360 degrees. Fry parsnip strips in batches until golden brown, transferring with a slotted spoon to paper towels to drain. Season fried parsnip with salt. Serve soup topped with fried parsnip.

Makes 6 servings

Chicken Velvet Soup

6 tablespoons butter
⅓ cup flour
1 cup skim milk
3 cups fat-free chicken broth
1 cup cooked chicken, finely
    chopped
½ teaspoon basil
½ teaspoon salt
1 tablespoon Worcestershire sauce

Melt butter in saucepan. Blend in flour. Over medium heat, gradually stir in milk and chicken broth until mixture thickens or just comes to a boil.

Add chicken, basil, salt and Worcestershire sauce, and continue to cook on low heat until all ingredients are heated.

Makes 4 servings

Red Curry Carrot Soup

1 tablespoon canola oil
6 large carrots, peeled (4 thickly
    sliced and 2 cut into fine
    matchsticks)
2 thin slices peeled fresh ginger
1 medium white onion, finely
    chopped
4 cups chicken stock or canned low-
    sodium broth
2 cups water
⅓ cup unsweetened coconut milk
¾ teaspoon red curry paste
salt
freshly ground pepper
1 scallion, cut into matchsticks
1 tablespoon cilantro leaves
1 tablespoon finely chopped basil

Heat oil in a large saucepan. Add sliced carrots and ginger and cook over moderately high heat, stirring, until carrots are crisp-tender and lightly browned, 6 to 7 minutes. Add onion and cook until softened but not browned, about 2 minutes.

Add chicken stock, water, coconut milk and curry paste to saucepan and bring to a boil. Simmer over moderate heat until carrots are tender, about 25 minutes. Strain cooking liquid into another saucepan, reserving the solids; discard ginger. Transfer carrots to a blender and purée with 1 cup of cooking liquid until very smooth. Return purée to cooking liquid, add the carrot matchsticks and cook until tender, about 3 minutes. Season with salt and pepper. Ladle soup into bowls, sprinkle with scallion, cilantro and basil and serve.

The soup may be refrigerated for up to 1 day.

Makes 4 servings

Soups

Stage Styles

Cabaret	*Conventional stage but patrons seated at table and chairs.*
Promenade	*Both stage and patron seating are on the same level.*
Theater in the Round	*Audience is seated around the performance area, on all four sides.*
Thrust Stage	*Stage is built-out into the auditorium (seating is on three sides of the stage).*

Butternut Squash and Garlic Soup

1 large butternut squash
 (approximately 4 pounds)
1 medium head garlic cloves
 separated but unpeeled
¼ cup olive oil, divided
¼ cup water
2 medium onions, finely chopped
4 cups chicken stock
½ teaspoon salt
½ teaspoon white pepper
1 teaspoon Chipotle chilies in
 adobo sauce, more to taste, finely
 chopped
½ cup sour cream

Makes 8 servings

Preheat oven to 325 degrees. Slice squash in half lengthwise and remove pulp and seeds with a spoon. Carefully slice peel off and then cut into 3-inch thick slices. In a medium roasting pan, combine squash and unpeeled garlic cloves. Drizzle with 2 tablespoons olive oil and mix until well coated. Pour water over vegetables. Roast in middle of oven for about 1 hour or until squash and garlic cloves are soft and slightly caramelized. (This will depend on how thick squash slices are.) Cool slightly.

While squash is roasting, heat remaining 2 tablespoons olive oil in a medium skillet on medium heat. Add onions and sauté slowly for about 20 minutes or until slightly caramelized. Reserve.

Spoon roasted squash into food processor fitted with metal blade. Squeeze pointed end of each garlic clove into squash. Add caramelized onions and purée mixture in food processor for 1 minute or until very smooth.

Pour squash into a large saucepan. Add chicken stock, salt and pepper to squash and bring to a simmer. Taste for seasoning.

In a small bowl combine sour cream with Chipotle sauce (more to taste) and blend well. When ready to serve, ladle soup into individual soup bowls or mugs and swirl in a teaspoon of the chipotle chili and sour cream mixture.

Serve immediately.

Split Pea Soup with Tomatoes

3 cups dry green split peas
1 bay leaf
2 teaspoons salt
7 cups water
2 tablespoons oil
1 cup minced onion
3 cloves garlic, crushed
1 cup minced celery
2 cups sliced carrots
1 small potato, thinly sliced
¼ cup dry red wine
¼ teaspoon dry mustard
¼ teaspoon thyme
a few drops of sesame oil
3 tablespoons vinegar
1 cup chopped tomatoes
¼ cup chopped parsley

In a large stock pot, simmer split peas, bay leaf, salt and water for 3 to 4 hours. Remove bay leaf at end of cooking time.

About 25 minutes before soup base is done cooking, heat oil in pan. Sauté onion, garlic, celery, carrots and potato. If necessary, add a small amount of water to help steam vegetables. Add vegetables to soup pot and continue cooking.

About 15 minutes before serving, add wine, dry mustard, thyme and sesame oil to pot. Continue to simmer. Add vinegar, tomatoes and parsley just before serving.

Makes 4-6 servings

Carl Selin

The Main Staircase (Arlene Schnitzer Concert Hall)

*Back in 1928, the old Publix Movie Theatre's interior design was described as Northern Italian Rococo Revival, and ornate beyond all reason. The décor included five different kinds of marble and life-sized statues, including **Surprise.** (see page 136 for photo).*

Roasted Garlic Soup

4 large heads of garlic
2 tablespoons olive oil
1 cup onion, diced (one medium)
3 cups potato, peeled and diced (3 large potatoes)
4 cups vegetable broth
2 bay leaves
2 cups dairy-free creamer (instead of heavy cream)
seasonings to taste

Roast garlic in oven or in microwave. Separate garlic cloves and peel. Heat oil in a large soup pot and sauté onion and garlic together for 5 minutes over medium heat. Do not brown.

Add potatoes, broth and bay leaves. Simmer for 20 to 30 minutes or until potatoes are soft. Remove bay leaves. Purée the soup. Add creamer and seasoning to taste.

Reheat gently (do not boil). Serve with croutons.

Makes 4 servings

Savory Cheese Soup

3 (14½-ounce) cans chicken broth
1 small onion, chopped
1 large carrot, chopped
1 stalk celery, chopped
¼ cup sweet red pepper, chopped
2 tablespoons butter or margarine
1 teaspoon salt
½ teaspoon pepper
⅓ cup flour
⅓ cup cold water
1 (8-ounce) package cream cheese, cubed and softened
2 cups Cheddar cheese, shredded
1 (12-ounce) can beer (optional)

In a slow cooker, combine chicken broth, onion, carrot, celery, red pepper, butter, salt and pepper. Cover and cook on low for 7 to 8 hours or until vegetables are well cooked and soft. Combine flour and water until smooth; stir into soup. Cover and cook on high 30 minutes until soup is thickened. Stir in cheeses until blended. Stir in beer, if desired. Cover and cook through.

Serve with your choice of toppings, such as croutons, crumbled bacon, or sliced green onions.

Makes 6 servings

Soups

Watercress Soup

4 (14-ounce) cans chicken broth
3 medium onions, chopped
2 medium white or red potatoes,
    peeled and cut into 1-inch cubes
2 tablespoons butter
1 bunch watercress
milk to thin the soup before serving
plain yogurt
salt
pepper

In a heavy-bottomed pan, melt butter and sauté onions over medium heat until tender but not browned . Add chicken stock and potatoes. Cover and simmer for 25 minutes or until potatoes are very tender. Add salt and pepper to taste. Pull watercress leaves off stems. Immerse watercress leaves in boiling water, drain at once, and immerse in ice water just long enough to chill; drain again. This will give the watercress a deep green color. Purée broth mixture and watercress using a blender or food processor. Return to pan and heat through. May prepare up to this point a day ahead. Thin to the right consistency with milk and a little yogurt when ready to serve. Whisk until smooth.

Makes 6 servings

Broccoli Vegetable Soup

4 slices bacon, cut in 1-inch pieces
12 ounces mushrooms, sliced
1 cup onion, chopped
1 tablespoon garlic, minced
1 tablespoon fresh parsley, minced
3 (14½-ounce) cans chicken broth
3 cups broccoli florets
1 (14½-ounce) can whole tomatoes
½ teaspoon dried thyme
½ teaspoon salt
¼ teaspoon pepper
2 tablespoons freshly grated
    Parmesan cheese
1 cup fresh spinach, chopped

In a stainless steel or enameled kettle, cook bacon over moderate heat until crisp. Add mushrooms, onion, garlic and parsley. Cook mixture, stirring, for 5 minutes, or until onion is translucent. Add chicken broth, broccoli florets, tomatoes (which have been chopped), dried thyme, salt and pepper, and cook mixture over moderately low heat for 25 minutes. Add spinach and Parmesan cheese, and cook, stirring, for 5 minutes. Ladle soup into heated bowls and serve.

Makes 8-10 servings

Chicken Tortellini Soup

2 (50-ounce) cans chicken broth
1 (9-ounce) package tortellini
1 pound boneless, skinless chicken
    breast, cut in 1-inch pieces
½ pound mushrooms, sliced
1 cup cooked rice
2 teaspoons dried tarragon
red pepper flakes, to taste (optional)
1 red bell pepper, cut in chunks
1 pound spinach leaves, chopped
grated fresh Parmesan cheese

In large saucepan, bring broth to a boil. Add tortellini and cook according to directions, just until tender. Add chicken, mushrooms, rice and tarragon and return to boil.

Reduce heat and cover; simmer until chicken pieces are no longer pink. Add red pepper flakes, red bell pepper, and spinach. Heat through, but avoid overcooking so as to retain color and texture.

Sprinkle with cheese and offer additional cheese to taste.

Makes 10-12 servings

Curried Seafood Chowder

1 (10½-ounce) can cream of
    mushroom soup
1 cup milk
1 large potato, baked and diced
½ medium onion, chopped
1 clove garlic, minced
1 (15¼-ounce) can whole kernel
    corn, drained
1 (4-ounce) can sliced mushrooms
1 (3¾-ounce) tin oysters
1 (3¾-ounce) tin smoked mussels
1 (3¾-ounce) tin clams
2 teaspoons curry powder, to taste
1 teaspoon black pepper, to taste
fresh chives, chopped

Partially drain all seafood. In medium large pan, combine soup with milk. Slowly heat to simmering. In small skillet, sauté the onion and garlic for 10 to 15 minutes, or until soft. Add to soup mixture.

When soup is heated through, add potatoes, corn, mushrooms, oysters, mussels, clams, curry powder and pepper. Stir in chives just before serving.

May substitute milk with half milk and half water, if desired.

Makes 4-6 servings

Easy Taco Soup

1 pound ground beef
2 (14½-ounce) cans tomatoes, with
　　liquid
2 (15-ounce) cans hominy, with
　　liquid
2 (16-ounce) cans kidney beans,
　　with liquid
1 package taco seasoning mix
1 package ranch-style dressing mix

In a large saucepan, brown beef, then drain the fat. Add tomatoes, hominy, kidney beans, taco seasoning and ranch-style dressing; mix well and cook until hot. Thin with water if soup is too thick.

This soup is even better the next day. May substitute beef with turkey, as desired.

Makes 6 servings

Hamburger Barley Soup

1½ pounds ground beef
6 cups water
3 beef bouillon cubes
2 cups carrots, sliced
1½ cups onion, chopped
1 (28-ounce) can tomatoes,
　　chopped
2 bay leaves
1½ cups celery, sliced
½ cup green pepper, diced
⅓ cup pearl barley
salt
pepper
¼ cup ketchup
1 (8-ounce) can tomato sauce

In large saucepan, brown ground beef; drain fat.

Add remaining ingredients and bring to a boil. Reduce heat and simmer for 1 hour, or until the barley is tender.

Makes 6-8 servings

Mathew's Bar is located on the 2nd level of the New Theatre Building and is open for pre-show and intermission refreshments for patrons attending a performance in the Newmark Theatre.

Smoked Sausage Soup with Potatoes and Kale

1 pound dried kidney beans
10 cups water
2 tablespoons olive oil
1½ pounds smoked linguiça or
    smoked kielbasa sausage
2 large onions, chopped
¾ pound red potatoes
1 large bunch kale, tender leaves
    coarsely chopped
2 tablespoons (or more) red wine
    vinegar
salt
freshly ground pepper
1 bay leaf, whole

Place beans in a heavy large pot. Add water and soak overnight. Add bay leaf. Cook beans in soaking liquid over medium heat until tender, stirring occasionally, about one hour.

Heat oil in a heavy large skillet over medium heat. Add sausage and cook until just beginning to brown, stirring occasionally, about 10 minutes. Add sausage to beans, using a slotted spoon; reserve drippings in skillet. Add onions to skillet and cook over medium heat until softened, stirring occasionally, about 10 minutes. Add onions and potatoes to beans and simmer until potatoes are tender, about 20 minutes.

Can be prepared 1 day ahead up to this point. Cool, cover and refrigerate.

Bring soup to a simmer before continuing with recipe.

Add kale and vinegar to soup and simmer 15 minutes, stirring occasionally.

Season with salt, pepper and more vinegar. Serve hot.

Makes 6 servings

Sweet Potato Salmon Chowder

2 medium red onions, diced
4 stalks celery, diced
4 carrots, diced
1 green pepper, diced
1 large sweet potato, peeled and
    diced
1 bunch cilantro, chopped
1 tablespoon garlic, roasted and
    diced
1 tablespoon oregano, to taste
1 tablespoon rosemary, to taste
1 tablespoon thyme, to taste
1 tablespoon basil, to taste
1 (8-ounce) can tomato paste
1 (8-ounce) can tomatoes and
    chilies
¼ cup olive oil plus a little more if
    needed
1 (8-ounce) can diced tomatoes
1 (32-ounce) can crushed tomatoes
1 (6-ounce) can tuna in water --
    drained and flaked
2 (6-ounce) cans salmon -- drained,
    deboned and flaked
½ cup balsamic vinegar
½ cup soy sauce
3 cups okra (frozen is fine)

Cover bottom of Dutch oven with olive oil. Sauté red onion, celery, carrots, green pepper, sweet potato. Add cilantro and garlic. Add your choice of green herbs (oregano, thyme, basil, rosemary) to taste.

Add tomato and chilies, diced tomatoes and crushed tomatoes to the vegetable mixture. Dilute the tomato paste with enough water to form a medium sauce consistency. Add to the pot. Add tuna and salmon to the pot.

Stir in the balsamic vinegar and soy sauce. Add okra. Allow to simmer until all ingredients are tender.

May add gumbo filé, turkey sausage, other vegetables, chili powder, cumin or hot peppers.

Makes 4-6 servings

Split Pea Soup

1 pound dry split peas, well washed
1 or 2 ham hocks
2 quarts water
1 onion stuck with 2 - 3 cloves
1 rib celery, chopped
1 or 2 carrots, chopped
2 garlic cloves
1 bay leaf
salt to taste

Combine washed peas, ham hock, water, vegetables, garlic and bay leaf in a soup pot. Do not include salt. Bring to a boil. Cover pot tightly, reduce heat, and cook for 2 to 3 hours - stirring occasionally.

Remove ham bone. Cut off any bits of meat and cut them into small dice. Strain soup. Return to pot with ham bits. If necessary, dilute with heavy cream, broth or water. Add salt to taste.

Serve it hot with thinly sliced sausages, crisp croutons or bits of bacon.

Makes 8 servings

Super Salmon Soup

2 (14½-ounce) cans Italian
    seasoned stewed tomatoes
2 cups stock (vegetable, fish or
    chicken) or water
2 cups vegetables cut into bite-sized
    pieces
1 tablespoon oregano
2 tablespoons lemon juice
1 teaspoon chopped garlic
1 pound salmon fillet, cubed into
    1-inch pieces
Italian parsley for garnish
Suggested vegetables: broccoli,
    green beans, asparagus, peppers,
    mushrooms or onions

Mix tomatoes, stock, vegetables and oregano in a pot and simmer for 30 minutes or until vegetables are cooked.

Just before serving, add garlic, lemon juice and salmon. Cook for 2 to 4 minutes taking care not to overcook. Serve with croutons or crackers.

Substitute any firm fish, shellfish, meat or sausage for the salmon.

Makes 4-6 servings

Soups

Wild Rice and Ham Soup

5½ cups water, divided
¾ cup wild rice
½ cup flour
¾ cup chopped onion
3 cloves garlic, minced
¼ cup margarine
4 cubes chicken bouillon
1½ cups potato, cubed
¾ cup carrots, cut up
½ teaspoon thyme
½ teaspoon nutmeg
¼ teaspoon pepper
1 bay leaf
1 (15¼-ounce) can whole kernel
    corn, undrained
2 cups half and half
3 cups ham, cubed
2 tablespoons parsley, chopped

Makes 6-8 servings

Combine 1½ cups water and wild rice. Bring to boil, cover, cook on low heat for 35 minutes. Do not drain. Set aside.

While wild rice is cooking, melt margarine, sauté onions and garlic until tender. Stir in flour and cook 1 minute. Gradually stir in 4 cups water and chicken bouillon. Add potatoes, carrots, thyme, nutmeg, pepper and bay leaf. Cook for 30 minutes, until thick. Add corn, cover and simmer 20 minutes.

Stir in half and half, ham and wild rice. Cook until heated. Remove bay leaf. Garnish with parsley.

On March 8, 1928, opening night for the Portland Publix Theatre, patrons enjoyed orchestra music, a live revue, a newsreel, an organ recital, and the first run comedy, Feel My Pulse - all for 60 cents. The usual ticket price after the opening is thought to have been about 25 cents.

Carl Selin

*A Crystal Chandelier
(Arlene Schnitzer Concert Hall)
All three chandeliers have been
restored to their former glory.*

Taco Soup

1 pound ground beef, browned and
    drained of fat
½ cup onion, chopped
2 cans stewed tomatoes
2 cans kidney beans
3 cups water
1 packet dry taco seasoning mix
1 (8-ounce) can tomato sauce

Toppings:
grated cheddar cheese
sour cream
sliced avocado
tortilla chips
chopped jalapeño peppers
chopped green onions
chopped black olives

Mix ground beef, onion, tomatoes, beans, water, taco seasoning and tomato sauce and simmer until the beans are soft.

Serve in bowls and top with toppings of your choice.

Variations:
1. Add one can of corn.
2. Use black, ranch or pinto beans instead of or in addition to kidney beans.
3. Use canned diced tomatoes or coarsely chopped canned whole tomatoes instead of stewed tomatoes.
4. Add one can chopped green chilies.

Makes 6 servings

The Newmark Theatre is Edwardian in style and offers continental seating (no middle aisle). The horseshoe balconies curve close to the stage, which creates an intimate space, even with three seating levels. Cherry paneling, teal velour seats, shining brass railings and rich blue walls create a sense of luxury.

Soups

Salads

Carl Selin

The Newmark Theatre (New Theatre Building)
This 900-seat theater is modeled after a typical Broadway venue.

Warm Hood River Asparagus with Dungeness Crab

PASCAL SAUTON - CARAFE RESTAURANT - PORTLAND, OR

1 bunch Hood River asparagus,
    trimmed and peeled
1 tablespoon extra virgin olive oil
1 cup Dungeness crabmeat
4 duck eggs
2 tablespoons white wine vinegar
1 tablespoon chives, finely minced
sea salt
black pepper

Vinaigrette:
2 tablespoons aged sherry vinegar
6 tablespoons walnut oil
1 teaspoon truffle oil
1 tablespoon chopped Oregon
    truffles
Fleur de Sel
black pepper

For the vinaigrette, combine sherry vinegar, walnut oil, truffle oil, Oregon truffles, Fleur de Sel and black pepper. Whisk vigorously to blend well together. Set aside.

Blanch the asparagus in salted boiling water until bright in color and still crunchy (1 to 2 minutes). Once done, cool in an ice bath, and drain on paper towels and lightly brush with olive oil.

For the poached ducks eggs, bring two quarts of water to a boil in a saucepan with the vinegar. Turn the heat down and keep on a simmer. Crack the eggs and add in the water. Cook until the white is firm but the yolk still runny.

While the eggs are cooking, warm the asparagus lightly under the broiler or in a hot oven.

Place the asparagus on 4 plates and place ¼ cup of crabmeat on top of each serving. When the eggs are done, remove from water with a slotted spoon and place on top of the crabmeat. Sprinkle a little bit of Fleur de Sel on top and some crushed black peppercorns. Drizzle with the vinaigrette and garnish with the chives.

Marinated Tomato Salad with Fennel, Carrots and Arugula

Cory Schreiver - WILDWOOD RESTAURANT - Portland, OR

Vinaigrette:
¼ cup extra virgin olive oil
2 tablespoons red wine vinegar
1 teaspoon coriander seeds, toasted
    and ground or cracked with the
    broad side of a knife
¼ cup picked whole cilantro leaves

Salad:
6 ripe tomatoes of any variety cut in
    half, core removed and cut into
    sixths or eighths, depending on
    their size
1 fennel bulb, trimmed, cut in half,
    core removed and thinly sliced
    crosswise
1 small red onion, peeled and thinly
    sliced crosswise
1 carrot, peeled and thinly sliced at
    an angle
1 teaspoon salt
½ teaspoon freshly ground black
    pepper
8 ounces young tender arugula
    leaves

Vinaigrette:
In a small bowl, whisk together the oil, vinegar, cilantro leaves and coriander seeds. Set vinaigrette aside.

Salad:
In a medium bowl, combine the sliced tomatoes, sliced fennel, red onion, and carrot. Toss with the vinaigrette and marinate for one hour. Just before serving, stir in the arugula, salt and pepper. Spoon onto plates or bowls and serve.

"Every March, I subscribe to Gathering Together Farm Box, a community supported agriculture (CSA) project. The money goes to the farmers just when they need it most as they start up the farm for another season of planting. The ingredients in this salad all arrive in splendid color and peak flavor in mid-summer. They are great when tossed together raw in a salad. I recommend the Gathering Together Farm Box to anyone looking for a constant supply of summer produce and who enjoys the surprise of finding something different each week. Let the farmer do the shopping for you!"--Cory Shriver

Salads

A Healthier Spinach Salad

Salad:
1 (16-ounce) bag washed spinach
4 green onions, chopped (optional)
5 slices turkey bacon, cooked and
   crumbled
2-4 hard-boiled eggs, sliced or
   chopped

Dressing:
2 tablespoons red wine (or
   seasoned) vinegar
1 tablespoon lemon juice
1 teaspoon sugar
½ teaspoon salt
pepper
¼ cup olive oil

Dressing:
Whisk together the red wine vinegar, lemon juice, sugar, salt and pepper and olive oil.

Salad:
Prepare greens. Pour dressing over spinach and toss. Garnish with green onions, turkey bacon and egg just before serving.

Asian Chicken Salad

Salad:
½ head romaine lettuce
½ chicken breast
1 (3-ounce) package chicken-
   flavored ramen noodles
2 tablespoons almonds, sliced
1 tablespoon butter
1 (11-ounce) can Mandarin
   oranges, drained and reserve
   juice

Dressing:
2 tablespoons Mandarin orange
   juice
2 tablespoons rice wine vinegar
2 tablespoons pure sesame oil

Bake or grill chicken breast and cut into pieces.

Tear romaine lettuce into bite-size pieces.

Break ramen into pieces and saute with almonds in butter until light brown. Cool and add to lettuce. Mix oranges into lettuce mixture.

Dressing:
Mix Mandarin orange juice, rice wine vinegar and sesame oil.

Add dressing to salad and toss.

Bok Choy Salad

Salad:
1 (4-ounce) package slivered
    almonds
2 packages ramen noodles
½ cup sesame seeds
½ cup margarine
2 heads bok choy or cabbage
5 green onions, sliced

Dressing:
½ cup oil
¼ cup vinegar
¾ cup sugar
2 tablespoons soy sauce

In a medium pan, brown almonds, ramen, sesame seeds and margarine. Set aside to cool.

Cut green parts of bok choy leaves into salad size. Cut white part of bok choy into small pieces.

In a large bowl, toss together ramen mixture, bok choy and onions.

Dressing:
Mix together oil, vinegar, sugar and soy sauce. Toss salad at least 20 minutes before serving.

This makes a large party salad.

Chicken Cilantro Pasta Salad

1 (12-ounce) package bow tie pasta
6 ounces chicken breast, grilled and
    in strips
1 green pepper, sliced
3 green onions, chopped
1 cup cherry tomatoes
¼ cup fresh cilantro, finely chopped
1 (16-ounce) bottle Bernstein's
    Herb Garden French dressing

Cook pasta according to package directions. While cooking, cut chicken strips into bite-sized pieces.

After pasta is cooked, drain and rinse with cold water. Add chicken and vegetables. Stir. Add dressing and stir to mix well.

Chill before serving.

Salads

Chicken Cobb Salad

Salad:
1 head cabbage, chopped
1 bunch green onions, chopped
2 chicken breasts, boiled and cooled
1 (2¼-ounce) package sliced
    almonds
1 (3¾-ounce) package sunflower
    seeds

Dressing:
½ cup salad oil
3 tablespoons vinegar
2 tablespoons sugar
½ teaspoon pepper
1 teaspoon salt
1 teaspoon Accent seasoning mix

Salad:
Shred chicken and mix with cabbage, green onion, almonds and sunflower seeds. Place in bowl and set aside.

Dressing:
Combine oil, vinegar, sugar, pepper, salt and Accent; blend well. Pour over chicken mixture and mix well. Chill until served.

Chicken Coleslaw

1 cup prepared coleslaw dressing
1 tablespoon soy sauce
8 cups coleslaw, prepared
2 cups chicken breast, cooked and
    cut into bite-sized pieces
1 cup green onion, chopped
1 (8-ounce) can pineapple, grated
    and drained
½ cup sliced almonds, toasted

In a large bowl, mix all salad ingredients. Stir well and serve.

May substitute crisp Oriental noodles for almonds. Makes a wonderful lunch. Serve with good bread rolls.

Chinese Chicken Salad

1 head lettuce, shredded
3 chicken breasts, cooked and
    shredded
3 stalks green onion, thinly sliced
    on a diagonal
½ (12-ounce) package won ton
    skins, deep fried and crushed
1 (2¼-ounce) package sliced
    almonds

Dressing:
¼ cup sugar
¼ cup vinegar
½ cup oil
2 teaspoons salt
⅓ teaspoon pepper

Dressing:
In a small bowl, mix all dressing ingredients and whisk vigorously before pouring.

Salad:
To serve, toss all salad ingredients in a large bowl and add dressing.

May substitute chopped walnuts for the sliced almonds.

Curried Chicken Salad

½ cup mayonnaise
½ teaspoon garlic salt
1 teaspoon curry powder
⅛ teaspoon cayenne
½ teaspoon prepared mustard
2 teaspoons fresh lemon juice
2 tablespoons Major Grey's Mango
    Chutney, finely chopped
3½ cups cold cooked chicken, cut
    into ½-inch cubes
⅔ cup celery, thinly sliced
2 green onions, thinly sliced
1 small apple, diced
3 tablespoons sliced almonds,
    toasted
lettuce leaves

In a medium sized bowl, combine mayonnaise, garlic salt, curry powder, cayenne, mustard, lemon juice and chutney; mix well. Add chicken, celery, green onions and apple, and stir to blend.

Cover and chill. Just before serving, sprinkle top with almonds. Serve on lettuce leaf.

Salads

Mandarin Chicken Salad

Salad:
2 pounds chicken breast, cooked and shredded
1 head iceberg lettuce, shredded
3 green onions, chopped
2 tablespoons sesame seeds, toasted
2 tablespoons sliced almonds, toasted
1 (11-ounce) can Mandarin oranges, drained
4 ounces chow mein noodles

Dressing:
2 tablespoons sugar
2 teaspoons salt
1 teaspoon pepper
2 tablespoons sesame oil
⅓ cup canola oil
¼ cup rice vinegar

Salad:
In a large bowl, combine chicken, lettuce, green onion, sesame seeds, almonds, Mandarin oranges and noodles.

Dressing:
In a small mixing bowl, combine all dressing ingredients and toss over salad.

Anansi is also known as the original Spider Man! This trickster can be found in many West African tales.

Jester is very recognizable as the fool, entertainer and storyteller found in the courts of Europe.

El Viejito is often used as a ceremonial buffoon of feast days and dances throughout many regions of Mexico.

The **Folly Bollards** - Valerie Otani, artist (Main Street Mall)

Photos: Carl Selin

Salads

Curried Spinach Salad

Curry Dressing:
½ cup white wine vinegar
⅔ cup salad oil
1 tablespoon Major Grey's Mango
    Chutney, finely chopped
1 teaspoon curry powder
1 teaspoon salt
1 teaspoon dry mustard
¼ teaspoon Tabasco sauce

Salad:
2 pounds spinach
3 red or golden delicious apples,
    chopped
⅔ cup dry roasted Spanish peanuts
½ cup raisins
⅓ cup green onions, sliced
2 tablespoons sesame seeds, toasted

Dressing:
In a small bowl, combine all dressing ingredients. Whisk well and let stand at room temperature at least 2 hours.

Salad:
Assemble salad ingredients in a large bowl. Toss with dressing and add sesame seeds on top.

Mongi Koyemsi is affectionately called Mudhead. In traditional Pueblo ceremonies, clowns wearing mud-colored masks such as his present a comical appearance.

Each character represents a particular culture and the universal appreciation for laughter. The five shown here are the perennial favorites with school children who tour the facilities.

Nulamal may be his official Kwakiutl name, but his name translated into English tells it all after a closer look - Mucous Man! His huge runny nose and uncouth behavior is always a hit at a winter potlatch.

Salads

Dungeness Crab Fruit Salad

Salad:
1 whole dungeness crab (2 to 3
    pounds), thawed if necessary
2 cups fresh pineapple chunks
2 apples, cut into chunks
1 orange, peeled, sliced and halved
lettuce leaves

Dressing:
½ cup mayonnaise
2 tablespoons lime juice
1 ½ teaspoons honey
⅛ teaspoon ground ginger
lime wedges, as garnish

Lift off back shell of crab. Remove and discard viscera and gills. Rinse crab thoroughly under cool, running water. Break off legs; crack along edges. Cut into serving-sized pieces. Break body section into several pieces. Microwave or steam crab until thoroughly heated; cool. Remove meat from body.

In mixing bowl, combine crab meat from body with fruit.

Dressing:
In small bowl, blend mayonnaise, lime juice, honey and ginger.

Arrange fruit mixture and cracked crab legs on lettuce-lined platter. Garnish with lime wedges.

May substitute pears for the apples.

French Salad

Salad:
1 cup brown rice, cooked and
    chilled
1 pound fresh green beans
4 hard-boiled eggs, halved
1 ear corn on the cob, cooked, with
    corn removed from cob
lettuce
2 (6-ounce) cans tuna, drained and
    flaked
2 tomatoes, cut in wedges
2 medium avocados, cut in wedges
    or chunks
½ cup mild cheese, cubed
1 (2¼-ounce) can whole black
    olives
fresh basil leaves

Dressing:
4 teaspoons Dijon mustard
4 teaspoons balsamic vinegar
olive oil

Salad:
Cook the green beans whole, until tender and crisp.

Line a large bowl with leaves of lettuce. Put rice in the bottom of the bowl. Add the salad items in an artistic manner and in the following order: green beans, tuna, tomatoes, avocados, cheese, corn, olives, eggs, and basil leaves.

Dressing:
In a small bowl, combine the mustard, balsamic vinegar and plenty of olive oil. Drizzle on the salad once it has been placed on the serving plates.

This is a wonderful salad for a hot summer day, accompanied with fresh French bread.

Salads

The PCPA is happy to arrange free tours of the New Theatre Building and the Arlene Schnitzer Concert Hall for your group. Most tours are one hour in length. The minimum size of the group is 10 or more. Special tours for groups of children may also be pre-arranged. Call 503-274-6552 for more information.

Green Salad with Shrimp and Ginger

¾ pound salad mix
½ pound small shrimp, cooked
3 tablespoons crystallized ginger, minced
¼ cup rice vinegar
3 tablespoons salad oil
1 tablespoon Oriental sesame oil
1 ½ tablespoons golden calendula flower petals

Rinse and crisp salad mix. Rinse and drain shrimp. Place salad mix and shrimp into a wide salad bowl. Add petals from a few calendula flowers. Add ginger, vinegar and oils at the last minute and toss carefully.

May substitute calendula with lavender or bachelor button petals, if desired.

The cookbook title going up on the marquee for the front cover photo shoot. (Arlene Schnitzer Concert Hall)

The volunteer program is an integral part of the PCPA's operational budget. On average, the volunteer corps donates a total of 50,000 man-hours each year. This cost savings is realized because of our close working relationship with Local 28 of the International Alliance of Theatrical Stage Employees (IATSA), District 1.

Hood River Romaine Salad

Dressing:
¼ cup salad oil
3 tablespoons ketchup
2 tablespoons red wine vinegar
1 tablespoon soy sauce
1 tablespoon sugar

Salad:
½ cup sliced almonds, toasted
6 slices bacon, cooked and crumbled
1 large head romaine lettuce,
    broken in bite-sized pieces
1 medium avocado, thinly sliced
½ cup golden raisins
salt
pepper

Preheat oven to 350 degrees. Toast almonds and set aside.

Dressing:
In a small bowl, combine oil, vinegar, ketchup, soy sauce and sugar. Stir well.

Salad:
In a large bowl, combine romaine, raisins, almonds and bacon. Add avocado. Add dressing and season to taste. Toss well.

Hot Shrimp Salad with Chipotle

½ pound shrimp, uncooked and
    peeled
½ cup vegetables, bite-sized
1 tablespoon olive oil
1 teaspoon garlic, chopped
2 tablespoons smoky Chipotle sauce
1 tablespoon lime juice
mixed salad greens

In frying pan or wok, saute vegetables in oil for 2 minutes. Add shrimp and saute until pink and curled (about 2 minutes). Add sauce. Serve over mixed salad greens.

Suggestions for vegetables: broccoli, asparagus, green beans, peppers, eggplant, or any combination.

Other sauce suggestions: garlic sauce, salsa, vinaigrette, or other salad dressings.

Italian Chop Salad

1 head iceberg lettuce, chopped
1⅔ cups cooked chicken, chopped
4 Roma tomatoes, chopped
5 ounces dry salami, chopped
¾ cup Mozzarella cheese, grated
½ cup Provolone cheese, grated
1 (15-ounce) can garbanzo beans,
    drained
1 bunch green onion, chopped
1 (2¼-ounce) can black olives,
    sliced and drained
⅓ cup fresh basil leaves, chopped
Italian oil and vinegar dressing

In a large bowl, mix all the salad ingredients together. Toss with Italian dressing and serve.

Serve with crusty French or garlic bread.

Janet's Famous Chicken Salad

2 chicken breasts, poached and
    cubed
2 cups bite-sized vegetables, raw or
    lightly steamed
5 tablespoons prepared salad
    dressing

In a salad bowl, combine chicken and vegetables. Add salad dressing and toss.

Suggested vegetables: broccoli, asparagus, peppers, green beans, carrots, mushrooms, or any combination.

May substitute salad dressing with vinaigrette, as desired.

Salads

Japanese Cabbage Salad

Salad:
2 chicken breasts, cooked and
    shredded
2 tablespoons toasted sesame seeds,
    (optional)
2 tablespoons slivered almonds
½ head cabbage, thinly sliced
2 green onions, chopped
1 (3-ounce)package Top Ramen
    Noodles, uncooked and crushed

Dressing:
½ teaspoon Accent seasoning mix
    (optional)
2 tablespoons sugar
1 teaspoon salt
½ cup salad oil
3 tablespoons vinegar
1 ½ teaspoons coarse pepper

In a bowl, combine all dressing ingredients. Blend well and set aside.

Combine salad items in a large salad bowl. Toss with the dressing.

May substitute 1 large can white chicken for the 2 chicken breasts.

Can be prepared ahead, but don't add Top Ramen Noodles or dressing until ready to serve.

Lila's Fantastic Chicken Salad

2 cups chicken, cooked and cubed
1 (6-ounce) package chicken-
    flavored Rice-a-Roni, prepared
    as directed
1 (5-ounce) can water chestnuts,
    sliced
4 green onions, sliced
1 (4-ounce) can mushrooms,
    drained
1 (2-ounce) jar pimiento
1 (6½-ounce) jar marinated
    artichoke hearts, save liquid
½ teaspoon curry powder

Mix reserved liquid from artichoke hearts and curry powder. Stir into prepared rice. Add the remaining ingredients.

Pour into shallow casserole and serve chilled as a salad.

Equally good hot or cold. If using as a side dish casserole, bake at 350 degrees for 30 minutes.

Overnight Layered Chicken Salad

6 cups shredded iceberg lettuce
1 (8-ounce) can sliced water
    chestnuts, drained
½ cup sliced green onions
    (including tops)
1 medium cucumber, sliced
4 cups cooked chicken, cubed
2 (6-ounce) packages frozen pea
    pods, thawed
2 cups mayonnaise
2 teaspoons curry powder
1 tablespoon sugar
½ teaspoon ground ginger
½ cup Spanish peanuts
16 cherry tomatoes, halved

Spread lettuce evenly in a 4-quart salad bowl. Top with a layer of water chestnuts, onions, cucumber and chicken. Pat pea pods dry and arrange on top.

In small bowl, stir together mayonnaise, curry powder, sugar, and ginger. Spread mayonnaise mixture evenly over pea pods. Cover and refrigerate for several hours or overnight.

Just before serving, garnish with tomato halves face down in a circle around the inside of the bowl. Sprinkle with peanuts.

Carl Selin

Reflection of the Arlene Schnitzer Concert Hall is visible across Main Street

Through these doors walk the patrons of PCPA (New Theatre Building)

Spinach Apple Salad

Salad:
2 (10-ounce) packages fresh
  spinach, washed and dried and
  torn into pieces
3 tart red apples, unpeeled, sliced
  and ½ inch diced
10 pieces bacon, fried crisp and
  crumbled

Dressing:
⅔ cup mayonnaise
⅓ cup frozen concentrated orange
  juice, undiluted

Combine the spinach, apples, and bacon in salad bowl. Mix the mayonnaise and orange juice. Pour over spinach mixture and toss lightly and serve.

Spinach Salad with Pistachio and Cranberries

1 bunch spinach, rinsed and torn
  into bite-sized pieces
¼ cup pistachio nuts
¼ cup orange-flavored dried
  cranberries
¼ pound Feta cheese, crumbled
raspberry vinaigrette

In a bowl, combine all ingredients. Toss with raspberry vinaigrette and serve.

See page 142 for raspberry vinaigrette recipe.

Salads

Spinach Salad with Sweet and Sour Dressing

1 pound fresh spinach, or more,
 washed

Sweet and Sour Dressing:
⅓ cup cider vinegar
½ cup sugar
¼ cup ketchup
2 tablespoons Worcestershire sauce
¼ medium onion, cut into chunks
1 cup salad oil
salt
pepper

Garnishes:
water chestnuts, sliced
hard-boiled egg, chopped fine
bacon, cooked and crumbled

Using a food processor, blend vinegar, sugar, ketchup, Worcestershire sauce and onion until smooth. Slowly add the oil while the food processor is running.

Place washed spinach in salad bowl. Dress with the sweet and sour dressing. Garnish with egg, water chestnuts, bacon, salt and pepper.

Village Salad

½ pound Feta cheese, diced into
 ½-inch squares
2 large sweet onions, coarsely
 chopped
1 long English cucumber, coarsely
 chopped
½ pound tomatoes, coarsely
 chopped
1 ½ cups large black olives
2 tablespoons red wine vinegar
1 tablespoon dried oregano
2 tablespoons chopped fresh basil
olive oil

Mix onions, cucumbers, tomatoes and cheese in a large bowl. Add olives, vinegar, oregano and basil; toss gently. Drizzle with olive oil, toss again and serve.

May substitute 1 large regular cucumber, with seeds removed and coarsely chopped.

Salads

Tuna with Pasta and Frisée

½ pound pasta such as fusilli,
    quadrefiore or radiatore
⅓ cup plus 1 tablespoon extra-
    virgin olive oil
8 large fresh water chestnuts, peeled
4 large scallions, thinly sliced
¼ cup fresh lemon juice
3 garlic cloves, minced
salt and freshly ground pepper
6 cups (10-ounces) chopped
    frisée, packed
1 (10-ounce) jar imported tuna
    packed in olive oil, drained and
    broken into large chunks with a
    fork

In a large pot of boiling salted water, cook the pasta until al dente. Drain well and toss with 1 tablespoon of the extra-virgin olive oil.

In a saucepan of boiling salted water, blanch the water chestnuts for 1 minute. Drain and slice ¼ inch thick.

In a large bowl, mix the remaining 1/3 cup of olive oil with the scallions, lemon juice and garlic. Season with salt and pepper. Add the pasta, frisée, tuna and the water chestnuts; toss well and serve.

May substitute water chestnuts with 1 small Granny Smith apple (peeled and in ½-inch chunks), if desired.

Carl Selin

The lighting tracks of Brunish Hall (New Theatre Building)

Brunish Hall received a $1 million renovation in early 2000. The new 4th floor lobby area was linked to the Park Blocks stairway and a glass wall above Main Street was added. The wood floor space matches the performance area of the Newmark Theatre, making Brunish Hall the perfect place to rehearse.

Salads

Warm Spinach Salad with Honey Mustard Dressing

¼ teaspoon minced garlic as
   minimum amount
1½ teaspoons minced shallot
2 tablespoons Dijon mustard
¼ cup honey
¼ cup red wine vinegar
½ cup vegetable oil
1½ (6-ounce) bags prepared
   spinach
½ pound lean bacon, cooked and
   crumbled (optional)
1 cup pecans, toasted lightly

Preheat oven to 325 degrees. Place pecans on cookie sheet and bake for 10 to 12 minutes, set aside. In a small saucepan whisk together the garlic, shallot, mustard, honey and vinegar. Add the oil in a stream, continue whisking until dressing is emulsified. Heat the dressing over moderate heat until it is warm. In a large bowl toss together the spinach, the bacon, the pecans and the dressing.

Very tasty with additional garlic.

Bleu Cheese Pear Salad

Salad:
1 head romaine lettuce, torn into
   bite-sized pieces
3 pears, cored and chopped
5 ounces Bleu cheese, crumbled
1 avocado, diced
½ cup green onion, sliced
¼ cup sugar
½ cup walnuts

Dressing:
⅓ cup olive oil
3 tablespoons red wine vinegar
1 ½ teaspoons sugar
1 ½ teaspoons prepared mustard
1 clove garlic, chopped
½ teaspoon salt
fresh ground pepper

In skillet over medium heat, stir sugar together with the walnuts. Continue stirring gently until sugar has melted and caramelized the walnuts. Carefully transfer nuts onto parchment paper. Allow to cool, and break into pieces.

Dressing:
In small mixing bowl, blend oil, vinegar, sugar, mustard, garlic, salt and pepper.

In a large serving bowl, layer lettuce, pears, Bleu cheese, avocado and green onions. Pour dressing over salad, sprinkle with walnuts, and serve.

May use pecans instead of walnuts, or Gorganzola cheese instead of Bleu cheese.

Salads

Oriental Salad

2 (11-ounce) cans Mandarin
    oranges, drained
1 head romaine lettuce, chopped
1 head red cabbage, chopped

Dry Dressing:
2½ ounces sesame seeds
½ cup sliced almonds
2 (3-ounce) packages Top Ramen
    Noodles
garlic salt
oil

Liquid Dressing:
2 tablespoons soy sauce
¼ cup cider or rice vinegar
¼ cup sugar
¾ cup oil

Sauté dry dressing ingredients in oil sprinkled with garlic salt until seeds start to brown (approximately 10 minutes). Mix liquid ingredients in a separate saucepan and boil one minute, stirring often. Allow both dressings to cool. Toss dry dressing and liquid dressing with lettuce, cabbage and oranges in salad bowl.

Serve immediately.

Dressings may be made in advance and stored separately until serving time. Always a favorite at potlucks.

A fly loft is the space above the stage where scenery and lights are hoisted to keep them out of the audience's line of sight. The fly loft has to be at least as tall as the set plus tall enough to hide the rigging. As a rule of thumb, the fly loft is over twice the height of the proscenium arch. At the Keller the proscenium is 30 feet high and the highest travel of the pipes is 72 feet. Line sets are used to support backdrops, scenery, lights and special effects. Pipes, called battens, run from one side of the stage to the other, suspended by a system of cables that connect at a counter weight arbor moving up and down at one side of the stage. The arbor is controlled by the flyman with a rope purchase line and may be raised or lowered quite quickly. With the aid of counter weights, the crew attempts to balance the weight of what is being suspended from the pipe batten. The Keller Auditorium has 76 line sets, whereas the Newmark Theatre has only 48 line sets in the fly loft.

Salads

Blueberry Salad

2 (3-ounce) packages blueberry
   Jello
2 cups boiling water
1½ cups fresh blueberries
1 (8 ½-ounce) can crushed
   pineapple, drained and reserve
   liquid
1 (8-ounce) package cream cheese
½ cup sugar
½ pint sour cream
½ teaspoon vanilla
½ cup chopped pecans

Dissolve Jello in boiling water. Measure blueberries and drain pineapple. Add water to pineapple liquid to make one cup. Add to Jello mixture. Stir in the blueberries and pineapple.

Pour into a 2-quart flat pyrex dish. Cover. Place in refrigerator until firm. Combine cream cheese, sugar, sour cream, vanilla and spread over the congealed salad. Sprinkle with chopped pecans.

Use 1 (15-ounce) can blueberries when fresh berries are not in season.

Cherry Jello Salad

1 (4-ounce) box cherry Jello
1 cup water, boiling
1 (12-ounce) can cherry pie filling
1 (15-ounce) can crushed pineapple
   in juice
½ cup pecan, chopped

Topping:
1 (8-ounce) package cream cheese,
   softened
1 cup sour cream
½ cup sugar
1 teaspoon vanilla

In a mixing bowl, dissolve Jello into boiling water; add pie filling, pineapple with juice, and pecans. Set until firm in either a bowl or a pan.

In a separate bowl, mix cream cheese, sour cream, sugar and vanilla. Spread mixture on top of set Jello.

Chill and cut into squares or serve by large spoonfuls.

Salads

Hazelnut Spinach Salad

½ cup cranberry juice, undiluted
  concentrate
⅓ cup olive oil
3 tablespoons raspberry vinegar
⅛ teaspoon salt
4 cups red apples, unpeeled and
  chopped
1 cup dried cranberries
8 cups fresh spinach
1 cup celery, thinly sliced
1 cup hazlenuts, toasted and
  chopped

In a small bowl, whisk together cranberry juice concentrate, olive oil, vinegar and salt. Place apples and cranberries in 2-quart shallow glass dish. Pour cranberry juice mixture over apple mixture. Refrigerate, covered, at least 3 hours or up to 24 hours. Stir occasionally.

When ready to serve, toss spinach and celery in a large bowl. Top with cranberry-apple mixture. If dressing mixture has been refrigerated several hours, allow to stand at room temperature about 15 minutes for olive oil to liquify.

Sprinkle nuts on salad after tossing with dressing.

Pecans may be substituted for hazelnuts.

Party Time on Main Street - Volunteer Recognition Night

Main Street Mall can be closed from Broadway to the Park Blocks by lowering the special gates and stopping the flow of traffic. The Mall can be transformed into a special outdoor event for groups and receptions.

Salads

Cranberry Freeze Salad

1 (16-ounce) can whole berry
    cranberry sauce
1 (8-ounce) can crushed pineapple,
    drained
1 cup dairy sour cream
⅛ cup chopped pecans
additional pecans, as garnish

In a mixing bowl, combine cranberry sauce, pineapple, sour cream and pecans. Mix well.

Pour into 8-inch square pan. Freeze until firm.

Cut into squares and garnish with additional pecans.

Geneva's Waldorf Salad

Salad:
4 cups apples, unpeeled and cut into
    small pieces
2 tablespoons lemon juice
1 cup celery, diced
½ cup golden raisins
1 cup miniature marshmallows
½ cup walnuts, chopped
¼ cup candied ginger, chopped

Dressing:
¾ cup reduced calorie mayonnaise
½ teaspoon ground nutmeg
½ teaspoon ground cinnamon
½ teaspoon ground ginger

In a large mixing bowl, combine apples, lemon juice, celery, raisins, marshmallows, candied ginger, and walnuts.

Dressing:
In small bowl, whisk mayonnaise, nutmeg, cinnamon, and ground ginger. Add to salad ingredients and toss until well-mixed.

Chill before serving.

Cranberry Salad

Salad:
12 ounces fresh cranberries
1 ½ cups water
¾ cup sugar
6 ounces red Jello
15 ounces crushed pineapple in
    juice
¾ cup celery, chopped
¾ cup nuts, chopped
1 large apple, chopped

Topping:
1 cup cranberry juice
2 eggs, beaten
⅓ cup sugar
2 tablespoons butter
2 tablespoons flour
1 cup Cool Whip

Salad:
In a saucepan, boil berries and water until berries pop. Add sugar and Jello; stir until dissolved, then remove from heat.

Stir in remaining ingredients and pour in 9 x 13-inch dish and chill.

Topping:
In a saucepan, cook cranberry juice, eggs, sugar, butter and flour over medium heat until it boils. Cool and stir in Cool Whip topping.

Spread topping over cranberries; garnish with additional chopped nuts.

May substitute orange juice for the cranberry juice in the topping.

Salads

Kiwi-Strawberry Spinach Salad

12 cups baby spinach
2 pints strawberries, sliced
4 kiwi fruit, peeled and sliced

Dressing:
⅓ cup sugar
¼ cup canola oil
¼ cup raspberry vinegar
¼ teaspoon paprika
¼ teaspoon worcestershire sauce
2 green onions, chopped
1 tablespoon poppy seeds
2 tablespoons sesame seeds, toasted

Place spinach, strawberries and kiwi fruit in very large salad bowl.

Mix dressing ingredients and add to salad immediately before serving.

Triple Apricot Pecan Salad

2 ½ cups apricot nectar
2 (3-ounce) packages apricot gelatin
1 ½ cups dry white wine
½ cup celery, sliced
½ cup pecan, chopped
1 (16 -ounce) can apricots, peeled
   and chopped

Bring apricot nectar to a boil in saucepan. Pour over gelatin and stir until gelatin is dissolved. Stir in wine. Chill until partially set.

Fold apricots, celery, pecans into gelatin. Pour into a 5 ½-6 cup mold. Chill until firm (approximately 2 hours).

Unmold onto platter. Garnish with greens if desired.

The wine can be replaced with apple juice or additional apricot nectar.

Orange Salad

1 (8-ounce) container Cool Whip
1 (8-ounce) container cottage
  cheese
1 (6-ounce) lemon yogurt
1 (3-ounce) package orange Jello
1 (11-ounce) can Mandarin oranges

Mix the Cool Whip, cottage cheese, yogurt, and orange jello. Arrange Mandarin oranges in a design of your choice.

Refrigerate until ready to serve.

Best Vegetable Salad

Salad:
1 (14½-ounce) can French-style
  green beans, drained
1 (15¼-ounce) can corn kernels,
  drained
1 cup green pepper, chopped
1 cup celery, sliced
½ cup green onion, sliced
2 tablespoons pimiento, diced

Dressing:
½ cup sugar
½ cup cider vinegar
½ cup salad oil
½ teaspoon salt
½ teaspoon pepper

Salad:
Place beans, corn, green pepper, celery, green onion and pimiento in a large mixing bowl.

Dressing:
In a small bowl, combine sugar, vinegar, oil, salt and pepper. Stir until sugar is dissolved. Pour over vegetables and toss to coat.

Let stand overnight in refrigerator.

Salads

Have you ever thought of becoming a PCPA volunteer? Training sessions for the various opportunities are conducted several times each year. Call 503-274-6552 for more information.

Orzo Salad with Vegetables

Salad:
6 ounces sugar snap peas, trimmed
    and cut into three 1-inch pieces
1⅓ cup orzo
1¼ cup, cubed tomatoes
¾ cup, cubed cucumber
½ cup, chopped green onions
¼ cup freshly chopped parsley
2 teaspoons lemon peel
salt and pepper

Dressing:
¼ cup lemon juice
2 teaspoons chopped lemon peel
1 teaspoon minced garlic
¾ cup olive oil

Salad:
Cook sugar snap peas for 1 minute in a large pot of boiling salted water. Remove with slotted spoon, rinse and cool. Add orzo to same pot and boil until tender, about 8 minutes. Drain and cool.

Mix orzo with peas, tomatoes, cucumbers, green onions, parsley, lemon peel. Season with salt and pepper to taste.

Dressing:
Combine all ingredients, using whisk to incorporate oil. Pour half over orzo/vegetables. Cover and chill. Bring to room temperature before serving and pour remaining dressing over salad. Line bowl with lettuce or other greens, mount salad in bowl. Garnish with parsley or other greenery.

Feel free to add your favorite vegetables to this salad.

Salads

Quinoa-Couscous Salad with Lemon-Cinnamon Dressing

Salad:
½ cup quinoa
1 cup water
½ cup hot water
½ teaspoon vegetable stock powder
½ cup couscous
¼ cup celery, chopped
1 green onion (green part), chopped
2 tablespoons freshly minced
    parsley
2 tablespoons currants

Dressing:
2 tablespoons lemon juice
2 teaspoons extra-virgin olive oil
2 teaspoons water
¼ teaspoon ground cinnamon
4 drops hot pepper sauce, or to
    taste
dash tumeric

*Garnish with Mandarin orange
    sections, toasted pine nuts*

Rinse quinoa thoroughly either by using a fine strainer or by running fresh water over it in a pan; drain.

Place rinsed quinoa and 1 cup water in a small saucepan. Bring to a boil over high heat. Reduce heat to low, cover and simmer until the water is absorbed, about 5 minutes. (When done, the grains will be translucent and the outer ring will separate.)

While quinoa is cooking, in a medium size bowl, dissolve stock powder in the hot water. Stir in couscous; cover and let stand until the liquid is completely absorbed, about 5 minutes.

Whisk together the dressing ingredients in a measuring cup. Taste; adjust seasonings. Set aside.

When the couscous has softened, fluff with a fork. Stir in quinoa; toss in celery, green onion, parsley, and currants. Add dressing and toss again. Allow the salad to cool or serve immediately. Garnish and serve.

Quinoa (keen-wah) is an ancient Peruvian grain which has been rediscovered in this country. Look for it in natural food stores, specialty food shops, and some large supermarkets. It has a distinctly sweet, nutty flavor and a light, fluffy texture.

Salads

Sweet and Sour Cucumber Salad

½ pound rotini (spiral) noodles
⅓ cup oil
¾ cup sugar
1 teaspoon salt
½ teaspoon garlic powder
1 teaspoon regular mustard
½ teaspoon Accent seasoning mix
¾ cup white vinegar
½ teaspoon parsley, chopped
2 medium cucumbers, sliced thin
1 medium red onion, sliced thin

Cook and drain noodles. Coat with oil while still warm. Place in bowl to cool.

Mix in remaining ingredients. Cover and place salad in refrigerator for at least 4 hours. Overnight is even better.

Personalize this salad by adding any chopped vegetables (such as olives, tomatoes, broccoli, carrots, etc), or beans (such as garbanzo or red kidney). It is not necessary to increase the dressing ingredients for these additions.

Anise Beet Salad

2 medium beets
6 tablespoons olive oil
3 tablespoons red wine vinegar
salt
freshly ground pepper
1 small onion, coarsely chopped
½ teaspoon anise seed

Place unpeeled beets in sauce pan; cover with water and bring to a boil. Simmer covered for 1 hour or until tender. Peel, cool, and cut into ¾-inch slices. Cut each slice in quarters.

In medium bowl, whisk the oil, vinegar, salt and pepper (to taste). Stir in onion, beets and anise. Cover and refrigerate.

This salad improves with age.

Salads

Asian Cole Slaw

½ cup sesame seeds
½ cup slivered almonds
2 (3-ounce) packages Top Ramen Noodles, any flavor, broken into pieces
1 head cabbage, grated
8 green onions, finely sliced

Dressing:
⅔ cup salad oil
2 tablespoons sesame oil
6 tablespoons seasoned Asian rice vinegar
1 teaspoon freshly ground pepper
3 tablespoons sugar

Preheat oven to 325 degrees.

Dressing:
Combine salad oil, sesame oil, rice vinegar, pepper and sugar. Some of the Top Ramen seasoning can be added to dressing if desired. Allow dressing to sit for one hour for sugar to completely dissolve. Occasional stirring will speed this up.

Toast sesame seeds on a baking sheet at 325 degrees for 6 minutes. Remove seeds and place slivered almonds on baking sheet. Bake at 325 degrees for 10 minutes. Set these aside. In a large bowl, combine Top Ramen pieces, onions and cabbage. Add the dressing and mix well. Add the almonds and sesame seeds and toss before serving. Can be served cold or at room temperature.

Baby Spinach Leaves with Dressing

2 cloves garlic
⅓ cup extra virgin olive oil
2 tablespoons balsamic vinegar
1 tablespoon red wine vinegar
1½ teaspoons Dijon mustard
1½ teaspoons dark brown sugar
½ teaspoon pepper
¼ teaspoon vanilla
½ teaspoon salt
6 quarts baby spinach leaves (about 1½ pounds)
1 cup Chèvre cheese, crumbled

In a food blender, combine garlic, olive oil, vinegars, Dijon mustard, brown sugar, pepper and vanilla. Blend well. Add salt and whirl briefly.

Rinse spinach. Wrap in paper towels and place in a plastic bag. Refrigerate until needed.

To serve, toss spinach with dressing and cheese.

Broccoli Salad

Salad:
4 cups broccoli florets, cut into bite-
    sized pieces
½ cup raisins, soaked and drained
1 medium red onion, chopped
10 slices bacon, cooked and
    crumbled

Dressing:
1 cup mayonnaise
⅓ cup sugar
2 tablespoons apple cider vinegar

In medium bowl, combine broccoli, raisins, onion and bacon.

Combine mayonnaise, sugar and apple cider vinegar, and blend in blender for a few seconds.

Add dressing to broccoli mixture just before serving.

Brown Rice and Vegetable Salad

1½ cups brown rice, cooked
    according to package directions
    and cooled
1 cup green onions, chopped
1 cup carrots, diced
1 cup red bell pepper, diced
3 tablespoons minced parsley
⅓ cup peanut oil
¼ cup rice vinegar
2 tablespoons honey
2 tablespoons Dijon mustard
½ teaspoon salt
¼ tablespoon pepper
1 cup roasted peanuts

In large bowl, combine cooled rice, green onions, carrots, red peppers and parsley. Set aside and chill.

In a small bowl, whisk together oil, vinegar, honey, mustard, salt and pepper.

When ready to serve, add peanuts to rice mixture. Add dressing and toss to blend.

Individual portion is served on a lettuce leaf.

Cold German Potato Salad

8 boiling potatoes
salt
1 medium onion, minced
1 ¼ cups beef stock
6 tablespoons white vinegar
5 tablespoons salad oil
prepared mustard (optional)
white pepper

In a medium sauce pan, place potatoes in their jackets, salt, and water to cover. Bring to a boil. Do not overcook or potatoes will fall apart in the salad. Peel while hot and cut in thin slices. Place in a bowl and add onion.

In a small sauce pan, bring beef stock to a boil with a little salt and the vinegar. Pour over the potatoes and marinate until almost all liquid is absorbed, about 20 to 30 minutes.

Pour excess liquid off and gently fold in the oil and mustard. Flavor with pepper. Cool the salad slightly and serve.

All kinds of interesting things flavor this salad in Germany. Add more vinegar, or use dry white wine throughout instead of vinegar. Minced green herbs are often added - especially parsley and chives - and so are chopped cucumber, diced peeled apple or diced cooked knob celery.

Leftover meats can be chopped or slivered, as can any kind of smoked ham, tongue or wurst. Chopped anchovies or salt herring, or dill pickle, is sometimes added. May also add ½ cup of mayonnaise or sour cream, though the Germans typically serve without either.

Salads

Cranberry Spinach Salad

6 ounces spinach salad greens,
    washed and cleaned
½ cup sweetened dried cranberries
1 small red onion, sliced
½ cup walnut pieces

Dressing:
4 slices bacon, fried crisp and
    crumbled
½ cup honey
½ cup lime juice
2 tablespoons Dijon mustard

In a large bowl, combine spinach, cranberries and onion slices. Toss well.

Dressing:
Combine dressing ingredients in small bowl and whisk together. Heat in microwave on high for one minute or until warm.

Toss with salad greens, add walnuts and serve.

Cucumbers with Yogurt

2 small green cucumbers
coarse cooking salt
2 teaspoons cumin seeds
2 green onions, chopped
1½ cups plain yogurt
1 tablespoon lemon juice

Peel cucumbers, cut lengthwise and scoop out seeds. Chop the cucumbers very finely and place in strainer. Sprinkle with salt and let them stand for 15 minutes. Rinse the cucumbers under cold water. Drain well.

Place cumin seeds in a small saucepan. Stir over a low heat until the seeds are well browned.

Combine half of the cucumbers, cumin seeds, onions, yogurt and lemon juice in a medium sized bowl. Sprinkle the remaining cucumbers on top.

Garnish with extra cumin seeds, if desired.

Easy Pea Salad

1 (16-ounce) package frozen petite peas
½ cup green onion, chopped
1 cup mayonnaise
1 (6-ounce) package dry chow mein noodles, crumbled

In a medium mixing bowl, combine peas, green onion and mayonnaise. Just before serving, add dry noodles.

Easy, crunchy salad. Great to take to potlucks.

Gorgonzola and Pecan-Crusted Tomato Slices

5 large tomatoes, cored
⅔ cup Gorgonzola cheese, crumbled
⅔ cup cream cheese, softened
2 tablespoons parsley, finely minced
ground black pepper
1 cup pecans, ground

Remove enough pulp from each tomato to make an opening for the cheese stuffing. Turn tomatoes upside down to let seeds and juices drain.

In a bowl, combine Gorgonzola cheese, cream cheese, parsley and pepper (to taste). Stuff each tomato with cheese mixture, packing it in firmly.

Refrigerate stuffed tomatoes for at least 1 hour.

When ready to serve, cut into thick slices. Sprinkle pecans over tomato slices, leaving cheese visible. Use 2 to 3 slices per portion.

Salads

The general public is able to rent the Dolores Winningstad Theatre space for private functions. The space is very flexible and can be used for meetings and social events as well as a performance venue.

Hot German Potato Salad with Bacon

8 boiling potatoes
salt
¼ pound bacon, diced
1 onion, minced
¾ cup vinegar
¾ cup beef stock
salt
white pepper
sour cream (optional)
minced parsley, as garnish

In a medium saucepan, place potatoes in their jackets, and salt. Cover with water and boil. Do not overcook or potatoes will fall apart in the salad. Peel while hot and cut in thin slices. Place potatoes in mixing bowl and set aside.

Fry bacon in a sauce pan and when golden but not yet brown or crisp, add onions. Sauté slowly until the onions become transparent but not golden.

Remove from heat and carefully pour in combined vinegar and stock. Bring to a boil and pour over sliced potatoes. Gently toss so potatoes are evenly covered with dressing.

Fold in a couple tablespoons of sour cream and sprinkle with minced parsley.

Carl Selin

*In 1975, John Haviland, the owner of the building at the time, organized an auction event from all the furnishings and trappings of the old Paramount movie house. Surprise has always been a special favorite of Portland residents. Her original purchase price was $10,000 back in 1928, but she was to be auctioned off to the highest bidder. The Landmarks Commission had gathered $2,700 for a bid, only to discover that someone from back east had placed a bid for $5,000. The hat was quickly passed among the 1,200 people at the auction and a winning bid of $ 5,233.97 was raised. **Surprise** was able to stay in Portland and in the building she has called home all these years.*

Surprise *(Arlene Schnitzer Concert Hall)*
Originally, Surprise stood in a fountain where she provided thousands of Portland youngsters with their first lesson in female anatomy.

Salads

Low Fat Potato Salad

6 cups red potatoes, cubed
¼ cup green onion, chopped
¼ cup vinegar (red wine, or any)
1 tablespoon olive oil
3 tablespoons chives, chopped
¾ teaspoon salt
¾ teaspoon pepper
½ teaspoon dry mustard

Optional garnishes:
sliced red, yellow or green peppers;
    tomato wedges

Bring potatoes to a boil and then simmer until tender but still firm. Drain.

In another bowl, mix vinegar, oil, onion, chives, salt, pepper, and dry mustard. Add to potatoes. Mix well.

Serve warm or cold. Garnish with peppers or tomatoes if desired.

Marinated Green Beans and Mushrooms

¼ teaspoon oregano
¼ teaspoon thyme
½ teaspoon salt
1 teaspoon onion, grated
1 clove garlic, crushed
¼ cup white wine vinegar
1 tablespoon salad oil
1 pound small, whole, fresh
    mushrooms
1 (14½-ounce) can whole green
    beans, drained

Combine seasonings, vinegar and oil. Pour over mushrooms and simmer for 10 minutes. Add green beans and heat through. Chill overnight. Serve cold.

Recipe doubles well. Keeps several days in refrigerator.

Salads

Rising Sun Salad

1 clove garlic, halved

Marinade:
¼ cup salad oil
1 ½ teaspoons sugar
1 tablespoon grated orange peel
¼ teaspoon red pepper flakes
1 teaspoon sesame oil
2 tablespoons tamari soy sauce (to taste)
juice of 1 orange
sesame seeds (garnish)
salt
pepper

Salad:
½ pound mushrooms, sliced
1 bunch radishes, sliced
2 medium avocados, peeled and diced
2 oranges, peeled and sliced. Add more orange slices if needed
1 bunch cilantro, minced
3 green onions including greens, sliced
1 (10-ounce) package spinach, torn
1 head lettuce

Rub large salad bowl with the garlic.

Marinade:
Combine salad oil, sugar, orange peel, red pepper flakes, sesame oil, tamari, salt and pepper, orange juice and sesame seeds in the salad bowl and mix well.

Salad:
Place salad items in the bowl in the order listed and without stirring, marinate the mushrooms, radishes, avocados and oranges, but not the greens.

Cover and store in a cool place until ready to toss and serve.

Tarragon Marinated Vegetables

1 pound small red potatoes, cooked and sliced ¼-inch thick
1 pound green beans, cooked 7 minutes; cut into 1-inch pieces
1 pound jicama, cut into 1-inch pieces
2 (10-ounce) packages frozen peas and carrots, thawed

Marinade:
½ cup olive oil
3 tablespoons white wine vinegar
1 teaspoon salt
1 teaspoon tarragon
2 teaspoons Dijon mustard
1 teaspoon pepper
1 tablespoon parsley, chopped
¼ cup green onion, chopped

Mix red potatoes, green beans and jicama. Add thawed peas and carrots (do not cook).

Marinade:
Mix oil, vinegar, salt, mustard, tarragon, parsley, and green onions. Pour over vegetables. Stir lightly. Refrigerate 8 to 24 hours. Serve chilled.

Three Bean Salad

1 (15-ounce) can French-style green beans
1 (15-ounce) can French-style wax beans
1 (15-ounce) can kidney beans
1 onion, chopped
¾ cup sugar
1 cup vinegar
½ cup olive oil
1 ½ teaspoons salt
1 teaspoon pepper

Mix everything together in a bowl. Refrigerate until ready to serve.

Allow salad to marinate overnight for best results.

Tomato, Mint and Lime Salad

4 medium tomatoes, chopped
6 green onions, chopped
½ cup fresh mint
¼ cup lime juice
2 teaspoons sugar
¼ teaspoon chili powder

Combine lime juice, sugar and chili powder in a small bowl. Stir in tomatoes and green onions. Toss with fresh mint.

Goes well with Chicken Curry (recipe on page 182).

Vegetable Potpourri Salad

1 head broccoli, broken into bite-
     sized pieces
1 head cauliflower, broken into bite-
     sized pieces
10 ounces frozen peas, thawed and
     drained
1 small onion, chopped

Dressing:
½ cup mayonnaise
½ cup sour cream
1 tablespoon sugar
1 teaspoon salt
¾ teaspoon garlic powder

Put vegetables in desired serving bowl.

Dressing:
Mix mayonnaise, sour cream, sugar, salt and garlic powder in medium bowl. Mix dressing with vegetables and let stand overnight.

May garnish with red peppers and/or cheddar cheese chunks to add color and texture.

Salads

Shoepeg Salad

Salad:
1 (15-ounce) can tiny peas, drained
1 (15-ounce) can French cut green
  beans, drained
1 (11-ounce) can shoepeg corn,
  drained
1 (4-ounce) jar diced pimiento,
  drained
1 cup onion, diced
1 cup celery, diced
1 red pepper, diced

Dressing:
1 cup sugar
½ cup canola oil
¼ cup cider vinegar
1 tablespoon water
1 teaspoon pepper

Place dressing ingredients in saucepan. Bring to boil then cool completely. Combine all vegetables in a bowl and pour cooled dressing over them.

Chill at least overnight. Twenty-four hours is even better.

Blender Salad Dressing

1 slice onion, chopped
1 teaspoon salt
1 teaspoon powdered mustard
1 teaspoon celery salt
1 teaspoon paprika
1 cup sugar
½ cup vinegar
1 cup oil

Using a blender, combine onion, salt, mustard, celery salt, paprika, sugar, and vinegar. Blend well.

Add oil, and blend again.

Shake before using. Refrigerate any unused portion.

Spiral's House Dressing

2 cups soybean oil
¾ cup filtered or bottled water
2 tablespoons rice wine vinegar
¾ cup white miso
2 tablespoons tamari soy sauce
½ cup onion, chopped

Place all ingredients in a blender in order listed. Blend until smooth and frothy, at least 2 minutes.

The original Spiral house salad was made with a bed of mixed salad greens, chopped celery, cucumber slices, cherry tomatoes, mung bean and soybean sprouts and sprinkled with shredded carrots. The dressing coats the salad well without tossing.

White miss is available in Asian groceries and some health food stores. Regular soy sauce may be substituted for tamari, but tamari produces a more mellow taste.

Raspberry Vinaigrette Dressing

½ cup raspberry vinegar
¼ teaspoon salt
¼ teaspoon pepper
4 teaspoons sugar
2 garlic cloves, finely chopped,
   about 2 teaspoons
2 teaspoons Worcestireshire sauce
1 tablespoon Dijon mustard

Combine all ingredients and mix well.

Refrigerate in a container with a tight fitting lid. Will keep for months.

The Dolores Winningstad Theatre accommodates approximately 300 patrons in a variety of seating arrangements. The main floor seats are on portable risers that may be reconfigured or removed entirely. The floor itself is on an elevator. It may be lowered to the basement or made level with the stage to create a large banquet space. The front of the stage is also an elevator. By lowering it to the level of the seating area, more seats may be added. If lowered a little more, an orchestra pit is created.

Entrées

Carl Selin

The Elizabethan-styled Winningstad Theatre (New Theatre Building)

The interior of the Winningstad is finished in tones of burgundy and red. These colors have the same light absorbing characteristics as black, but are far more cheerful and inviting.

Chicken Mireille

CHRISTOPHER HOWELL - **BRASSERIE MONTMARTRE RESTAURANT** - PORTLAND, OR

2 whole chickens (2-3 pounds
    each), boned, and separated into
    eight pieces
8 ounces morels
10 small fingerling potatoes, cut in
    half, lengthwise
3 sprigs rosemary, chopped
2 shallots, minced and divided
2 cloves garlic, minced
3 ounces olive oil
16 ounces white wine
20 stalks green asparagus
20 stalks white asparagus
½ cup butter (1 cube), divided
salt
pepper

Makes 4-6 servings

Preheat oven to 400 degrees.

Bring a pot of water to boil. Add fingerling potatoes and boil for 5 minutes. Remove potatoes from water and allow to cool until warm to the touch. In a large mixing bowl, toss together potatoes, ¼ cup butter, rosemary, garlic, one shallot, salt, and pepper. Place potatoes on a sheet pan and set aside.

In a pan large enough to fit the chicken, heat olive oil. Sprinkle chicken with salt and pepper. Brown chicken, skin side first, then add white wine, one shallot, and morels. If pan is also oven-proof, keep chicken as is. If not, switch chicken to oven pan.

Place chicken and potatoes in hot oven. Cook potatoes 15 minutes, or until golden brown. Cook chicken for 15 to 25 minutes, depending on size of chicken. Remove chicken and simmer remaining liquid over medium heat on stove top. Reduce cooking liquid to one quarter its original volume. Whisk ¼ cup butter into cooking liquid.

Drop asparagus in boiling water and cook for 3 to 5 minutes. Drain asparagus.

Place chicken (one breast and one leg) in center of each plate. Arrange asparagus and potatoes around each plate. Pour sauce and morels over chicken, and serve.

Entrées

Alsace Chicken

ALBERTINA'S RESTAURANT - PORTLAND, OR

8 chicken breast halves (about 4 ounces each), boned and skinned
5½ cups Panko crumbs or coarse bread crumbs
⅓ cup grated Parmesan cheese
¼ teaspoon paprika
⅓ cup dried parsley flakes, optional

Marinade:
½ cup butter (1 cube)
1 clove garlic, minced
5 teaspoons Dijon mustard

Dijon Sauce:
2 tablespoons Dijon mustard
¼ cup mayonnaise

Preheat oven to 350 degrees. Grease a 9 x 13-inch pan.

Make marinade by melting butter in a saucepan. Add garlic and sauté on medium-low heat for 5 minutes. Blend in Dijon mustard, stirring well. Cool enough to touch but not to solidify. Whip vigorously until mixture thickens.

Mix bread crumbs with Parmesan cheese, paprika and parsley to make a breading mixture.

Dip breasts in marinade, then in bread crumb mixture, packing crumbs to coat well. Place chicken in prepared pan. Can be refrigerated up to several hours at this point. Bake chicken at 350 degrees for 30 minutes, or until done. Spoon Dijon Sauce over top.

To prepare Dijon Sauce, blend remaining mustard with the mayonnaise.

Serve with parsleyed rice.

The flavor, the moistness, the aroma, the crust - words can't describe this delicious dish.

Makes 8 servings

Entrées

Spring Lamb Stew (Navarin d'Agneau Printanier)

PASCAL SAUTON - CARAFE RESTAURANT - PORTLAND, OR

1 ½ pounds boneless lamb shoulder,
   cut in 3 ounce cubes
2 tablespoons olive oil
4 tablespoons tomato paste
½ bottle dry white wine
1 quart veal stock
sea salt
black pepper to taste

Aromatics:
1 cup diced onions
4 cloves garlic, peeled and sliced
3 thyme sprigs
1 bay leaf
parsley stems

Garniture:
1 pound new potatoes
8 baby turnips
8 baby carrots

16 pearl onions
1 tablespoon butter
1 tablespoon sugar
3 tablespoons chopped parsley

Season the lamb cubes with salt and pepper. Heat the oil in a casserole and sear the lamb in it. Remove. Place the aromatics (onions, garlic cloves, thyme sprigs, bay leaf and parsley stems) in the casserole, and cook for a minute.

Add the meat and deglaze with white wine. Reduce the wine until almost dry, add the tomato paste and the veal stock. Cook covered at a simmer for 1 ½ hours. Check seasoning. Remove the vegetables, bay leaf and aromatics.

For the garniture:
Peel the turnips, carrots and potatoes, and cut in even sizes. Cook in salted boiling water to ¾ done. Add to the lamb for the last 15 minutes of the lamb cooking time.

Peel the pearl onions and glaze with butter and sugar for 5 minutes. Serve lamb with added pearl onions as garnish. Sprinkle with parsley.

Makes 4 servings

Rabbit Moutarde

Christopher Howell - **BRASSERIE MONTMARTRE RESTAURANT** - Portland, OR

4 rabbit hindquarters
1 (750 ml) bottle white wine
4 ounces Dijon mustard
2 shallots, minced
1 white onion, diced
2 cloves garlic, minced
6 ounces olive oil, divided
12 sprigs fresh thyme
¼ cup butter
12 small new red potatoes
6 sprigs fresh mint
1 zucchini, thinly sliced
1 yellow squash, thinly sliced
salt
pepper

Bring wine to a boil and ignite, then continue boiling until no alcohol remains. Chill wine. Cover rabbit with the wine and marinate for 24 hours.

Preheat oven to 350 degrees. Remove rabbit from wine, and place wine over medium-low heat. Skim the wine frequently, removing any scum that rises.

Sauté onion, shallots, and garlic in 2 ounces of olive oil until translucent. Place vegetables in a pan deep enough to hold the rabbit and wine. Sprinkle rabbit with salt and pepper and brown in 2 ounces of olive oil. Place in pan. Add wine, Dijon mustard and thyme to pan. Cover with foil and place in the oven. Cook the rabbit for 1½ to 2 hours, or until tender.

While rabbit is cooking, boil new potatoes in salted water with the fresh mint. Sauté zucchini and squash in remaining olive oil.

Remove rabbit from pan and reduce the cooking liquid to ¼ of its original volume. Whisk butter into cooking liquid to form sauce.

Place 3 potatoes in the center of pasta dishes and arrange vegetables around them. Place rabbit on top of potatoes and pour the sauce over the rabbit.

Makes 4 servings

Entrées

Salmon and Crab Tower

McCORMICK & SCHMICK'S SEAFOOD RESTAURANT
HARBORSIDE AT THE MARINA, PORTLAND, OR

4½ ounces salmon
herb oil
3 spears asparagus
2 artichoke hearts with stem
1 ounce russet potato sliced into
shoestrings with mandoline
(small julienne setting), hold in
water
seasoned salt
red pepper for roasting
extra-virgin olive oil, as needed
salt and pepper
1 ounce crab meat
lemon infused oil
pesto infused oil
sun dried tomato oil
chopped parsley for garnish

Seasoned oils:
Herb oil: Add 1 cup dried parsley
and 1 cup dried thyme to a
gallon of extra-virgin olive oil.
Add salt and pepper to taste.
Store in sealed container.
Lemon Oil: Blend 1 tablespoon
lemon juice with 12 ounces of
extra-virgin olive oil. Hold in
squeeze bottle.
Pesto Oil: Add ½ cup of pesto to 12
ounces of extra-virgin olive oil.
Strain the oil and pesto through
cheese cloth. Hold in squeeze
bottle.

Cut salmon into three medallions making sure they are very flat. Put salmon in herb oil until ready to cook. Just prior to assembly, sear on high heat until cooked to medium.

Trim asparagus to same length as salmon. Roast on a grill and hold in herb oil until ready for use.

Trim artichoke hearts to same length as salmon. Cut off rounded edge. Grill hearts and hold in herb oil until ready to use.

Rub pepper with extra-virgin olive oil, salt and pepper. Roast on a grill until skin is charred. Allow to steam in a paper bag for 10 minutes or so. Peel skin off. Remove seeds and membranes attached to pepper. Cut into 1-inch strips. Set aside.

Remove shoestring potatoes from water and fry until golden brown. Season with seasoned salt. Set aside.

Splash crabmeat with lemon oil and toss gently to infuse.

Assembly: Place fried shoestring potatoes in a tight nest in middle of plate. Place first piece of salmon on potatoes, followed by artichoke hearts and 2 roasted pepper strips. Add next piece of salmon, followed by 3 grilled asparagus pieces. Top with last piece of salmon. Crown with lemon oil infused crab meat. Garnish with other oils and parsley.
(See next page)

Entrées

Salmon and Crab Tower (continued)

Sundried Tomato Oil: Add 1 cup of sun dried tomatoes to 12 ounces of extra-virgin olive oil in a food processor. Pulse the tomatoes until blended, and pass through cheese cloth. Hold in squeeze bottle.

This dish is done in layers. Follow the instructions to build a tower that is sure to please your guests. The recipes for the various seasoned oils are also included for your convenience.

Makes 1 serving

Paella Valencia

RONNIE MACQUARRIE - **SOUTHPARK SEAFOOD GRILL** AND **WINE BAR** - PORTLAND, OR

1 pound paella rice
8 ounces diced chicken
3 prawns, peeled completely
12 clams
12 mussels
½ pound chorizo sausage
½ medium yellow onion, diced small
1 green bell pepper, diced small
1 red bell pepper, diced small
1 tablespoon Spanish paprika
1½ quarts chicken stock or water
½ tablespoon saffron, chopped
salt and pepper to taste
2 tablespoons butter
olive oil, as needed
chopped cilantro for garnish

In a large sauté pan with a little olive oil, sauté the onions until clear. Add the rice and cook until the rice is coated with the oil. Add stock to the pan and bring to a boil. Once it begins boiling, reduce heat to a simmer. Add the saffron and Spanish paprika to the rice. Stir the paella rice frequently as it continues to simmer.

In a separate pan with a small amount of olive oil, place the prawns, sausage and chicken. Sauté until slightly brown, then add the peppers, clams and mussels. Let cook until the clams and mussels begin to open. Combine the rice with the shellfish and chicken and stir until the mixture begins to thicken. Continue stirring until the rice is tender. Remove the paella from the heat and stir in the butter. Serve with a sprinkle of chopped cilantro.

Makes 4 servings

Entrées

Kells Shepherd's Pie

Ethan Light - KELLS RESTAURANT - Portland, OR

1½ pounds ground free-range beef
½ cup diced sweet onion
½ cup diced baby carrots
¼ cup Guinness stout
¼ cup Cabernet
1 teaspoons Worcestershire sauce
¼ teaspoon fresh basil
¼ teaspoon fresh oregano
¼ teaspoon fresh sage
¼ teaspoon fresh marjoram
1-2 teaspoons finely minced garlic
    (or crushed)
7 ounces beef broth
½ teaspoon salt
¼ teaspoon pepper
1 cups peas (fresh is preferred,
    frozen ok)
2 tablespoons melted butter
2 tablespoons flour

Simmer the ground beef in an appropriately sized saucepan until cooked throughout. Drain excess fat when cooked. Add all ingredients except the peas, butter and flour; these ingredients are reserved for later in the recipe. Stir and simmer ingredients over a low heat until all ingredients are tender and flavors have bloomed (about 15 minutes). This is a good time to add the peas.

Thicken the recipe with a roux (a mixture of equal parts flour and butter). Melt butter in a pan and stir in flour. Slowly add the roux in small amounts to the simmering mixture until desired thickness is achieved. You may not need the full amount. Cook 5 to 10 minutes to release roux into the recipe. Add salt and pepper to taste. Place in individual ovenproof serving bowls or a 9½-inch round casserole dish or, a deep pie dish.

Recipe is now ready for the potato topping. See next page.

Kells Shepherd's Pie is the ultimate comfort food, combining meat, potatoes and vegetables with the rich taste of Guinness! What makes this particular recipe especially tantalizing is Chef Ethan Light's addition of Irish White Cheddar in the potato topping.

Makes 6-8 servings

Entrées

Shepherd's Pie Topping (Ulster Champ Potatoes)

ETHAN LIGHT - **KELLS RESTAURANT** - PORTLAND, OR

1¼ pounds russet potatoes (4 medium sized potatoes)
2 ounces (¼ cup) milk
1 cup finely grated Irish white cheddar
2 ounces butter
¼ cup fresh parsley cleaned and chopped
⅓ cup scallion or chives
white pepper, to taste
¼ teaspoon salt (or to taste)

For the potato topping, wash, scrub and peel potatoes. Cut potatoes in large pieces – smaller pieces will deteriorate and cause loss of product. Cook potatoes by steaming or simmering in water. Do not boil. Cook until tender and drain well, leaving no moisture. Add butter, cream, scallion and fresh parsley. Season to taste and mix by hand or mixer until smooth and creamy. Add in grated Irish White Cheddar while whipping the potato mixture. If available, use a pastry bag and star tip to pipe the potatoes onto Shepherd's Pie. A pastry bag is not essential…the potatoes may also be spread on as a topping with a rubber spatula.

Bake at 350 degrees for 20 to 30 minutes or until hot and golden brown.

As an option, in the final 1 to 2 minutes of cooking, you may place the Shepherd's pie under a broiler, to achieve the perfect, crispy golden-brown crust! Serve hot, with HP sauce, steak sauce or pan gravy (thickened and flavored beef broth).

Entrées

Salmon Rillettes

PASCAL SAUTON - CARAFE RESTAURANT - PORTAND, OR

½ pound Fresh Wild Oregon
   Salmon
4 tablespoons sweet butter, room
   temperature
1 teaspoon Dijon Mustard
1 teaspoon chopped fresh tarragon
1 teaspoon chopped fresh chives
1 teaspoon chopped parsley
1 teaspoon lemon juice
Piment d'Espelette
sea salt
1 cup frisée lettuce or arugula
8 slices baguette, cut on the bias in
   1-inch pieces

Court- bouillon:
2 cups water
1 cup dry white wine
2 sprigs fresh thyme
1 bay leaf
1 small onion, peeled and diced
1 small carrot, peeled and diced
1 stalk celery, diced
1 tablespoon salt
olive oil to season lettuce
fresh radishes, sliced, for garnish
chopped chives for garnish

For the court-bouillon, place the water, white wine, thyme, bay leaf, onion, carrot, celery and salt in a sauce pot. Bring to a boil. Reduce heat and simmer for 10 minutes.

At that time, place the salmon on top of vegetables and cook through but fish still moist, about 5 to 7 minutes. Remove the salmon and refrigerate it.

Whip the butter with a whisk until light and fluffy. Add the herbs, mustard, and lemon juice and whip to mix thoroughly. Season with salt and Piment d'Espelette. With your fingers, flake the flesh of the salmon into small pieces. Add to the butter and fold in with a spatula. Refrigerate for at least one hour.

When ready to serve, grill the baguette slices. Season the lettuce with lemon, olive oil and salt and pepper. Place the lettuce on top of the bread. Use a spoon to place salmon mixture in an attractive manner. Garnish with radishes and chives for additional color.

Makes 4 servings

Baked Chicken with Bacon, Mushrooms, and Pearl Onions

3 pounds chicken breasts, cut into
    pieces
coarse salt
freshly ground black pepper
2 teaspoons olive oil
½ pound bacon, cut into ½-inch
    pieces
12 cloves garlic, unpeeled
16 pearl onions
24 white mushrooms, trimmed
1 cup dry white wine
15 sprigs assorted herbs
    such as parsley, rosemary, sage,
    thyme, marjoram or savory
1 to 2 tablespoons flour

Preheat oven to 325 degrees. Wash the chicken pieces under cold running water and pat dry with paper towels. Season chicken all over with salt and pepper, then set aside.

In a large, heavy bottomed pot large enough to hold the ingredients, heat olive oil and bacon over medium-high heat. Cook bacon for 5 minutes, or until it has browned and rendered enough fat to coat the bottom of pot. Transfer bacon to a paper-towel-lined plate to drain, leaving as much fat as possible in the pot.

Add chicken pieces to pan, skin side down, and brown all over in bacon fat, 4 to 5 minutes per side. Return bacon to pan, along with garlic, onions, mushrooms, wine and herb sprigs. Cover pot and transfer to the oven. Bake for 20 minutes, then remove cover and bake for another 20 minutes.

Transfer chicken and vegetables from pot to a warm platter, discarding herb sprigs. Skim any grease from surface of the sauce, and then whisk in the flour to thicken, if desired.

Divide chicken pieces among four plates, spoon a good assortment of vegetables over each portion, and top with sauce.

Serve alongside a tomato, onion and kalamata olive salad dressed in a fresh herb vinaigrette.

Makes 4 servings

Theatre	Year built	Year renovated
Keller	1917	1968
Schnitzer	1927	1983-84
Newmark	1987	-
Winningstad	1987	-
Brunish Hall	1987	2000

Entrées

Chicken and Garlic Stew

3 tablespoons olive oil
40 cloves garlic, peeled
12 pieces chicken legs and thighs
½ cup chopped parsley
½ cup chopped celery leaves
1 teaspoon dried tarragon
1 tablespoon salt
1 teaspoon ground white pepper
½ teaspoon allspice
¼ teaspoon cinnamon
1½ cups dry white wine

Makes 6 servings

Preheat oven to 375 degrees.

Place oil in ovenproof heavy pot which can be tightly covered. Add 1/3 of the garlic and 1/3 of the other ingredients, including the chicken pieces. Repeat layering two more times.

Cover pot tightly and bake at 375 degrees for 1¼ hours.

Serve with crusty bread to soak up the sauce. Spread softened garlic on the bread like a pâté.

Although this seems like a lot of garlic, it will not be overpowering after it is cooked. This recipe is even better served the next day!

Carl Selin

Sconce and Scagliola (Arlene Schnitzer Concert Hall)

Advertised as "an acre of seats in a palace of splendor", the Portland Publix Theatre was a movie theatre and vaudeville house of great opulence and scale. With 3034 seats, it was the largest movie theater in Portland. After the modifications made to the hall during the restoration, we now have 2776 seats.

Scagliola is hand-veined plaster that resembles marble. Much of the original lobby was done in scagliola. During the restoration, new scagliola was created to match the remaining pieces.

Chicken Breasts with Artichokes and Mushrooms

2 pounds skinless, boneless chicken
    breasts
onion powder, to taste
paprika, to taste
salt
pepper
1 (14-ounce) can artichoke hearts,
    drained
½ pound fresh mushrooms, sliced
1 bunch green onions, chopped
2 cloves garlic, minced
2 tablespoons butter
2 tablespoons flour
⅔ cup chicken broth
3 tablespoons sherry

Preheat oven to 350 degrees.

Season chicken with onion powder, paprika, salt and pepper. Place chicken in bottom of a 3-quart casserole. Cut artichokes and place around chicken.

In a small skillet, sauté mushrooms, green onions and garlic until tender. Place mushroom mixture on top of chicken. In same skillet, melt butter and add flour, stirring. Gradually add chicken broth and sherry, cooking until smooth. Pour sauce over all in casserole.

Bake covered at 350 degrees for 1 hour. Remove cover, and continue baking for 15 minutes to brown chicken.

Makes 4-6 servings

Chicken Breasts with Chipped Beef and Mushrooms

8 boned chicken breasts, halved
1 (5-ounce) jar chipped beef,
    shredded
½ pound mushrooms, sliced
1 pint sour cream
2 (10½-ounce) cans cream of
    chicken soup
2 tablespoons sherry
1½ teaspoons tarragon
paprika

Preheat oven to 350 degrees.

In a skillet, sauté the mushrooms. Set aside. Place chipped beef in the bottom of a large baking dish. Place chicken breasts on top of chipped beef.

In a mixing bowl, combine sour cream, soup, sherry, mushrooms and tarragon; mix well. Pour sauce over chicken and sprinkle with paprika.

Bake at 350 degrees for 1½ hours. Cover with foil if it is drying out. Serve with rice.

Makes 10 servings

Chicken Breasts with Fresh Green Herb Sauce

Chicken:
6 chicken breast halves, boned
1 teaspoon chili powder
1 teaspoon garlic powder
½ teaspoon cracked black pepper
½ teaspoon salt
½ teaspoon ground cumin

Sauce:
1 cup chopped parsley leaves
1 cup chopped cilantro leaves
1 cup chopped basil leaves
1 cup chopped dill leaves
   (all herbs loosely packed)
⅓ cup olive oil
¼ cup red wine vinegar
3 tablespoons roasted garlic
½ teaspoon salt
½ teaspoon cracked black pepper

Preheat oven to 400 degrees. Line a 9 x 13-inch baking dish with foil.

Sauce:
In medium bowl, stir together parsley, cilantro, basil, dill, oil, vinegar, garlic, salt and pepper. Let stand at room temperature for 30 minutes.

Chicken:
In a small bowl, mix chili and garlic powders, pepper, salt and cumin; rub mixture over both sides of the chicken. Arrange on prepared pan in single layer, cover and marinate in refrigerator 15 minutes.

Place oven rack in lowest position. Bake chicken 12 to 15 minutes, or until golden and cooked through.

Transfer chicken to serving plates and drizzle with sauce to serve.

Makes 6 servings

Chicken Cranberry Casserole

6 boneless chicken breasts
1 (16-ounce) can whole cranberries
1 package onion soup mix
½ cup creamy French dressing

Preheat oven to 325 degrees. Grease a 9 x 13-inch casserole dish.

Place chicken in prepared casserole dish, skin side up. In a mixing bowl, combine French Dressing, soup mix and cranberries together and pour over chicken. Bake at 325 degrees for 45 to 60 minutes. Serve with rice.

Makes 6 servings

Chicken Enchiladas

2 cups chicken, cooked and cut into
   small pieces
½ cup onions, finely chopped
½ cup mushrooms, sliced (optional)
1 (10½-ounce) can cream of
   chicken soup
¾ cup chicken broth
1 (4-ounce) can diced green chilies
13 (6-inch) corn tortillas
1½ cups Cheddar cheese, grated
¼ teaspoon pepper

Garnish:
diced fresh tomato
sour cream
avocado

Makes 6 servings

Preheat oven to 375 degrees.

In a saucepan, combine soup, broth, chilies and pepper. Cook over low heat until smooth. In a separate bowl, combine chicken, onions and mushrooms and add a small amount of soup mixture.

Spread 1/3 of the soup mixture in a 9 x 13-inch pan. Warm tortillas, two at a time in the microwave to soften (about 30 seconds). Put 2 tablespoons of chicken mixture on each tortilla, sprinkle with cheese, roll up and place seam side down in the pan.

Pour remaining soup mixture over all and sprinkle with remaining cheese. Bake at 375 degrees for 30 to 45 minutes, or until hot and bubbly.

Serve with diced fresh tomatoes, sour cream and avocados.

Chicken Poppy Seed Casserole

2 cups chicken, diced
1 (8-ounce) can water chestnuts,
   sliced and rinsed in boiling water
16 ounces frozen peas
1 (10½-ounce) can cream of
   chicken soup
1 cup sour cream
½ cup butter (1 cube), melted
1 tube Ritz crackers, crushed
2 tablespoons poppy seeds

Preheat oven to 350 degrees. Grease a 7 x 11-inch baking dish.

In a mixing bowl, combine chicken, water chestnuts, peas, soup and sour cream. Place in prepared baking dish. In a separate bowl, combine butter, crackers and poppy seeds. Place on top of chicken mixture.

Bake at 350 degrees for 30 minutes.

Makes 4-6 servings

Chicken Pot Pie

3 cups cooked chicken breasts,
   cubed
1¼ cups milk, divided
½ cup sour cream
¾ cup buttermilk baking mix
¼ cup cornmeal
1 egg
1 (16-ounce) package frozen peas
1 (10½-ounce) can cream of
   chicken soup
2 cups Cheddar cheese, shredded
paprika for color (optional)

Preheat oven to 375 degrees.

In a saucepan, heat chicken, ½ cup milk, sour cream, peas and soup to boiling. Spoon into 6 ungreased 10-ounce casserole custard cups or a rectangular 9 x 13-inch baking dish.

In a small bowl, beat baking mix, cornmeal, ¾ cup milk and egg with a wire whisk until almost smooth. Pour evenly over the hot chicken mixture. Sprinkle with cheese and paprika. Bake uncovered for 20 to 25 minutes until the top is set and the soup mixture bubbles around the edge.

Makes 6 servings

Creamy Chicken Enchiladas

4 cups cooked chicken breast,
   coarsely chopped
2 cups light sour cream
7 ounces diced green chilies
3 (10½-ounce) cans cream of
   chicken soup
¾ cup green onions, chopped
12 (8-inch) flour tortillas
½ cup Monterey Jack cheese, grated
1½ cups Cheddar cheese, grated

Preheat oven to 350 degrees. Lightly grease a 9 x 13-inch baking dish.

In a mixing bowl, combine sour cream, green chilies and soup to make a sauce. Divide in half. To one half add chicken and onions. Spoon chicken mixture equally onto tortillas. Roll tortillas and place seam down in prepared baking dish.

Cover with remaining sauce. Sprinkle with the cheeses. Bake at 350 degrees for 20 minutes, or until hot and bubbly.

Makes 6-8 servings

Chicken with Green Grapes

4 whole skinless, boneless chicken
   breasts
3 tablespoons flour
6 tablespoons butter, divided
⅔ pound mushrooms, sliced
1¼ cups chicken broth
1 cup dry white wine
½ teaspoon dried rosemary
3 tablespoons flour
⅓ cup water
2 cups seedless green grapes
salt
pepper

Lightly coat chicken with flour and shake off excess.

In a large skillet, melt 4 tablespoons butter over medium high heat. Add chicken pieces and cook, turning once until browned, about 10 minutes. Remove chicken from skillet and set aside.

Melt remaining 2 tablespoons butter in skillet, add mushrooms and cook, stirring, until lightly browned. Add chicken broth, wine and rosemary.

Return chicken to pan; cover and simmer, turning once, until meat is no longer pink, about 20 minutes.

With slotted spoon or tongs, transfer chicken to serving dish and keep warm.

In a small bowl, mix flour and water until smooth. Gradually stir into pan juices. Cook, stirring constantly, until thickened, about 2 to 3 minutes.

Add grapes; cook, stirring just until heated, about 3 to 4 minutes. Salt and pepper to taste. Pour over chicken.

Makes 4 servings

Entrées

*The Metropolitan Arts Commission administers a special fund, **1% for the Arts**. An ordinance requires that 1% of new construction or major alteration of public buildings is set aside for art purchases. The New Theatre Building received three pieces of art under this plan: the **Spectral Light Dome**, the **Portland Town** mural and the fireplace, **Muse, Gaze, Mirror, Maze.***

Basic Tomato Sauce

1 tablespoon olive oil
1 medium leek, white and green
    parts, cleaned and chopped
2 cloves garlic
1 (35-ounce) can Italian tomatoes
1 teaspoon sugar
1 teaspoon salt
½ teaspoon freshly ground pepper

Heat oil in skillet. Add leek and garlic, and sauté over low heat for 5 minutes or until leek is wilted.

Empty tomatoes with liquid into a bowl and mash thoroughly.

Add tomatoes, sugar, salt and pepper to leeks and garlic; stir to combine.

Simmer sauce, uncovered, over low heat until liquid is reduced by half (approximately 25 to 35 minutes).

Makes about 2 cups

Easy Paprika Chicken

1 tablespoon butter
4 skinless, boneless chicken breasts
2 (10½-ounce) cans cream of
    mushroom soup
1 teaspoon paprika
4 cups cooked bow tie pasta
1 cup sour cream
salt
pepper

In a 10-inch skillet, cook chicken in hot butter until browned on both sides. Remove and set aside. In the same skillet, combine soup and paprika. Heat to boiling. Return chicken to the skillet. Reduce heat to low.

Gradually add cooked bow tie pasta. Cover and cook 5 minutes, or until chicken is no longer pink, stirring occasionally. Stir sour cream into the mixture in the skillet. Heat through and serve.

Makes 4 servings

Entrées

Herbed Almond Chicken

4 boneless, skinless chicken thighs
    (about 1 pound)
¼ cup Dijon mustard
1 tablespoon packed brown sugar
1 teaspoon dried tarragon
½ teaspoon garlic powder
1 cup coarsely chopped almonds

Makes 4 servings

Preheat oven to 400 degrees. Lightly grease a baking sheet.

In a small bowl, blend mustard, brown sugar, tarragon and garlic powder.

Coat chicken thighs with mustard mixture, then roll in chopped almonds. Place on prepared baking sheet.

Bake at 400 degrees for 25 to 30 minutes, or until done.

Also good as an appetizer. Cut thighs to bite-sized pieces.

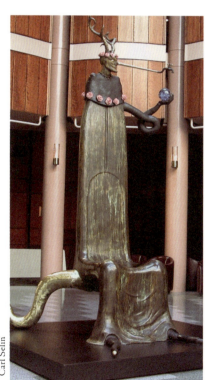

Carl Selin

Mago Hermano *- Alejandro Colunga, Artist*
(New Theatre Building)

Mago Hermano *means brother magician and represents a man, 10 feet tall, whose body serves as a bench. The bronze work was presented to the City of Portland by the City of Guadalajara, Mexico, under the Portland-Guadalajara Sister City Association program. The statue is meant to be sat upon, and the children love him.*

Hot Chicken Salad Casserole

2½ cups chicken breast, cooked and
    diced
1 cup celery, diced
1 cup fresh mushrooms, sliced
1 tablespoon lemon juice
½ teaspoon crushed rosemary
1 tablespoon minced onion
¼ teaspoon pepper
1 (8-ounce) can sliced water
    chestnuts
2 cups cooked rice
¾ cup mayonnaise
1 (10½-ounce) can cream of
    mushroom soup

Topping:
½ cup cornflakes
3 tablespoons butter
½ cup slivered almonds

Preheat oven to 350 degrees.

In a large mixing bowl, combine chicken, celery, mushrooms, lemon juice, rosemary, onion, pepper, water chestnuts and rice. In a separate small bowl, blend mayonnaise and soup, and add to chicken mixture. Pour into 2-quart casserole.

Topping:
In a saucepan, melt butter and combine with cornflakes and almonds. Top casserole with mixture.

Bake at 350 degrees for 30 minutes.

Makes 6 servings

Movie House to Concert Hall

1927	Ground broken on Broadway and Main for Portland Publix Theatre.
1928	In March, movie house was opened for business.
1929	Renamed Portland Paramount Theatre and was affiliated with Paramount Pictures.
1971	On August 15, last movie was shown, **Dr. Phibes Rides Again.**
1972	Building was declared an Historic Landmark.
1973	Structure was added to the National Historic Register.
1975	Paramount furnishings auctioned off by the owner to raise cash.
1975 - 1983	Theater's slow demise. Used for rock concerts and closed circuit television broadcasts.
1983	In September, ground was broken for refurbishing to create the concert hall.
1984	The Arlene Schnitzer Concert Hall opened its doors in September of that year.

Entrées

Mexican Chicken with Rice

4 boneless chicken breasts
1 cup salsa
1 package dry taco seasoning mix
2 cups water
2 cups uncooked Minute Rice
1 (15¼-ounce) can corn, drained
1 cup shredded cheese
chopped olives

Cut chicken into small pieces. Bring chicken, salsa, taco seasoning mix and water to a boil in a large skillet. Cover and simmer for 10 minutes. Return to a boil. Stir in Minute Rice, corn and cheese. Top with olives and cover. Cook on low heat for 5 minutes.

Makes 6 servings

Spectacular Chicken Casserole

4 cups cooked chicken, diced
3 cups French cut green beans
1 cup cooked white rice
1 cup cooked wild rice
½ cup canned water chestnuts,
    sliced and blanched in boiling
    water for 15 seconds
¼ teaspoon salt
2 (10½-ounce) cans cream of celery
    soup
½ teaspoon white pepper
½ cup onion, diced
Tabasco sauce, to taste
½ cup bread crumbs
paprika - for color

Preheat oven to 350 degrees. Mix all ingredients together except bread crumbs and paprika. Put the mixture in a 9 x 13-inch baking dish. Sprinkle with bread crumbs and paprika. Bake 25 to 30 minutes or until bubbly.

May substitute broccoli for green beans.

Makes 8 servings

Entrées

Sweet and Sour Chicken

8 boneless chicken breasts
1 cup orange marmalade
1 cup Russian salad dressing
1 package dry onion soup mix
2 green peppers, seeded and cut
   into small chunks
1 (15-ounce) can pineapple chunks
   in light syrup, drained

Preheat oven to 350 degrees. Place chicken in a greased 9 x 13-inch baking dish. Combine orange marmalade, Russian dressing and dry onion soup mix. Cover chicken with orange marmalade mixture.

Bake for 40 minutes. Remove from oven, and add green pepper and pineapple. Return to oven for 10 minutes or until heated through.

Makes 8 servings

Butterflied Leg of Lamb

1 (4 pound) butterflied, boneless
   leg of lamb
1 cup sour cream
1 teaspoon salt
¼ teaspoon coarsely ground pepper
1 teaspoon oregano
1 teaspoon parsley
1 teaspoon fresh garlic, finely
   minced

In a small bowl, mix sour cream, salt, pepper, oregano, parsley and garlic. Blend well.

Leaving the meat in a flat piece, coat both sides generously with the sour cream mixture.

Place in a plastic or glass dish, cover with plastic wrap and place in the refrigerator for about 8 hours.

Broil or grill to an internal temperature of 130 to 135 degrees, and it is done. Let stand 10 minutes before serving.

Ask the butcher to trim or pull the "fell" off the outside of the lamb. If the lamb is not butterflied, score through the thickest part of the lamb leg to open it up.

Makes 8 servings

Entrées

Italian Lamb Skillet Dinner

1 pound boneless lamb, cut into
    bite-sized pieces
5 cups cooked rotelle pasta
    (2 cups uncooked)
3 cups spaghetti sauce
4 cups chopped assorted vegetables
2 tablespoons water
1 teaspoon basil
1 teaspoon oregano
salt and pepper
2 tablespoons cooking oil
grated fresh Parmesan cheese

Heat oil in 10 to 12-inch skillet and sauté lamb until brown.

Add spaghetti sauce and stir. Add cooked pasta and stir. Add vegetables and water, stirring well.

Cover with lid, stirring occasionally for 10 minutes, or until vegetables are slightly cooked.

Serve on plates, topped with Parmesan cheese. Serve this with crusty bread, wine, and salad on the side. Makes a good leftover.

Makes 4 servings

Lamb Stew

2½ pounds lean lamb shoulder,
    cubed
1 cup flour
salt
freshly ground pepper
2 tablespoons butter
2 tablespoons vegetable oil
2 cups low-salt beef stock
3 large carrots, peeled and cut into
    ½-inch cubes
1 large turnip, peeled and cut into
    ½-inch cubes
1 large onion, thinly sliced

Makes 4 servings

Preheat oven to 350 degrees. Put the flour, salt and pepper in a large plastic sealable bag. Dredge lamb cubes in flour and shake off any excess.

In a large skillet, melt butter and oil. Raise temperature to medium high. Add lamb and cook, turning often, until browned on all sides (5 to 7 minutes). Transfer to a large oven-proof casserole.

Pour off any remaining fat from skillet. Add beef stock and increase heat to high. Bring to a boil, stirring to pick up any browned bits left in bottom of skillet. Pour over lamb in casserole, cover, and bake in preheated oven for 1 hour. Add vegetables and cook for an additional 45 minutes until vegetables are cooked.

This is great the second day.

Entrées

Lamb Tagine with Dates and Pearl Onions

1 pound pearl onions
¾ cup golden raisins
¾ cup dry sherry
1½ cups fresh orange juice
6 cloves garlic, minced
4½ pounds boneless lamb
  shoulder or stew meat cut
  into 1½ to 2- inch pieces
¾ cup dry red wine
1½ tablespoons flour
¾ cup halved pitted black olives
8 tablespoons chopped fresh
  parsley
¼ cup chopped fresh cilantro or
  1 teaspoon ground coriander
1½ teaspoons ground
  cinnamon
1½ teaspoons ground ginger
¾ cup pine nuts
⅛ teaspoon crushed saffron
  threads (may add up to ¼
  teaspoon in total)
2¼ cups water
12 ounces pitted dates
3 tablespoons slivered almonds,
  toasted
1 (14-ounce) can tomatoes, well
  drained or fresh tomatoes
  (optional)

Makes 8 servings

Soak raisins in ¾ cup sherry for 3 hours. Cook onions in boiling water for 2 minutes. Drain, rinse under cold water and peel.

Place lamb, orange juice, and garlic in large bowl. Marinate at room temperature for at least 2 hours, turning lamb occasionally. Drain, reserving marinade. Heat oil in Dutch oven over medium-high heat. Brown lamb a few pieces at a time - about 4 minutes per batch. Return to bowl as browned.

With lamb still in bowl, add ¾ of the pearl onions to Dutch oven, sauté lightly. After a few minutes add parsley, cilantro/coriander, cinnamon, ginger, saffron, and pine nuts to Dutch oven. Cook 5 minutes more. Add flour and stir. Cook 1 minute. Add raisins, sherry and reserved marinade to Dutch oven. Stir to mix.

Return lamb to Dutch oven. Add olives, remaining pearl onions and tomatoes. Reduce heat, cover and simmer until lamb is tender, about 1 hour to 1 hour 20 minutes. Using slotted spoon, transfer lamb and pearl onions to bowl. Reserve 5 dates for garnish. Adjust consistency of sauce at this point. Add water if too thick, or reduce if too thin. Add remaining dates to sauce in Dutch oven. Simmer 5 minutes, mashing dates to coarse purée with back of fork. Return lamb mixture to Dutch oven; simmer until heated through, about 5 minutes. Season tagine to taste with salt and pepper. Top with slivered almonds and reserved dates.

Serve with Couscous.

Entrées

Chinese Barbecued Pork

2 pounds boneless center-cut pork
    loin, cut into 3-inch slices

Marinade:
2 tablespoons Hoisin sauce
2 tablespoons soy sauce
1½ tablespoons rice wine
2½ tablespoons sugar
1 teaspoon salt
1 tablespoon ketchup
1½ tablespoons minced garlic
2 to 3 slices fresh ginger, chopped

Preheat oven to 375 degrees.

In a mixing bowl, combine all ingredients. Place meat in the marinade for 4 hours or overnight, turning occasionally.

Arrange the meat on a rack in a roasting pan. Roast at 375 degrees for 45 minutes. Cool slightly, slice thin, and serve.

This freezes well.

Makes 6-8 servings

Chinese Red-cooked Pork Bites

2 pounds boneless pork loin, cut
    into ¾-inch cubes
2 tablespoons brown sugar
2 tablespoons Hoisin sauce
2 tablespoons soy sauce
1 tablespoon Worcestershire sauce
1 tablespoon toasted sesame oil
1 shallot, chopped
2 teaspoons five spice
2 teaspoons grated ginger root
2 cloves garlic, minced

Makes 6-8 servings

In a 1-gallon self-sealing plastic bag, combine the cubed pork, brown sugar, Hoisin sauce, soy sauce, Worcestershire, sesame oil, shallot, five spice, ginger and garlic. Mix well. Seal bag and marinate in the refrigerator 8 to 12 hours or overnight.

When ready to continue, preheat oven to 350 degrees.

Remove pork cubes from marinade, discarding marinade. Pat pork dry with paper toweling. Place cubes in a single layer in a shallow baking dish, taking care not to allow cubes to touch.

Bake at 350 degrees for 25 to 30 minutes, until pork is just tender and lightly browned. Remove to serving platter or chafing dish and serve hot.

Hoisin sauce and five spice can be found in the Asian food section of most grocery stores.

Entrées

Galotsie Polonaise

1 pound pork tenderloin, cut in ½-inch slices
½ pound ham steak, cut in 2-inch strips
1 pound thin sliced bacon, cut in 3-inch pieces and partially cooked
½ pound smoked bratwurst, cut in small pieces
1 pound mushrooms, cleaned and sliced
½ pound green pitted olives, sliced thin
½ cup butter (1 cube)
1 (14½-ounce) can stewed tomatoes
1 pound fresh sauerkraut, washed in cold water and drained
2 cups tomato juice
3 Granny Smith apples, cored and sliced
2 large white onions, peeled and sliced thin
1 small white cabbage, sliced and par-boiled in salted water
salt
freshly ground pepper
2 bay leaves
1 teaspoon sugar

Mustard Sauce:
2 cups sour cream
3 tablespoons imported mustard
fresh chives, as garnish

Preheat oven to 375 degrees. Due to the large number of ingredients, use the largest Dutch oven available. It will cook down considerably. Grease the Dutch oven with butter or a bit of the bacon grease.

Except for the butter and tomato juice, add all ingredients in layers. Bury half the butter in the middle of the pot. Pour the tomato juice over all. Mix well. Place remaining butter on top.

Cover and place in oven for at least 2 hours. (It is better to overcook than undercook!) The blending of the flavors is essential here. Remove the cover for the last 20 minutes to allow dish to brown slightly on top.

If it is too juicy, remove some of the juice and reduce separately. If too dry, add more tomato juice or canned consommé.

Mustard Sauce:
In a small bowl, fold mustard into the sour cream. Sprinkle the top with finely chopped fresh chives. Serve mustard sauce separately to be added on top.

Serve with boiled potatoes.

May be assembled a day ahead and refrigerated. Plan on a longer cooking time if it is cold. This dish is even better the next day (or the day after).

Makes 8-12 servings

Entrées

Pork Medallions with Port and Dried Cranberry Sauce

½ cup dried cranberries or cherries
1 cup water
1 teaspoon vegetable oil
1 pound pork tenderloin, trimmed
    of fat and membrane and cut
    into 12 medallions
salt
freshly ground black pepper
1 shallot, finely chopped
½ cup tawny port
¼ cup balsamic vinegar
1 cup low-fat, reduced sodium
    chicken stock
½ teaspoon dried thyme
1 teaspoon cornstarch
1 tablespoon water

In a small saucepan, combine dried cranberries and 1 cup water. Bring to a simmer and cook for 3 minutes. Drain, reserving both fruit and cooking liquid. Set aside.

In a large nonstick skillet, heat oil over medium heat. Season pork with salt and pepper and add to skillet; cook until browned on the outside and no longer pink on the inside, about 3 minutes per side. Transfer to a platter, cover loosely and keep warm. (Do not wash the skillet.) Add shallots to the skillet and cook, stirring, for 30 seconds. Pour in port and vinegar and bring to a boil, stirring to scrape up any brown bits. Boil until reduced by half (3 to 5 minutes).

Add chicken stock, thyme and reserved cranberry cooking liquid; boil until reduced again by half (5 to 7 minutes). In a small bowl, dissolve cornstarch in 1 tablespoon water. Whisk into the sauce and cook, stirring, until slightly thickened and glossy. Stir in the reserved cranberries and season with salt and pepper. Spoon the sauce over the medallions and serve.

Serve with Rice and Noodle Pilaf (see page 70 for recipe).

Makes 4-6 servings

Entrées

The PCPA is nestled between the busiest street (Broadway) and the quietest street (Park) in downtown Portland. The Park Blocks were established very soon after the founding of Portland and originally stretched from Portland State University through the downtown area. Over time, several blocks have been lost to private development. But the three blocks behind PCPA were slated for renewal at the same time the performing arts complex was being planned. The Park Blocks facelift was designed to compliment the PCPA.

Pork Tenderloin with Rosemary and Thyme

2 (½-pound) pork tenderloins or 1
    pound boneless pork loin roast
cooking spray
2 tablespoons Dijon mustard
1 tablespoon honey
1 teaspoon chopped fresh rosemary
½ teaspoon chopped fresh thyme
¼ teaspoon pepper
thyme sprigs (optional)

Preheat oven to 350 degrees. Trim fat from pork; place on a broiler pan coated with cooking spray. Combine mustard, honey, chopped rosemary, thyme, and pepper in a bowl; brush over pork. Insert a meat thermometer into the thickest part of the pork. (Use a heat resistant thermometer, not an instant-read one.) Bake at 350 degrees for 50 minutes or until thermometer registers 160 degrees (slightly pink), basting frequently with mustard mixture.

Allow meat to rest 15 minutes before carving. It will continue to cook slightly. Garnish with thyme sprigs, if desired.

Makes 4 servings

Spicy Pork Tenderloin with Ginger Maple Sauce

2 teaspoons chili powder
1 teaspoon cinnamon
1 teaspoon salt
1 teaspoon pepper
2 (1-pound) pork tenderloins
1 tablespoon butter
½ cup diced onion
1 tablespoon grated or minced
    ginger root
½ cup chicken stock
¼ cup maple syrup
cooking spray

Makes 4 servings

Preheat oven to 375 degrees. Combine chili powder, cinnamon, salt and pepper. Coat the tenderloins with this mixture. Let stand for 30 minutes at room temperature.

In a skillet over medium heat, melt butter and caramelize the onions (stirring constantly for 20 minutes). Add ginger. After 5 minutes add chicken stock and simmer for 10 minutes. Add maple syrup and simmer for an additional 5 minutes.

In a separate oiled skillet, sear the tenderloins on high heat until browned on all sides. Transfer to a 9 x 13-inch baking dish. Bake 20 to 30 minutes. Pour sauce over meat and return to oven for 5 minutes. Remove from oven and stir to deglaze. Slice the meat on the diagonal, spoon sauce over the top.

Entrées

Barbeque Brisket of Beef

1 (1 to 8 pound) brisket of beef
garlic powder
onion salt
celery salt
3 ounces Liquid Smoke flavoring
black pepper
Worcestershire sauce

Sauce:
1 cup ketchup
1 cup beef broth
1 teaspoon salt
2 dashes Tabasco sauce
1 teaspoon chili powder
3 tablespoons Worcestershire sauce

Prepare sauce by mixing ketchup, beef broth, salt, Tabasco, chili powder and Worcestershire sauce. Sprinkle brisket with garlic powder, onion salt and celery salt. Pierce with a fork and pour on Liquid Smoke seasoning. Cover and refrigerate overnight. When ready to bake, sprinkle on black pepper and Worcestershire sauce.

Bake at 250 degrees for 5 hours, covered.

After baking meat, cool and slice. Return to pan, add the sauce, and bake at 250 degrees for 30 to 45 minutes longer.

Beef Bravado

4 pounds pot roast
1 tablespoon seasoned salt
¼ cup cooking oil
4 tablespoons butter, divided
3 cloves garlic, pressed
1 cup onion, chopped
¾ cup celery, thinly sliced
¼ cup flour
2 (8-ounce) cans tomato juice
2 cups 7-Up
1 beef bouillon cube
2 tablespoons chopped parsley
1 tablespoon brown sugar
1 teaspoon marjoram
1 teaspoon thyme
¼ teaspoon black pepper
1 pound mushrooms, quartered
pitted ripe olives, for garnish

Cut meat into 1½-inch cubes and sprinkle on all sides with seasoned salt. In large skillet, heat oil and 2 tablespoons butter. Brown meat, and add garlic, onion and celery. Cook 3 to 5 minutes. Blend in flour, then stir in the remaining ingredients except for butter, mushrooms and olives. Cover and bring to a boil. Reduce heat and simmer until tender. Remove excess fat.

Approximately 15 minutes prior to the end of cooking, melt 2 tablespoons butter in a skillet and sauté mushrooms, stirring occasionally. Mix mushrooms into beef mixture and turn onto a heated platter. Garnish with olives.

Makes 6-8 servings

Beef Ai Raifoid

4 pounds beef, trimmed and cubed
½ cup butter (1 cube), divided
2 large onions, thinly sliced
3 teaspoons curry powder
2 teaspoon ground ginger
3 tablespoons Worcestershire sauce
1 teaspoon salt
1 teaspoon black pepper
1 cup white wine
1 cup sour cream
5 tablespoons horseradish
3 tablespoons chopped parsley

Preheat oven to 300 degrees.

In large skillet, melt half of butter over medium high heat. Working in batches, brown beef on all sides. Add additional butter as needed. Transfer beef to a large, covered ovenproof dish or pot. Set aside.

In the original skillet, brown onions and sauté until limp. Transfer onions and any remaining pan juices to the pot with the beef. Add curry powder, ginger, Worcestershire, salt, pepper and wine.

Cover and cook at 300 degrees for 3 hours, stirring occasionally.

In a small bowl, mix the horseradish with the sour cream and parsley. Add to the pot and stir to blend. Serve over prepared egg noodles.

Makes 6 servings

The area back stage where performers wait to go on is traditionally called the Green Room. There are many stories telling how this name came into being. One story claims that the term began with the first waiting area of London's famed Covent Garden that just happened to be painted green. Another story tells of the early spotlights giving off a green cast on the performers (hence the saying, in the limelight). After staring into these lights during the performance, everything began to take on a greenish hue. Consequently, when the performer left the stage and returned to the waiting area, that room looked "green".

Beef Stew in Red Wine

4 strips bacon, cut in 1-inch pieces
2 ½ pounds beef stew meat
salt
pepper
½ pound boiling onions
3 tablespoons flour
1 ½ cups dry red wine
3 tablespoons brandy
1 medium onion
4 whole cloves
2 cloves garlic, minced
⅛ teaspoon dried marjoram
⅛ teaspoon dried thyme
1 strip orange peel, zested
1 tablespoon beef bouillon granules
1 cup water
½ pound mushrooms, quartered
2 tablespoons butter
fresh parsley, finely chopped

Makes 4-6 servings

Preheat oven to 325 degrees.

In a heavy frying pan, brown bacon. Remove bacon. Season beef with salt and pepper, and add to hot bacon drippings and brown on all sides. Transfer meat and crisp bacon to a 3-quart casserole.

Add boiling onions to drippings and brown lightly; set aside. Sprinkle flour into drippings and let brown slightly. Gradually add wine and brandy to flour mixture. Stud the onion with cloves. Add onion, garlic, marjoram, thyme, orange zest, beef bouillon granules and water to wine mixture. Bring to a boil and pour over meat.

Cover casserole and cook at 325 degrees for 2 to 2½ hours, or until meat is almost tender enough to serve. Add browned onions and cook 30 minutes longer, or until meat is very tender when pierced.

Sauté mushrooms in butter. Add mushrooms to the meat for the last 10 to 15 minutes of cooking.

Sprinkle with parsley.

May substitute brandy with cognac, if desired.

Entrées

Beef Stroganoff

2 pounds round steak, trimmed and
    cubed
4 tablespoons flour
4 tablespoons butter
¼ pound fresh mushrooms, sliced
¼ teaspoon garlic salt
1 tablespoon flour
1 teaspoon Worcestershire sauce
½ cup onions, chopped
⅛ teaspoon pepper
1 cup hot water
1⅔ cups evaporated milk
1 tablespoon lemon juice
2 cups cooked rice or noodles

In a skillet, melt the butter. Dredge meat in flour and brown in butter. Add onions, mushrooms, garlic salt and pepper.

In a small bowl, mix Worcestershire sauce and flour. Add to meat mixture. Add hot water, cover and cook on low heat for 1 hour, or until meat is tender. Stir in evaporated milk.

Just before serving add the lemon juice.

Serve over fluffy rice or wide noodles.

Makes 4 servings

Peach Glazed Corn Beef

1 (3-pound) corned beef brisket
2 cups water
salt
½ cup hot water
2 acorn squash, quartered and
    seeded
4 apples, cored and quartered
½ cup peach preserves
½ teaspoon ground ginger

Preheat oven to 350 degrees. Rinse meat in cold water. Place fat side up on a rack in a roasting pan. Add water and cover. Bake at 350 for 2 hours. Drain. Add squash and apples. Sprinkle squash with salt. Place apples skin side down. Add ½ cup hot water. Cover and bake an additional 45 minutes. Mix preserves and ginger. Spoon over all. Bake uncovered for 10 minutes more.

Makes 6-8 servings

Carol's Applesauce Meatballs

1 egg
½ cup milk
1½ cups herbed seasoned croutons
1½ pounds ground chuck
⅔ cup thick applesauce
3 tablespoons onion, chopped
1½ teaspoons salt
⅛ teaspoon pepper
¼ teaspoon crumbled sage
1 (10½-ounce) can cream of celery
    soup
½ cup water

Preheat oven to 350 degrees.

In a large bowl beat egg, blend in milk and add croutons. Let stand for 10 minutes until croutons have absorbed liquid. Stir until mixture is smooth. Add meat, applesauce, onion, sage, salt and pepper.

Shape mixture into 24 balls and place in a shallow baking pan, or two 10-inch pie plates. In a small bowl, blend soup with water and pour over meatballs. Bake at 350 degrees for 45 minutes.

Serve with boiled potatoes or noodles.

Makes 4 servings

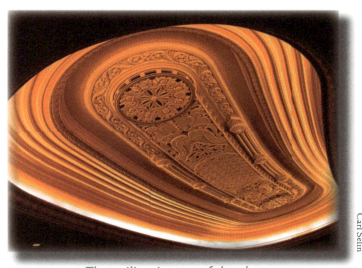

Carl Selin

The ceiling is part of the show.
(Arlene Schnitzer Concert Hall)

The original color scheme of the old movie house utilized shades of gold, green, and red with quantities of gold leaf as accents. The windows and doorways were heavily draped in red velvet. The plasterwork was detailed and beautiful in its own right.

Entrées

Hamburger Stuffed Zucchini

6 small zucchini
1 pound ground beef
1 cup onion, minced
1 egg, slightly beaten
½ cup cracker crumbs
½ cup Parmesan cheese
1 (15-ounce) can tomato sauce
salt
pepper
garlic salt

Makes 6 servings

Preheat oven to 350 degrees. Cut zucchini in half lengthwise. Scrape out insides and reserve, leaving shell with ¼-inch thick walls. In a skillet, brown beef and onions. Add squash pulp. Cover and cook for 5 to 10 minutes, or until squash pulp is soft. Remove beef mixture from heat; stir in egg, cracker crumbs, half of the cheese and enough tomato sauce to moisten. Season with salt, pepper and garlic salt (to taste).

Season squash shells with salt and pepper. Stuff with filling, mounding to use all the filling. Place in shallow baking pan. Spoon a small amount of tomato sauce on squash halves; pour remaining sauce around them. Cover pan and bake at 350 degrees for 30 minutes. Remove cover and top with remaining cheese. Bake 15 minutes longer, until cheese is toasted.

Indonesian Beef Curry

6 pounds cubed beef
1½ cups flour
½ tablespoon salt
1 teaspoon pepper
5 tablespoons curry powder
1 (49-ounce) can beef broth

Assorted Toppings:
   celery, fried bacon, onion, green
   and red peppers, black olives,
   parsley, chopped tomatoes, diced
   peanuts, chopped hard cooked
   eggs, chopped apple, raisins,
   coconut, chutney, yogurt

In a gallon bag, mix flour, salt, pepper, and curry. Shake beef cubes in bag to coat thoroughly. In a skillet with oil, brown the beef. Once thoroughly browned, place beef in a heavy oven-proof pan. Cover with beef broth. Simmer for 1 to 2 hours on very low heat. Stir occasionally to avoid scorching.

Serve over hot rice with assorted toppings.

Makes 8-10 servings

Entrées

Joe's Special

2 tablespoons onion, chopped
1 tablespoon olive oil
1¾ pounds lean ground beef
½ pound fresh mushrooms, sliced
1 (10-ounce) package frozen
   chopped spinach, cooked and
   drained
salt
pepper
4 eggs
½ teaspoon oregano
Parmesan cheese (optional)

In a skillet, sauté onion in olive oil until limp. Add ground beef and cook until still a little pink. Add mushrooms and cook for 10 minutes. Add spinach and heat through completely. Season with salt and pepper to taste. Break eggs into mixture, one at a time. Stir after addition of each egg. Season to taste with oregano. Sprinkle with Parmesan cheese. Serve immediately.

Serve this with crusty bread, wine, and salad on the side. Makes a good leftover.

Makes 4 servings

Non-layered Lasagna

1 pound mini lasagna or bowtie
   noodles, cooked and drained
1 pound lean ground beef
1 (26-ounce) jar spaghetti sauce
8 ounces Mozzarella cheese,
   shredded
1 (5½-ounce) container Chèvre
   goat cheese with herbs
¼ cup fresh Parmesan or Romano
   cheese, grated
oregano

Preheat oven to 375 degrees. While noodles are cooking, brown ground beef and pour off any excess fat. Add spaghetti sauce to beef. Mix in cooked noodles, Chèvre and half the Mozzarella.

Place meat, sauce and cheese mixture in a greased 9 x 13-inch baking dish. Top with remaining Mozzarella and Parmesan. Sprinkle with oregano.

Bake 25 to 30 minutes.

Serve with a crisp green salad and French or Italian bread.

Makes 8-10 servings

Entrées

Broccoli and Beef Stir Fry

¼ cup oil, divided
1½ cups broccoli florets, trimmed, washed, and patted dry
1 pound flank steak, sliced into thin strips
4 tablespoons sherry
4 tablespoons soy sauce
1 teaspoon salt (optional)
1 tablespoon sugar
¼ teaspoon ground ginger
4 tablespoons cornstarch
1½ cups beef broth, divided
pepper

Makes 4 servings

In large skillet or wok, heat 2 tablespoons oil on high heat. Add broccoli and stir rapidly to prevent burning. Reduce heat, cover, and steam for 4 to 5 minutes.

Remove broccoli from pan and set aside. In same skillet, heat remaining oil until hot and stir fry meat until cooked. Remove meat and set aside. Remove any residue still in pan, then add the sherry, soy sauce, sugar and ginger, mixing well. In a small bowl, add ½ cup beef broth to the cornstarch and stir until all lumps are dissolved. Add remaining broth, cornstarch mixture, salt and pepper to sherry mixture. Heat until sauce begins to come to a boil so it can thicken, stirring constantly. Return broccoli and beef to pan and mix well with sauce. Toss until well mixed. Serve with rice.

Peking Roast Beef

1 (3-5 pound) beef roast, boneless
1 cup vinegar
2 cups strong coffee
2 cups water
1 medium onion, diced
6-8 cloves garlic, slivered
oil

Makes 6-8 servings

Cut slits into meat. Insert pieces of onion and garlic in slits all around roast. Place in a bowl and pour vinegar over roast. Cover. Marinate in refrigerator for 24 to 48 hours, turning from time to time. Discard vinegar. Brown roast in oil in a heavy pot until it is very well browned. Pour strong coffee over roast. Add 2 cups of water and cover. Slowly simmer for 6 hours. Add more water if necessary but never more than 1 cup at a time.

This is a good crockpot recipe.

Perfect Prime Rib

1 aged standing prime rib roast
salt
pepper

Makes 2 servings per pound

Preheat oven to 375 degrees. Let roast stand at room temperature for 1 hour or until it reaches room temperature. Rub meat with salt and pepper. Place the meat fat side up in a shallow roasting pan.

Do not cover and do not add water. Put roast in oven. Cook one hour. Turn off heat. Do not open oven door at any time until ready to serve, regardless of the length of time the roast is in the oven. Then, 30 to 40 minutes before serving time, turn the oven back on to 375 degrees. Cook for 30 to 40 minutes. The roast beef will be medium rare.

Yes, this really works!

Six Layer Casserole

1 cup uncooked rice
2 cups whole kernel corn
1 medium onion, chopped
½ cup chopped green pepper
2 (8-ounce) cans tomato sauce
water
1 pound lean ground beef
1 clove garlic, chopped
Italian seasoning (oregano, basil, thyme), to taste
salt and pepper

Garnish:
cooked crumbled bacon bits

Makes 6 servings

Preheat oven to 350 degrees and grease a 9 x 13-inch pan. Add ingredients layer by layer in the following order: uncooked rice on bottom, then corn, onion, and green pepper. Pour 1 can of tomato sauce and a ½ can of water over pepper layer, then add ground beef, followed by the second can of tomato sauce. Mix garlic, salt and pepper, and any Italian seasoning into ¼ can of water and pour over the top.

Cover with foil and bake at 350 degrees for 90 minutes. Sprinkle bacon bits over casserole just before serving.

This recipe originated with Hunt-Wesson Foods back in the early 60's. It's great for pot lucks.

Entrées

Stack-a-Roll-Stroganoff

1½ pounds ground beef, browned
1 (4-ounce) can mushrooms, drained
1 (3½-ounce) can French fried onions
1 (10½-ounce) can cream of mushroom soup
½ cup sour cream
1 (8-ounce) tube refrigerated biscuits

Topping:
½ cup sour cream
1 egg, beaten with a fork
1 teaspoon celery salt
1 teaspoon salt

Preheat oven to 375 degrees. Combine cooked ground beef, mushrooms, soup, sour cream and most of the French fried onions. (Save a few of them for the final touches.) Place meat mixture into a casserole dish.

Cut each biscuit in half and arrange in a circle over meat mixture, leaving center portion open. (Hint: Use a round mixing bowl to make a circle impression on the meat.) Place remaining fried onions in the center of the circle.

Topping:
Mix sour cream, beaten egg, celery salt and salt. Pour topping over biscuits. (This will prevent them from getting too dark.) Bake at 375 degrees for 25 to 30 minutes.

Makes 4 servings

Myrt's Meatloaf

1½ pounds ground beef
½ pound mild Italian pork sausage
1 (10½-ounce) can chicken with rice soup
1 cup quick oatmeal
1 egg
2 teaspoons salt
¼ teaspoon paprika
¼ teaspoon pepper
1 onion, chopped
3 bay leaves

Preheat oven to 350 degrees. Mix all ingredients except bay leaves. Place bay leaves on bottom of a greased loaf pan. Add meat mixture on top of bay leaves.

Bake at 350 degrees for 1 hour and 30 minutes.

Makes 8 servings

Entrées

True Lasagna

8 ounces lasagna noodles
12 ounces Mozzarella cheese, sliced

Meat Sauce:
1 pound bulk Italian sausage
½ pound lean ground beef
2 cloves garlic, minced
3 (14½ -ounce) cans Italian plum
    tomatoes with basil, chopped
    (save juice)
2 teaspoons crushed dried basil
1 teaspoon crushed dried oregano
1 teaspoon salt
1 (10¾-ounce) can tomato purée
½ teaspoon sugar

Cheese Filling:
3 eggs
1 cup whole milk Ricotta cheese
1 cup dry cottage cheese
⅔ cup grated Romano or Parmesan
    cheese
¼ cup minced fresh parsley
½ teaspoon freshly ground black
    pepper
salt

Meat Sauce:
Preheat oven to 375 degrees. In a large skillet or Dutch oven, brown sausage, ground beef and garlic. Drain off excess fat. Add tomatoes with juice, basil, oregano, salt, tomato purée and sugar to skillet mixture. Bring to a boil; stir well and simmer, partially covered for 30 minutes stirring often until very thick. Remove from heat.

Cook noodles according to package directions. Set aside.

Cheese Filling:
In a medium bowl, beat eggs and blend in the remaining ingredients. Set aside.

Assembly:
Spread a thin layer of meat sauce in the bottom of a greased 9 x 13-inch baking dish. Layer half of lasagna noodles over sauce, cover with half of the cheese filling, half of remaining meat sauce and half of Mozzarella slices. Repeat layers adding the last of the Mozzarella on top. Bake at 375 degrees for 30 to 40 minutes or until bubbly. Let stand approximately 10 minutes before cutting into serving pieces.

The meat sauce can be made a day ahead and refrigerated until time to assemble the dish.

Makes 8-12 servings

Entrées

Marinated Chicken Curry

2 pounds chicken thighs
1 tablespoon oil
¼ cup (½ cube) unsalted butter
1 medium onion, minced
1 tablespoon grated ginger root
2 teaspoons cumin seeds
6 medium tomatoes, peeled and
    chopped
1 tablespoon tomato paste
1 teaspoon sugar
½ cup sour cream
2 teaspoons garam marsala
½ cup chopped cilantro

Marinade:
½ cup plain yogurt
⅓ cup lime juice
1 clove garlic, crushed
1 teaspoon ground cardamom
1 teaspoon ground coriander
½ teaspoon ground cinnamon
½ teaspoon chili powder
¼ teaspoon ground cloves

Prepare marinade by combining yogurt, lime juice, garlic, cardamon, coriander, cinnamon, chili powder and cloves. Mix well.

Place chicken in a large bowl, prick chicken all over with a fork. Add marinade. Cover, refrigerate for several hours or overnight stirring occasionally. Remove chicken, but reserve remaining marinade.

Heat butter and oil in a large saucepan, add chicken in batches. Cook over high heat for about 5 minutes or until browned all over. Remove chicken from pan.

Add onion and ginger to same pan, stir over medium heat for 2 minutes or until onion is soft. Stir in cumin seeds, stir over medium heat for 1 minute. Stir in tomatoes, tomato paste and sugar. Bring to a boil and reduce heat, cover and simmer for about 15 minutes or until sauce is thick.

Stir in chicken, reserved marinade and sour cream. Bring to a boil, reduce heat, cover, simmer for about 15 minutes or until chicken is tender, stirring occasionally.

Stir in garam marsala and cilantro, mix well.

Serve with white rice, tomato, mint and lime salad (recipe on page 140), or yogurt with cucumbers. This dish can be made two days ahead and refrigerated, but do not freeze.

Makes 6-8 servings

Entrées

Curried Shrimp, Chicken and Vegetable Stew

3 onions, halved and sliced thin
2 cloves garlic, minced
3 carrots, sliced
2 stalks celery, sliced
2 parsnips, sliced
2 red bell peppers, chopped
½ cup unsalted butter (1 cube)
3 tablespoons curry powder
1 bay leaf
½ teaspoon cayenne pepper
1 teaspoon cinnamon
½ teaspoon allspice
½ teaspoon cumin
½ teaspoon ground coriander
½ teaspoon black pepper
1 teaspoon salt
1 tablespoon tomato paste
1 (35-ounce) can plum tomatoes
5 cups chicken stock
3 cups water
1 (5-6 pound) roasting chicken
⅓ cup long-grain rice
1 small head cauliflower, cut into
    florets
1 pound green beans, 1-inch pieces
2 small zucchini, sliced
1½ pounds shrimp
½ cup minced parsley
¼ cup minced coriander (cilantro)

In an 8-quart kettle, sauté onions, garlic, carrots, celery, parsnips and bell peppers in butter, over moderate heat, until onions are golden. Stir in curry, bay leaf, cayenne, cumin, cinnamon, allspice, ground coriander, salt and pepper and cook over moderately low heat for 3 minutes.

Stir in tomato paste; add tomatoes (with juice, chopped), stock and water. Bring to a boil, stirring occasionally. Add chicken and simmer, covered, for 1½ hours.

Transfer chicken to cutting board. Skim off fat from kettle. Discard skin and bones from chicken. Cut chicken into 1-inch pieces. Reserve meat. Bring mixture in kettle to boil and stir in rice. Simmer for 10 minutes. Add cauliflower and beans; simmer 5 minutes. Add zucchini and simmer 2 minutes. Add reserved chicken and shrimp and simmer just until shrimp are pink.

Just before serving, stir in minced parsley and coriander. Adjust salt and pepper to taste.

May be made one day in advance, kept covered and chilled. Reheat before serving.

Serve with your choice of crumbled bacon, green hot chili peppers, roasted salted peanuts, golden raisins, onions (sliced thin), lime wedges, or plain yogurt.

Makes 6-8 servings

Barbeque Salmon Fillet

1 (3-4 pound) salmon fillet

Marinade:
2 cloves garlic, crushed
1 tablespoon garlic salt
1 tablespoon onion powder
4 teaspoons seasoned salt
¼ cup lemon juice
¼ teaspoon liquid smoke flavoring
¼ cup brown sugar

Marinade:
In a bowl, combine all marinade ingredients and mix well. Marinate the salmon for at least 2 hours, or overnight.

Preheat oven to 350 degrees. Place marinated salmon fillet on aluminum foil. The foil should be large enough to cover and seal the fillet. Bake at 350 degrees for 15 to 20 minutes, or barbeque for 10 to 20 minutes.

May substitute brown sugar with honey, if desired.

Makes 6-8 servings

Grilled Malaysian Shrimp

1 pound medium sized shrimp in the shell
½ teaspoon crushed red pepper flakes
1 teaspoon minced garlic
¾ cup red onion, finely minced
2 teaspoons tumeric
2 teaspoons ground coriander
1 teaspoon ground cumin
4 teaspoons grated lemon rind
1 tablespoon lemon juice
1 tablespoon soy sauce
⅓ cup peanut oil
wooden skewers

In a medium mixing bowl, combine all ingredients except shrimp and set aside.

Peel shrimp, leaving tails on. Butterfly each shrimp by cutting halfway through along vein on outer curve. Devein shrimp. Open shrimp and thread a wooden toothpick or skewer lengthwise through it.

Toss shrimp with marinade and refrigerate for one hour.

To cook shrimp, shake off any excess marinade and grill them quickly over glowing coals or mesquite, or broil them 3 inches from the heat source for 2 minutes without turning.

Remove the wooden skewers. Serve hot.

Makes 4 servings

Entrées

Pasta with White Clam Sauce

¼ cup butter
3 large cloves garlic, chopped fine
2 tablespoons flour
2 cups clam juice
¼ cup chopped parsley
1½ teaspoons dried thyme leaves
2 cups minced clams - fresh or
    canned
salt
freshly ground pepper
linguini or angel hair pasta, cooked

Heat butter in a saucepan. Add chopped garlic and cook for one minute over moderate heat. Whisk in flour. Add clam juice while stirring. Add parsley, salt, pepper, thyme and simmer gently for 10 minutes. Add clams and heat. Be careful not to overcook.

Serve over linguini or angel hair pasta.

Makes 4 servings

Penne with Creamy Basil Tomato Sauce

1 tablespoon chopped garlic
1 tablespoon olive oil
2 cups tomato sauce, preferably
    home made
2 tablespoons white wine
¼ cup half and half
¼ cup oil-packed sun dried
    tomatoes, drained
2 teaspoons salt
½ pound penne or other short
    circular pasta
½ cup torn fresh basil leaves
¼ cup grated Parmesan cheese

Makes 2-4 servings

In a medium skillet, sauté garlic in olive oil over low heat until light brown, 1 to 2 minutes. Add tomato sauce and simmer for 1 minute. Add wine and simmer a few seconds. Stir in half and half and simmer until warmed through. Add tomatoes and stir well.

Sauce can be made one day ahead and refrigerated at this point. Heat well before continuing.

Cook penne as directed on package, until tender but firm. Drain.

Add basil to simmering sauce. Add drained penne. Remove from heat. Add half of the Parmesan cheese to sauce. Sprinkle remaining cheese as a garnish before serving. Serve immediately

Add cooked Italian sausage for extra flavor.

Entrées

Salmon en Croute with Wine and Shallot Sauce

2 (17¼-ounce) packages frozen
    puff-pastry sheets (4 sheets)
8 salmon fillets approximately ½ to
    ¾-inch thick and 4 inches long
    by 2 inches wide.
4 tablespoons olive oil
1 tablespoon chopped fresh parsley
    (or 1 teaspoon dried parsley)
1 tablespoon chopped fresh
    tarragon (or 1 teaspoon dried
    tarragon)
1 tablespoon chopped fresh chervil
    (or 1 teaspoon dried chervil)
salt and pepper, to taste
2 eggs beaten

Wine and Shallot Sauce:
4 tablespoons unsalted butter
4 teaspoons finely minced shallots
1 cup dry white wine
2 cups heavy cream
salt
cayenne pepper
2 tablespoons finely chopped fresh
    chervil or dried for garnish

Makes 8 servings

Preheat oven to 375 degrees. Thaw puff-pastry according to package directions. Season salmon fillets with olive oil, parsley, tarragon, chervil, salt and pepper.

On floured surface roll out 2 puff-pastry sheets to 10 x 14-inches. Lightly score each pastry sheet in half lengthwise and crosswise, forming 4 rectangles on each sheet of dough. You will use these guidelines to center a fillet on each one of these rectangles. Roll out remaining sheets of pastry to same size and place over fillets. Press down with side of hand between each portion of fillets. Cut each pastry in half lengthwise and crosswise, forming 8 rectangles of dough each stuffed with a salmon fillet.

Using as much of the pastry around each fillet as possible, trim the pastries into a fish shape with head and tail. Press edges together to seal. Simulate fish scales by using a knife. Brush with egg. Place on baking sheets. Refrigerate 15 to 30 minutes. Bake pastries in oven for 20 to 25 minutes until golden brown and puffed.

Wine and Shallot Sauce:
While salmon is chilling, melt butter in small saucepan over medium-high heat. Stir in shallots and cook, stirring often until soft. Add wine and boil gently until most of the liquid evaporates. Reduce heat to medium. Gradually whisk in cream, salt and cayenne to taste. Boil gently until thickened, whisking often. Remove from heat and keep warm. Serve on heated plates and spoon sauce around the fish. Sprinkle with additional chervil.

Entrées

Sautéed Scallops with Lime

3 tablespoons olive oil
1½ pounds sea scallops
2 tablespoons finely chopped
    cilantro
1 garlic clove, minced
1 teaspoon fresh lime juice
salt
freshly ground pepper, to taste

Heat oil in a large nonstick skillet until almost smoking. Add scallops and cook over moderately high heat until browned on bottom, about 2 minutes. Turn scallops and cook until just opaque throughout, about 2 minutes longer. Add cilantro, garlic and lime juice, season with salt and pepper to taste. Toss to combine.

Serve with crusty bread.

Makes 4 servings

Scallops in Ginger Cream Sauce

24 sea scallops (about 2 pounds)
salt
pepper
2 tablespoons unsalted butter,
    divided
1 tablespoon olive oil
1 tablespoon minced ginger
1 clove garlic, minced
2 tablespoons minced scallion
2 tablespoons rice wine vinegar or
    white wine vinegar
½ cup dry white wine
½ cup heavy cream
2 tablespoons chopped cilantro

Season scallops with salt and pepper. Heat 1 tablespoon butter and oil in heavy skillet on high heat. When melted, sear scallops approximately 1 minute on each side. Remove with slotted spoon to a bowl.

Add garlic, ginger, scallions and vinegar to pan and stir until fragrant, about 30 seconds. Add cream and wine and cook for 2 minutes. Stir in remaining tablespoon of butter and stir until melted. Add scallops and cook until opaque (about 1½ minutes). Sprinkle with chopped cilantro before serving.

Makes 4 servings

Entrées

Seafood with Pistachio Orange Sauce

Pistachio Orange Sauce:
1 tablespoon sliced garlic (3 cloves)
¼ cup chopped thyme, tarragon,
    rosemary or savory
½ cup diced onion
1½ cups dry white wine
½ cup fresh orange juice
2 tablespoons butter
2 tablespoons flour
½ cup whipping cream
1 tablespoon zest of orange
⅓ cup chopped pistachios
salt and freshly ground pepper

Seafood:
1 pound scallops
½ pound medium prawns, shelled
1 tablespoon butter or margarine
2 tablespoons pistachios, chopped
    (garnish)

Sauce:
Combine garlic, herbs, onion, wine and juice in a non-aluminum saucepan. Bring to a boil and boil uncovered at high heat for about 10 minutes. Strain into a measuring cup and add water, if necessary, to make 1 cup of liquid.

Melt butter in saucepan and stir in flour. Then gradually stir in cream, hot wine mixture and orange peel. Cook, stirring constantly, until sauce comes to a boil and is thickened. Stir in pistachios. Season with salt and pepper.

Seafood:
In a skillet, gently sauté scallops and prawns in butter about 4 to 6 minutes, or until cooked through but still tender. Divide into four warmed, individual ramekins or a single shallow baking dish. Spoon Pistachio Orange Sauce over seafood and garnish with chopped pistachios.

Makes 4 servings

Shrimp Scampi in Wine

1 pound large shrimp, deveined,
    shelled with tails left on
¼ cup butter (½ cube)
1 large clove garlic, finely chopped
2 teaspoons finely chopped fresh
    parsley
3 tablespoons fresh lemon juice
⅓ cup dry white wine
salt and pepper

In a skillet, melt butter, add garlic and parsley and brown lightly. Blend in lemon juice, wine, salt and pepper to taste. Add shrimp and sauté them quickly - about 1 to 2 minutes per side maximum. Do not overcook. Serve the sauce over the shrimp.

Rice makes a good accompaniment.

Makes 4 servings

Shrimp with Linguini

¼ cup butter (½ cube)
2 cloves garlic
3 green onions, chopped
1 teaspoon dry basil
½ cup white wine
½ pound pre-cooked shrimp
1 (16-ounce) package frozen peas,
    thawed and cooked
3 tablespoons fresh chopped parsley
⅓ cup whipping cream
fresh grated Parmesan cheese
linguini, cooked

In a saucepan, heat butter, garlic, onions, basil and white wine. Remove from heat and add shrimp, peas, parsley and cream. Heat through and pour over linguini. Dust with freshly grated Parmesan cheese.

Makes 2-3 servings

White Clam Sauce with Linguini

¼ cup butter
3 large cloves garlic
2 tablespoons flour
2 cups clam juice
¼ cup chopped parsley or 3
    tablespoons of dried parsley
1½ teaspoons dried thyme leaves
2 cups minced clams, fresh or
    canned
salt
pepper
linguini or angel hair pasta, cooked

In a saucepan, melt the butter. Add the garlic and cook for one minute over moderate heat. With a wire whisk, stir in the flour. Add the clam juice, while stirring. Add the parsley, salt, pepper, and thyme and simmer gently for 10 minutes. Add clams and heat thoroughly. (Pasta may be cooked while you prepare the sauce.)

Serve over linguini or angel hair pasta noodles.

Makes 4 servings

Entrées

Eastern Shore Crab Cakes

¾ pound all purpose potatoes,
    peeled and diced
¼ cup celery, finely chopped
½ cup onion, finely chopped
2 tablespoons butter
3 eggs, lightly beaten
3 tablespoons lemon juice
½ teaspoon pepper
¾ teaspoon salt
1 teaspoon Old Bay Seasoning
½ teaspoon Tabasco sauce
2 tablespoons minced parsley
2 tablespoons minced dill (optional)
1 pound crabmeat (lump, backfin,
    or claw), picked over for shells
¼ cup fine dry bread crumbs
additional bread crumbs for coating
vegetable oil for deep frying

Preheat oven to 250 degrees.

In a large mixing bowl, combine all ingredients. Form the crab mixture into 12 patties, each about 3-inches in diameter and ½-inch thick. Coat patties with the additional bread crumbs. Using a mini-fryer or deep saucepan, heat at least a 2-inch depth of vegetable oil to 350 degrees. Deep-fry crab cakes, several at a time for 5 minutes, or until they are a deep golden brown. Drain on paper toweling and keep warm in the oven while cooking the rest.

Serve with lemon wedges, parsley, and your choice of cocktail, chili, or tartar sauce or with pimiento mayonnaise.

Makes 4 servings

From 24 to 84

PCPA volunteers may be of all different ages, but they all love the theater.

Anna's Spannakopita

14 sheets phyllo dough
3 tablespoons extra virgin first cold-
    pressed olive oil
1 medium yellow onion, diced
kosher salt
1 pound fresh spinach or one
    (10-ounce) package, frozen
4 ounces Feta cheese, crumbled or
    chopped
¼ cup Parmesan cheese
5 cloves garlic, minced
1 egg
⅓ cup plain bread crumbs
1 dash nutmeg
1 teaspoon paprika
1 teaspoon cinnamon
ground black pepper
⅛ cup pine nuts

Makes 6-9 servings

Preheat oven to 350 degrees. Line the bottom of a 9-inch square baking dish with 5 to 7 sheets of phyllo dough.

Add olive oil to a cold sauté pan, add onion and warm to medium heat. Once onion becomes fragrant, sauté on medium for one minute. Add salt to taste. Add fresh spinach and continue to sauté until spinach is just wilted. (For frozen spinach, sauté until warm.)

In another bowl, combine Feta cheese, Parmesan cheese, garlic, egg, bread crumbs, nutmeg, paprika, cinnamon and pepper (to taste). Add cooked spinach and combine thoroughly.

Spread mixture over phyllo dough in baking dish. Cover mixture with another 5 to 7 sheets of phyllo dough. Brush additional olive oil on top of phyllo dough. Loosely sprinkle pine nuts on top.

Bake at 350 degrees for 25 to 30 minutes.

Serve alongside a tomato, onion and kalamata olive salad dressed in a fresh herb vinaigrette.

This is a Greek-inspired recipe, which can be easily modified. Have fun experimenting with different spices, using chard instead of or in addition to spinach, adjusting garlic, or adding/deleting/trying different cheeses.

Entrées

Egg Foo Yong

2 tablespoons salad oil
3 eggs
1 cup bean sprouts, drained
1 cup pork, cooked and chopped
2 green onions, chopped
2 tablespoons soy sauce

Sauce:
1 teaspoon cornstarch
1 teaspoon sugar
1 teaspoon vinegar
2½ teaspoons soy sauce
½ cup water

Heat oil in large skillet. In a bowl, beat eggs until thick and lemon colored. Stir in bean sprouts, pork, onion and soy sauce.

Pour ¼ cup of the mixture at a time into the skillet. With a broad spatula, push cooked egg up and over meat to form a patty. When patties are set, turn to brown the other side. Serve hot with sauce.

Sauce:
Combine the sauce ingredients in a small saucepan. Cook stirring constantly, until mixture thickens and boils. Boil and stir for one minute.

Makes 2-4 servings

Ma Po Tofu

2 tablespoons oil
3 green onions, chopped
3 cloves garlic, minced
1 tablespoon grated ginger root
1½ pounds zucchini, sliced
¼ cup red miso
2 tablespoons brown sugar
2 tablespoons soy sauce
¼ cup ketchup
dash of cayenne
12 ounces firm tofu, cubed

Sauté onion, garlic and ginger in the oil. Add zucchini and cook until tender. Combine miso, sugar, soy sauce, ketchup and cayenne. Add this mixture to the cooked vegetables and heat through. Add the tofu. Mix to coat and heat through. Serve on rice.

Will last in the refrigerator for several days and is good cold.

Makes 4 servings

Entrées

Quinoa Pilaf with Peas

½ pound mini-carrots, chopped
2 tablespoons olive oil
1 medium onion, chopped
½ teaspoon cumin
1 teaspoon of your favorite herb
    seasoning mix
3 cups water
1½ cups uncooked quinoa
1 medium red bell pepper, chopped
2 tablespoons slivered almonds
2 tablespoons golden raisins
1 cup frozen peas, thawed
½ pound tofu marinated in
    balsamic vinegar (optional),
    cubed and sautéed

Croutons:
1 tablespoon virgin olive oil
2 large cloves garlic, minced
1 slice of your favorite bread, 1-inch
    cubes

Preheat oven to 425 degrees

Pilaf:
Heat oil in a large skillet over medium heat. Add onion and carrots and stir, cooking, until onions are translucent. Stir in seasonings. Add water and bring to a boil. Add quinoa, stirring to push it under the water. Place red pepper, raisins, and almonds on top.

Cover and simmer until all the water is absorbed and quinoa is light and fluffy. It puffs into little spirals after about 20 to 25 minutes. Add peas and optional tofu during the last 5 minutes of cooking and fluff into the mixture with a fork.

Croutons:
Heat oil and garlic in a small pan until simmering. Brush olive oil onto bread cubes, patting garlic bits on top. Bake at 425 degrees until brown on top, about 6 to 9 minutes.

Place quinoa in a serving dish. Garnish with croutons. Quinoa is pronounced Keen-wah.

Makes 4-6 servings

Theatre	Distance from the Last Row to the Stage
Schnitzer	154 feet
Keller	142 feet
Newmark	65 feet
Winningstad	32 feet

Entrées

Carl Selin

The only remaining tower is a symbol for the South Park Blocks. It has stood its ground well over 100 years.

The Bell Tower of the First Congregational Church of Portland

Desserts

Carl Selin

If this is Portland, that must be Mt. Hood.

Lemon Chiffon Cake

Natasha Ohlman - PAPA HAYDN'S RESTAURANT - Portland, OR

Lemon Filling:
2 teaspoons unflavored gelatin
3 tablespoons water
1 cup crème fraîche
2 cups lemon curd

Cake:
2 cups cake flour
1⅓ cups granulated sugar, divided
2 teaspoons baking powder
½ teaspoon salt
8 eggs, separated
⅔ cup vegetable oil
½ cup freshly squeezed lemon juice
    (about 2 medium lemons)
1 teaspoon cream of tartar

Chiffon Frosting:
½ cup egg whites
2⅔ cups powdered sugar
1⅓ cup plus ½ cup unsalted butter,
    softened, divided
⅔ cup lemon curd

Filling:
Sprinkle gelatin over water in a metal measuring cup and let sit for 5 minutes. Place cup over medium heat until gelatin has melted. Cool slightly. Place crème fraîche in the bowl of an electric mixer. Whip on high speed until thick and fluffy. Add lemon curd and whip until combined. Slowly pour in melted gelatin while mixing. Refrigerate for 2 hours or until set. Makes 3½ cups filling.

Cake:
Preheat oven to 325 degrees. Grease and flour two 8-inch cake pans. Line cake pans with parchment paper. Set aside. Sift together the cake flour, 2/3 cup sugar, baking powder and salt.

In a large bowl, whisk together 8 egg yolks, oil and lemon juice until well combined. Add the sifted dry ingredients and whisk until smooth.

In another bowl, combine the egg whites and cream of tartar. Whip on high speed until soft peaks form. Add remaining 2/3 cup sugar and continue whipping until stiff peaks form, about 1 to 2 minutes more. Gently fold the egg whites into the batter, being careful not to overmix the batter.

Divide batter between prepared pans and bake for 40 to 45 minutes or until cake springs back when lightly touched in the center. Remove from oven and cool on a wire rack for 10 minutes. Remove from pans and cool completely.

(continued on next page)

Desserts

Lemon Chiffon Cake

Frosting:
In a large bowl of an electric mixer, whip egg whites until stiff. Reduce speed to low and gradually add powdered sugar. Continue mixing for 15 minutes while adding sugar. Add 1 1/3 cups butter in chunks. Add lemon curd and continue mixing. Add remaining ½ cup butter and mix until well-combined. Reserve until ready to frost the cake.

Assembly:
Split each cake layer in half. Place one split layer on a cake plate and spread with one-third of the filling. Repeat with remaining layers. Frost top and side with frosting. Store in the refrigerator.

This is the ultimate cake - moist and flavorful with a delicious filling and a creamy frosting. The big flavor and beautiful presentation make it worth every bit of the effort it takes to make.

Use pasteurized egg whites, available in the refrigerated section of most stores.

Makes 8 servings

Crème Fraîche

Crème fraîche is available at some supermarkets and specialty food stores. To make your own, use one of these foolproof methods:

Method 1:
Whisk together ½ cup sour cream and ½ cup whipping cream in a small bowl. Pour into a jar and cover. Let stand in a warm place until thickened, about 12 hours. Stir well and refrigerate, covered, 36 hours before using.

Method 2:
Pour 1 cup heavy or whipping cream and 1 teaspoon buttermilk into a glass jar. (Instant buttermilk can be used to prepare buttermilk.) Cover and shake vigorously for 1 minute. Let stand in a warm place until thickened, about 12 hours. Stir well and refrigerate covered at least 24 hours before using.

Crème fraîche will keep 7 to 10 days.

Both methods make 1 cup

Cheese Dumplings in Milk Custard (Ras Malai)

PLAINFIELDS' MAYUR RESTAURANT - PORTLAND, OR

40 ounces Paneer Indian cheese
½ teaspoon baking powder

Syrup:
16 cups sugar
⅓ teaspoon cream of tartar
18 cups water plus additional water
    to maintain boil
3 tablespoons cornstarch, dissolved
    in 6 tablespoons water
12 cups warm water

Milk Sauce (Rabdi):
3 gallons whole milk
sugar
crushed pistachio
silver leaf (optional)

Caution: restaurant proportions

Using a mixer, combine Paneer and baking powder. Mix until soft, moist and sticky. Roll into ½ ounce balls, making sure that there are no cracks on surface of ball. Flatten into patties. Set cheese patties aside.

Syrup:
In large pot, combine sugar, cream of tartar and water. Boil rapidly at 220 degrees. Add cornstarch. Reduce heat to a slow boil and gently slip cheese patties into syrup. Let simmer for 1 minute.

Bring the syrup to a rapid boil, cover and boil 20 minutes. (Keep temperature at 220 degrees by adding 3 tablespoons water every three minutes.)

Remove 6 cups syrup to a hotel pan. Add warm water to thin the syrup. Gently transfer cooked dumplings to the diluted syrup. (Dumplings will look like little pillows.) Cool, cover and refrigerate until ready to put into milk sauce.

Milk Sauce:
Pour milk into jacketed kettle. Bring to boil. Adjust heat to maintain a constant boil without allowing milk to boil over. Stir every few minutes to break up crust that forms on top.

Continue this process until consistency is that of thickened cream sauce. Run reduced sauce in blender with a little sugar to taste. Blend until smooth. Strain through a sieve, cool and refrigerate.

(continued on next page)

Cheese Dumplings in Milk Custard (Ras Malai)

Assembly:
Remove dumplings from diluted syrup one at a time and gently squeeze syrup from dumpling. Be careful not to break surface of dumpling. Gently submerge dumplings into the cream sauce. Let sit at least one hour before serving. Garnish with crushed pistachio nuts and silver leaf (optional).

This is an amazing dessert with only two main ingredients-milk and sugar. The flavor and texture are wonderful. The little puffy milk balls will just melt in your mouth. If you are successful at making this dish, you will be admired by any Indian cook.

Paneer is available in most Asian grocery stores.

Angel Dessert

3 egg whites
1 teaspoon baking powder
1 cup sugar
⅔ cup nuts, chopped
14 crackers (Ritz or saltines),
   crushed

Topping:
½ pint whipping cream
fresh fruit of the season

Preheat oven to 325 degrees. Grease a 9-inch pie pan.

Beat egg whites until they form peaks. Add baking powder and then gradually add sugar. Gently fold in nuts and crackers. Pile into prepared pie pan. Bake at 325 degrees for 30 minutes. Cool for 3 hours before cutting into slices. Serve topped with fresh fruit and whipped cream.

Try this for fresh strawberry or peach shortcake instead of the traditional bases.

Makes 6-8 servings

Desserts

Semolina Corn Meal Cake with Citrus Syrup

Cory Schreiver - WILDWOOD RESTAURANT - Portland, OR

Simple Syrup:
1 cup sugar
1 cup water
half of one vanilla bean
juice of 1 lemon (optional)
juice of 1 orange (optional)

Cake Batter:
2¾ cups unsalted butter
3 cups sugar
9 whole eggs
18 egg yolks
zest of 3 lemons
zest of 3 oranges
1½ cups corn meal
2¼ cups flour
¾ teaspoons salt
3¾ teaspoons baking powder

Simple Syrup:
Combine sugar and water and bring to a boil, let simmer for five minutes and then cool with scraped vanilla bean. Add lemon and orange juice.

Cake:
Preheat oven to 350 degrees. Cream the butter and sugar together. Slowly add the egg yolks, whole eggs and orange and lemon zest. Blend well.

Sift together the corn meal, flour, salt and baking powder, and slowly incorporate it into the wet mixture. Blend thoroughly into a batter.

Line 2 (9 or 10-inch) spring form pans with parchment or wax paper on the bottom, and lightly oil with a pan spray. Pour the batter into the spring form pans and bake at 350 degrees for 50 to 60 minutes or until a knife or toothpick comes out of the center clean. Allow cake to cool and then baste lightly with the simple syrup until the syrup is absorbed.

Slice and serve with whipped cream or fruit sorbet.

Makes 2 cakes

Desserts

Apple Cake

Dough:
1½ cup flour
1 egg
½ cup sugar
⅓ cup butter
1 teaspoon baking powder

Filling:
5 pounds Granny Smith apples,
    peeled and sliced
1 teaspoon cinnamon
¼ cup sugar
½ teaspoon lemon juice

Makes 9 servings

Preheat oven to 350 degrees. Grease an 8-inch square cake pan.

In a large bowl, sprinkle apple slices with sugar, cinnamon, and lemon juice. Set aside.

In a mixing bowl, combine flour, egg, sugar, butter and baking powder. Mix well. Form a ball and wrap in plastic wrap and refrigerate for at least 1 hour. Divide dough in half and roll out each half on a well-floured board. Dough will be sticky. Line the pan with half of the dough. Add the prepared apples. Cover with the remaining dough. Bake for 45 to 60 minutes or until golden brown.

This cake is almost a pie.

Applesauce Cake

½ cup shortening
1 cup sugar
1 egg, well beaten
1 cup raisins
1 cup water
1¾ cups flour
½ teaspoon baking soda
¼ teaspoon salt
1 teaspoon cinnamon
½ teaspoon cloves
1 cup applesauce, heated

Makes 8-10 servings

Preheat oven to 350 degrees. Grease and flour a loaf pan. In large mixing bowl, beat shortening and sugar until fluffy. Add egg and beat some more. Set aside.

In medium mixing bowl, sift together the flour, soda, salt, cinnamon and cloves. Set aside. Bring raisins to a boil in the water, then drain.

Alternately add to the shortening mixture, one-third of the flour mixture and one-half of the applesauce. Beat well after each addition. Fold in raisins. Pour mixture into prepared pan. Bake at 350 degrees for 1 hour.

Desserts

Apricot Brandy Cake

Cake:
1 cup butter (2 cubes)
3 cups sugar
6 eggs
3 cups flour, sifted
½ teaspoon salt
¼ teaspoon baking soda
1 cup sour cream
1 teaspoon orange extract
¼ teaspoon almond extract
½ teaspoon rum extract
½ teaspoon lemon extract
½ cup apricot brandy
1 cup nuts, finely chopped

Frosting:
2 cups powdered sugar, sifted
3 tablespoons butter, melted
½ tablespoon vanilla
⅛ cup apricot brandy
½ cup nuts, finely chopped

Preheat oven to 325 degrees. Grease and flour a bundt pan. Cream butter until light and fluffy. Add sugar, one cup at a time, creaming after each addition. Add eggs, one at a time, beating until fluffy. Beat combined mixture for three minutes. In a mixing bowl, sift flour with salt and soda. In a separate bowl, combine sour cream and extracts. Alternately add flour mixture and sour cream mixture to the batter. Blend well. Fold in brandy Pour into bundt pan. Bake at 325 degrees for 1 hour and 10 minutes, or until it tests done. Remove and let cool. Turn out onto cake plate.

Frosting:
Blend powdered sugar, butter and vanilla until creamy. May thin the frosting with apricot brandy, if desired. Pour frosting over cooled cake and allow frosting to drip down the sides of the cake.

Makes 8 servings

Audrey's Gooey Bars

1 (18½-ounce) package yellow cake mix
½ cup butter (1 cube), melted
1 egg

Topping:
1 (8-ounce) package cream cheese, softened
1 pound powdered sugar
2 eggs, beaten

Preheat oven to 350 degrees. Grease a 9 x 13-inch baking dish.

In mixing bowl, combine cake mix, butter and egg. Pat this mixture into prepared baking dish.

Topping:
Beat cream cheese, powdered sugar and eggs. Pour this on top of the first mixture and sprinkle with reserved powdered sugar over the top. Bake at 350 degrees for 45 minutes.

Makes 10-12 bars

Desserts

Best Ever Chocolate Cake

1 (18¼-ounce) package Dark Fudge
    Cake Mix
1 (3.4-ounce) instant chocolate
    pudding mix
4 eggs
1 cup sour cream
½ cup warm water
½ cup vegetable oil
1½ cups semisweet chocolate chips

Makes 12 servings

Preheat oven to 350 degrees. Spray a 12-cup bundt pan.

In mixing bowl, blend cake mix, pudding mix, eggs, sour cream, water, and vegetable oil on low speed for 1 minute. Scrape the sides and bottom of the bowl. Increase speed to medium and mix for another 3 minutes. The batter will be thick. Fold in chocolate chips, making sure they are evenly distributed through the batter. Pour into bundt pan. Bake at 350 degrees for 45 to 50 minutes, or until it starts to pull away from the sides.

Cool for 30 minutes and remove from the pan. Store at room temperature for one week or freeze.

Philippine Dessert (Bi Bing Ka)

1 package sweet rice flour (Mochiko
    Brand)
1½ cups sugar
4 eggs
½ cup butter (1 cube), melted
1 (12-ounce) can evaporated milk
1½ cups water

Preheat oven to 350 degrees. Grease an 8 x 12-inch pan.

In mixing bowl, combine all ingredients and mix well. Pour into prepared pan and bake at 350 degrees for 50 minutes.

Stage Directions

Stage Left	The performer's left as they face the audience.
Stage Right	The performer's right as they face the audience.
Upstage	The rear portion of the stage.
Downstage	The area of the stage nearest the audience.
House Left	The audience's left as they face the stage.
House Right	The audience's right as they face the stage.

Desserts

Cheesecake

1 package graham crackers -crushed
⅓ cup sugar
¼ cup nuts, finely chopped
dash cinnamon, (optional)
½ cup butter (1 cube), melted

Filling:
1½ (3-ounce) packages cream
    cheese
3 eggs
¾ cup sugar
1½ teaspoons vanilla
1 teaspoon lemon juice
¾ teaspoon almond extract
1½ pints sour cream

Preheat oven to 350 degrees. In medium bowl, mix together all crust ingredients. Press firmly into bottom and up sides of a 10-inch springform pan.

Filling:
In mixing bowl, cream together filling ingredients. Mix thoroughly and pour into prepared pan. Bake at 350 degrees for 40 minutes. Insert knife blade, and if it comes out clean it is done. Cool in pan then remove outer ring. Chill in refrigerator.

May be topped with fresh fruit.

Makes 8 servings

Chocolate Buttermilk Cake

¼ cup butter
1¼ cups water
¼ cup oil
2 cups flour
1½ cups sugar
4 tablespoons cocoa
2 eggs, beaten
½ cup buttermilk
1½ teaspoons baking soda
1 teaspoon vanilla

Frosting:
½ cup butter (1 cube)
⅓ cup buttermilk
1 (16-ounce) box powdered sugar
1 teaspoon vanilla
4 tablespoons cocoa
1 cup walnuts, chopped (optional)

Cake:
Preheat oven to 350 degrees. In a small saucepan, bring to a boil the butter, water and oil. In mixing bowl, combine flour, sugar, cocoa and beaten eggs. Pour the melted mixture over the flour mixture and mix. Add buttermilk, baking soda and vanilla. Bake in a jelly roll pan, at 350 degrees for 20 minutes.

Frosting:
In small saucepan, heat butter and buttermilk until butter is melted. Pour mixture over powdered sugar, vanilla and cocoa. Mix together and frost the cake while it is still warm.

Makes 8 servings

Desserts

Chocolate Cherry Bars

1 (18¼-ounce) package chocolate
    fudge cake mix
1 (21-ounce) can cherry pie filling
1 teaspoon almond extract
2 eggs, beaten

Frosting:
1 cup sugar
⅓ cup milk
5 tablespoons butter
1 (6-ounce) package semisweet
    chocolate chips

Makes 8 serving

Preheat oven to 350 degrees. Grease and flour a 9 x 13-inch pan.

Cake:
In a large bowl, combine cake mix, cherry pie filling, almond extract and eggs. Mix by hand until well blended. Pour into prepared pan and bake at 350 degrees for 30 minutes, or until toothpick comes out clean. While bars are cooling, make frosting.

Frosting:
In small saucepan, combine sugar, butter, milk and bring to a boil for 1 minute. Remove from heat; add chocolate chips and stir until smooth. Pour over partially cooled bars.

Chocolate Eclair Squares

2 (3.4-ounce) packages Jello vanilla
    instant pudding
3 cups milk
1 (9-ounce) container Cool Whip
1 pound graham crackers

Frosting:
5 tablespoons unsweetened cocoa
2 tablespoons salad oil
2 tablespoons Karo syrup
3 tablespoons milk
1 teaspoon vanilla
1½ cups powdered sugar

Makes 24 bars

In a mixing bowl, beat pudding and milk for 2 minutes. Fold in Cool Whip.

In a 9 x 13-inch pan, make a single layer of whole graham crackers. Spread half of pudding mixture over crackers. Add another layer of crackers and the remainder of the pudding. Place crackers on top.

Frosting:
In mixing bowl, beat cocoa and salad oil until almost smooth. Add Karo syrup, milk, vanilla and powdered sugar. Beat until smooth and then spread over the top layer of crackers. Refrigerate for 10 hours or overnight. Cut into squares.

Desserts

Chocolate Ice Box Cake

1 large angel food cake, torn in
   pieces
2 (6-ounce) packages semisweet
   chocolate chips
4 eggs, separated
1 teaspoon vanilla
1 pint heavy cream, whipped
2 tablespoons sugar
1 cup nuts

Makes 12-15 servings

Melt chocolate in double boiler. Beat egg yolks and slowly add to melted chocolate. Allow to cool. Beat egg whites until stiff and add vanilla and sugar. Fold this into the chocolate mixture.

Fold whipped cream and nuts into chocolate. In a 9 x 13-inch pan, place half of the cake pieces. Cover with half of the whipped cream and chocolate mixture. Repeat, ending with the chocolate mixture. Refrigerate overnight.

Chocolate Sheet Cake "To-Die-For"

Cake:
2 cups flour
2 cups sugar
1 teaspoon baking soda
1 cup butter (2 cubes)
4 tablespoons cocoa
1 cup water
½ cup buttermilk
2 eggs
1 teaspoon vanilla

Frosting:
½ cup butter (1 cube)
4 tablespoons cocoa
⅓ cup buttermilk
1 (16-ounce) package powdered
   sugar
walnuts, chopped (optional)

Preheat oven to 400 degrees. Grease an 11 x 14 x ¾-inch pan.

Cake:
In large mixing bowl, sift together flour, sugar, and baking soda. Set aside. In saucepan, combine butter, cocoa and water, and bring this mixture to a rapid boil. Remove from heat and pour over dry ingredient mixture and mix lightly. Add buttermilk, eggs and vanilla and beat. Pour into prepared pan. Bake at 400 degrees for 15 to 20 minutes, or until it tests done.

Frosting:
In another saucepan, combine butter, cocoa and buttermilk, and bring to a boil. Remove from heat and add powdered sugar and stir until smooth. Add nuts. Spread frosting over the hot cake.

Makes 16-20 servings

Desserts

Easy Chocolate Torte

Cake:
1 cup boiling water
3 (1-ounce) squares unsweetened
    chocolate squares
2 eggs
1 cup sugar
1 cup light brown sugar
2 cups sifted flour
2 teaspoons baking soda
1 teaspoon salt
1 cup sour cream
1 teaspoon vanilla

Whipped Cream Filling:
1 cup whipping cream
3 tablespoons powdered sugar

The PCPA volunteers have a Speakers Bureau. They go to various meetings around the greater Portland area and tell the PCPA story. Their multi-media presentation covers the history of the buildings, current happenings in the theaters and interesting facts about the arts in Portland. This service is free to organizations. Call 503-274-6552 for more information.

Preheat oven to 350 degrees. Grease two 8 or 9-inch round cake pans. Pour boiling water over chocolate in a microwave safe bowl. Heat in microwave to boiling and cook until thickened, stirring occasionally. Remove and cool.

Cake:
In mixing bowl, beat together eggs, sugar, and brown sugar until thick and creamy. In bowl, sift together flour, soda, and salt. In a separate bowl, combine sour cream and vanilla. Add flour mixture to egg mixture alternately with sour cream mixture, beginning and ending with flour.

Blend in cooled chocolate mixture (batter will be thin). Turn into prepared cake pans. Bake at 350 degrees for 25 to 30 minutes, or until toothpick comes out clean. Don't over bake. Cool 10 minutes before removing from pan. Cool completely and then split each layer in half.

Filling:
Beat whipping cream and powdered sugar until stiff. Spread whipped cream filling between layers, stacking one on top of the other to form a torte.

Place a paper doily over the top of the cake and sprinkle with additional powdered sugar. Remove doily carefully to leave a design. Or, simply sift powdered sugar over the top of the cake.

Makes 8-10 servings

Desserts

Fourteen Carrot Cake

Cake:
2 cups flour
2 teaspoons baking powder
1½ teaspoons baking soda
1 teaspoon salt
2 teaspoons cinnamon
2 cups sugar
1½ cups oil
4 eggs
2 cups carrots, grated
1 (8-ounce) can crushed pineapple, drained
½ cup shredded coconut meat
½ cup nuts, chopped

Frosting:
¾ cup butter
8 ounces cream cheese
2 teaspoons vanilla
1 (16-ounce) box powdered sugar

Preheat oven to 350 degrees. Grease and flour three 8-inch cake pans.

Cake:
In mixing bowl, sift together flour, baking powder, baking soda, salt and cinnamon. Add sugar, oil, eggs and mix well. Add carrots, pineapple, coconut and nuts. Mix, then pour into prepared pans. Bake at 350 degrees for 35 to 40 minutes. Test for doneness by inserting a toothpick in the center - if it comes out clean, cake is done. Cool cake then frost.

Frosting:
In mixing bowl, blend butter, cream cheese and vanilla. Beat in powdered sugar. Spread on the layers of cake.

Makes 8-10 servings

German Apple Cake

4 cups apple, chopped
2 cups walnuts, chopped
2 cups flour
2 teaspoons baking soda
1 teaspoon salt
2 cups sugar
2 teaspoons cinnamon
2 eggs
½ cup oil
2 teaspoons vanilla

Preheat oven to 375 degrees. Line a 9 x 15-inch pan with foil, or line two 8-inch square pans.

In mixing bowl, sift flour, soda, salt, sugar and cinnamon together. Mix dry ingredients with the apples and nuts. Add the eggs, oil and vanilla. Pour mixture into prepared pan(s).

Bake at 375 degrees for 45 minutes.

No frosting needed for this dessert!

Makes 16 servings

Desserts

Orange Yogurt Cake (Tourta Me Portokali Ke Yaourt)

Cake:
2½ cups flour
2 teaspoons baking powder
1 teaspoon baking soda
½ teaspoon salt
1 teaspoon cinnamon
3 eggs
1 cup sugar
¾ cup butter, melted
2 teaspoons orange peel, grated
1 teaspoon vanilla extract
1 cup plain, lowfat yogurt
½ cup orange juice
1 cup walnuts, finely ground

Syrup:
1 cup sugar
½ cup water
½ cup orange juice
1 cinnamon stick
2 pieces orange peel, 1 x 2-inches
   each

Makes 10-12 servings

Preheat oven to 350 degrees. Butter a 9 x 13-inch cake pan and lightly flour the bottom and sides.

Cake:
In a medium bowl, combine flour, baking powder, baking soda, salt, and cinnamon. In a large bowl, beat together eggs and sugar until they are light and foamy. Add melted butter, orange peel and vanilla extract. Mix well. Add yogurt, orange juice and combined dry ingredients a little at a time. Beat well after each addition. Fold in walnuts.

Pour batter into baking pan and smooth the top. Place on middle oven rack and bake for 45 minutes, or until cake pulls away from the side of the pan. Cake is done when toothpick inserted into the center comes out clean.

Syrup:
While cake is baking, combine ingredients in a small saucepan. Bring syrup to a boil over high heat. Lower the heat and simmer for 10 minutes. Remove from heat and cool. Remove peel and cinnamon stick. Pour syrup over cake while cake is still warm. When cake cools, cut into diamonds or squares, and serve.

It is very important that the cake pan is properly prepared with butter and flour.

Desserts

Hot Apple Cake with Caramel Rum Sauce

Cake:
1 cup butter (2 cubes)
1 cup sugar
2 eggs
1½ cups flour
1 teaspoon nutmeg
1 teaspoon vanilla
1 teaspoon cinnamon
1 teaspoon baking soda
½ teaspoon salt
3 medium tart apples, finely
   chopped
¾ cups walnuts, chopped

Caramel Rum Sauce:
½ cup sugar
½ cup brown sugar
½ cup whipping cream
½ cup butter (1 cube)
¼ cup rum

Preheat the oven to 350 degrees. Prepare pie or tart pan.

Cake:
In a mixing bowl, blend sugar, butter, and eggs. Add flour, nutmeg, cinnamon, baking soda, and salt. Add apples, nuts, and vanilla. Mix thoroughly. Pour into pie or tart pan. Bake at 350 degrees for 45 minutes, or until lightly browned.

Sauce:
In a double boiler, combine sugars and whipping cream. Cook for 30 minutes. Add butter and continue cooking for 30 minutes. Remove from heat and beat well. Add rum and blend thoroughly.

Serve warm topped with vanilla ice cream and caramel rum sauce.

Makes 6-8 servings

The PCPA and the First Congregational Church share the same city block and enjoy a partnership in the arts. When the New Theatre Building was designed, concerns for the church were taken into consideration. The original fly tower of the Newmark Theatre was placed so it would not block the light from the church's beautiful stained glass window. The window is visible from the alleyway that divides the two buildings.

Inside-Outside Chocolate Cake

1 (18¼-ounce)package chocolate
    cake mix
1 (4.3-ounce) package instant
    chocolate pudding
2 eggs
1¾ cups milk
1 (12-ounce) package chocolate
    chips

Makes 6-8 servings

Preheat the oven to 350 degrees. Grease a bundt cake pan.

In mixing bowl, combine cake mix, eggs, milk and pudding mix, and mix for 2 minutes. Stir in chocolate chips.

Pour into prepared bundt cake pan. Bake at 350 degrees for 50 to 55 minutes. Cool for 15 minutes before turning out onto cake plate or wire rack.

Serve plain or dusted with powdered sugar or drizzle with chocolate frosting. Great with ice cream.

Jolly Jam Bars

1 cup butter (2 cubes)
1 cup sugar
2 egg yolks
2 cups flour
1 cup nuts, chopped
½ cup jam

Makes 12-16 bars

Preheat the oven to 325 degrees. Grease a 9-inch square pan.

In a mixing bowl, cream butter and sugar until light and fluffy. Add egg yolks and blend well. Gradually add flour and mix thoroughly. Mix in chopped nuts. Divide the dough in half. Put half the dough evenly into pan. Spread with jam. Cover with remaining dough. Bake at 325 degrees for 1 hour, or until lightly browned. Cool then cut.

Desserts

Italian Cream Cake

Cake:
½ cup butter (1 cube)
½ cup shortening
2 cups sugar
5 eggs, separated
2 cups flour
1 teaspoon baking soda
1 cup buttermilk
1 teaspoon vanilla
1 cup pecans, chopped
1½ cups Angel Flake coconut

Frosting:
1 (8-ounce) package cream cheese,
    softened
¼ cup butter, softened
1 (16-ounce) package powdered
    sugar
1 teaspoon vanilla
pecans, chopped, as garnish
toasted coconut, as garnish

Preheat oven to 350 degrees. Grease and flour three 8-inch round cake pans.

Cake:
In mixing bowl, cream the butter and shortening. Add sugar and beat until smooth. Add egg yolks and beat well.

Sift flour and baking soda together. Add to creamed mixture alternately with buttermilk. Stir in vanilla. Add nuts and coconut. In separate bowl, beat egg whites until they form stiff peaks. Fold egg whites into buttermilk mixture. Pour this batter into the three prepared cake pans. Bake at 350 degrees for 25 minutes, or until toothpick inserted in center comes out clean. Cool and then frost with cream cheese frosting.

Frosting:
In mixing bowl, combine cream cheese, butter, powdered sugar, and vanilla. Blend well. Frost cooled cake and garnish it with chopped nuts or toasted coconut.

May substitute pecans wtih pistachios, as desired.

Makes 6-8 servings

Jo's Coffee Cake

½ cup shortening
¾ cup sugar
1 teaspoon vanilla
3 eggs
2 cups flour
1 teaspoon baking powder
1 teaspoon baking soda
1 cup sour cream
6 tablespoons butter
1 cup brown sugar, firmly packed
2 teaspoons cinnamon
1 cup nuts, chopped

Makes 12 servings

Preheat oven to 350 degrees. Grease and line with wax paper, one 10-inch tube pan.

In a mixing bowl, cream shortening, sugar and vanilla. Add eggs, one at a time, beating well after each addition. In a medium bowl, sift flour, baking powder and baking soda together. Add to creamed mixture alternately with sour cream, blending after each addition.

Spread half of batter in the tube pan. In mixing bowl, cream butter, brown sugar and cinnamon together. Add nuts. Dot batter in pan evenly with half of the nut mixture. Cover with remaining batter and dot with remaining nut mixture.

Bake at 350 degrees for 50 minutes. Cool cake 10 minutes before removing from pan.

Kate Hepburn's Brownies

2 ounces unsweetened baking
   chocolate squares
½ cup butter (1 cube)
1 cup sugar
2 eggs
½ teaspoon vanilla
¼ cup flour
¼ teaspoon salt
1 cup walnuts, chopped

Makes 9 servings

Preheat oven to 325 degrees. Melt chocolate, cool slightly. Beat butter, sugar, eggs, vanilla and chocolate until fluffy. Add the flour, salt and mix well. Add chopped walnuts, mix well.

Spread batter into a buttered 8 x 8-inch pan. Put the pan on the middle shelf and bake for 40 minutes. Cool in the pan then cut and eat.

This recipe came from Saybook, CT. Kate lived near there. She gave the recipe to a reporter who then published it in a local newspaper.

Jo's Kahlua and Cream Cheesecake

Crust:
1½ cups chocolate wafer cookies, coarsely chopped
½ cup butter (1 cube), melted
3 tablespoons sugar

Filling:
3 (8-ounce) packages cream cheese, softened
2 cups sugar
3 eggs
½ cup Kahlua
1 teaspoon vanilla
1 cup sour cream

Glaze:
1 cup powdered sugar
¾ cup sour cream
3 tablespoons Kahlua

whipped cream, optional

Makes 8 servings

Preheat oven to 350 degrees.

Crust:
Mix cookie crumbs, butter and sugar together until moistened. Press mixture against the bottom and sides of a 10-inch spring form pan. Bake at 350 degrees for 5 minutes. Cool.

Filling:
In a mixing bowl, beat cream cheese until fluffy. Add sugar slowly and beat after each addition. Add eggs, one at a time and continue beating until very smooth. Add Kahlua, vanilla and sour cream. Mix well. Pour filling into pie crust and bake at 350 degrees for 55 to 60 minutes. At the end of the baking time, with the heat turned off, leave cake in the oven and the oven door open, for 45 to 60 minutes. Remove and refrigerate until cool.

Glaze:
Combine powdered sugar, sour cream and Kahlua making sure it is of a consistency that can be poured easily. Spread the glaze on top of the cheesecake and return the cake to the refrigerator. Refrigerate at least six hours but preferably overnight.

Cut and serve with whipped cream for a garnish.

Kahlua Brownies

Brownies:
1 (18¼-ounce) package Fudge
    Brownie Mix
½ cup oil
¼ cup Kahlua
2 eggs
1 cup white baking chips
1 cup semisweet chocolate chips,
    chopped
½ cup nuts, chopped

Frosting:
¼ cup butter, melted
4 tablespoons Kahlua, warmed
2 cups powdered sugar, sifted
¼ cup cocoa powder
¾ cup nuts, chopped

Brownies:
Preheat oven to 350 degrees. Grease the bottom of a 9 x 13-inch baking pan. Mix together brownie mix, oil, Kahlua and eggs until dry mix is moistened. Stir in white baking pieces, chocolate chips and nuts. Spread batter in prepared pan. Bake at 350 degrees for about 30 minutes or until center is set. Cool.

Frosting:
In a small bowl, combine butter and Kahlua. Stir in powdered sugar and cocoa. Beat by hand until smooth. Spread over brownies and top with ¾ cup nuts. Cool until frosting is set.

Makes 24 brownies

Carl Selin

Portland - the City of Roses

Desserts

Lemon Lush

1½ cups flour
¾ cup butter (1½ cubes)
¼ cup pecans, chopped
1½ cups powdered sugar
3 (3-ounce) packages cream cheese
1½ cups Cool Whip (13-ounce tub)
4 cups cold milk
3 (3.4-ounce) packages instant
   lemon pudding

Makes 4-6 servings

Preheat oven to 375 degrees. Mix flour, butter and pecans to form a dough and spread it into a 9 x 13-inch pan. Bake at 375 degrees for 10 to15 minutes. Mix powdered sugar, cream cheese, and Cool Whip together and spread on the warm crust.

Mix cold milk and lemon pudding together and pour over crust and filling mixtures. Top with remaining Cool Whip.

You can also use 2 (8-ounce) containers of Cool Whip. Use 1½ cups in the middle layer, but add the rest to top.

Lemon Poppy Seed Cake with Rum Drizzle

1 cup butter (2 cubes), softened
4 ounces cream cheese, softened
1¾ cups sugar
3 eggs
1 tablespoon grated lemon peel
1½ cups flour
1 teaspoon baking powder
2 tablespoons poppy seeds
¼ cup light rum

Makes 12 servings

Preheat oven to 375 degrees. Grease a 10-inch tube or bundt pan. In a large bowl, beat together the butter and cream cheese until well blended, then beat in sugar, eggs and lemon peel, beating until mixture is light and fluffy.

In a separate bowl, sift together the flour and baking powder, then beat this into butter mixture. Stir in poppy seeds. Spoon batter into prepared pan and bake until cake is light golden brown and springs back firmly when pressed, 55 to 60 minutes. Cool for 15 minutes in pan, then invert onto a wire rack to cool.

Drizzle rum over cake a little at a time, allowing it to be absorbed by cake before adding more. Transfer to a cake plate or cake stand, cover and let stand 2 to 3 hours before serving.

Desserts

Mints

1 (8-ounce) package cream cheese
2 (16-ounce) packages powdered
   sugar
½ drop mint flavoring oil
small amount of desired food
   coloring
sugar for rolling

Mix together all the ingredients except granulated sugar. Knead with hands until resembles pie dough. Roll into small balls. Dip in granulated sugar (prevents sticking). Press into candy molds. Pop out immediately.

Store in covered container. Keeps indefinitely in refrigerator.

Makes 200 mints

Lemon Squares

Crust:
2 cups flour
½ cup powdered sugar
1 cup butter (2 cubes)

Filling:
4 eggs, beaten
2 cups sugar
⅓ cup lemon juice
¼ cup flour
½ teaspoon baking powder

Preheat oven to 350 degrees.

Crust:
Mix flour, powdered sugar and butter and press into ungreased square or 9 x 13-inch pan. Bake in 350 degree oven for 20 minutes or until edges are browned.

Filling:
Mix eggs, sugar, lemon juice, flour and baking powder and pour over crust. Bake at 350 degrees for 25 minutes.

Sprinkle powdered sugar over top and let cool before cutting into squares.

Makes 24 bars

Desserts

Mary's Chocolate Trifle

1 (18¼-ounce) package chocolate
    cake mix plus required
    ingredients
2 (4.3-ounce) packages chocolate
    flavored Jello Instant Pudding
    prepared according to package
    directions, chilled and set
6 regular sized Heath candy bars,
    frozen until needed
1 cup Kahlua, divided
2 small containers Lite Cool Whip

Preheat oven to 350 degrees. Prepare chocolate cake according to package directions. Use square pans. Let it cool completely then cut into 1-inch cubes. Break frozen candy bars into small pieces.

Using a large glass bowl, assemble by starting with a little less than half of cake cubes. Pour half of Kahlua over cake. Spread half of chocolate pudding on cake. Spread half of Cool Whip on top of pudding layer. Sprinkle half of Heath bar crumbs on top of Cool Whip. Repeat sequence once more, using all remaining ingredients. Refrigerate until serving time.

It's a great make-ahead dessert. This cake can be assembled 1 to 3 days ahead and kept refrigerated until serving time.

Makes 24 servings

Desserts

Mississippi Mud

Cake:
4 eggs
2 cups sugar
1½ cups flour
1 teaspoon vanilla
⅓ cup cocoa
1 cup coconut
1 cup butter (2 cubes)
1 cup nuts, chopped
1 (7-ounce) jar marshmallow cream

Frosting:
¼ cup butter, melted
3 tablespoons cocoa
½ teaspoon vanilla
3 tablespoons milk
½ box powdered sugar (½ pound)
½ cup nuts, chopped

Cake:
Preheat the oven to 350 degrees. Grease and flour a 9 x 13-inch pan. Beat the eggs and sugar until thick. Set aside. Melt butter and add flour, vanilla, cocoa, coconut, and chopped nuts. Combine both mixtures and pour into the pan. Bake at 350 degree for 30 minutes. After removing the cake from the oven, spread marshmallow cream on top while cake is still warm.

Frosting:
Combine melted butter, cocoa, vanilla, milk, and powdered sugar. Spread over marshmallow cream. Sprinkle frosting with nuts.

Makes 16-20 bars

Orange Cake

2 egg yolks
½ cup sugar
½ cup orange juice (or the juice of 1 orange)
¾ cup almonds, finely ground
¾ cup flour
2 egg whites
whipped cream for garnish

Makes 6 servings

Preheat oven to 325 degrees. Beat egg yolks and sugar until pale and thick. Gradually beat in juice. In a separate mixing bowl combine ground almonds and flour. Add flour mixture to egg yolk mixture. Beat egg whites until stiff. Fold this into flour batter.

Grease an 8-inch pan and line with parchment paper. Pour batter into pan. Bake at 325 degree for 30 minutes. Unmold on a wire rack and cool completely.

A small amount of whipped cream on the side is a nice touch.

Desserts

Phillippine Egg and Milk Flan (Leche Flan)

Flan:
8 egg yolks
¾ cup sugar
1 (12-ounce) can evaporated milk
12 ounces cold water
1½ teaspoons pure vanilla extract
    or lemon extract
½ teaspoon lime or lemon peel,
    finely grated

Caramel Sugar Sauce:
1 cup sugar
¼ cup water

Preheat oven to 350 degrees. In a bowl, beat egg yolks until well blended. Add ¾ cup sugar gradually and mix thoroughly. Pour milk and water slowly into yolk mixture, stirring constantly. Add lime or lemon rind and vanilla. Mix well. Strain with a fine wire strainer or cheese cloth and set aside.

Prepare Caramel Sugar Sauce. Mix 1 cup sugar with ¼ cup water in a small pan. Heat over medium-low heat until light golden brown, taking care not to burn it. Pour into a flan or 10-inch pie pan. Swirl caramelized sugar to line the pan.

Pour egg and milk mixture into the caramel lined plan. Place it in a large shallow baking pan and set it in the middle rack of the oven. Pour enough hot water into the bigger pan to come half-way up the sides of the flan pan. Bake for 1 hour and 15 minutes to 1½ hours or until toothpick or knife inserted in the middle comes out clean.

Let cool to room temperature. Chill for several hours or overnight before serving. Run a knife around the sides and unmold it to a serving dish. Pour caramel sauce over it.

Makes 12 servings

All the beautiful cherry wood used in the New Theatre Building was grown in the Southeastern part of the United States, but was milled and finished here in the Northwest. The wood is used in the Newmark Theatre and rotunda area.

Desserts

Orange Pineapple Cake

Cake:
1 (18¼-ounce) package yellow cake
    mix
3 eggs
¾ cup oil
1 (11-ounce) can Mandarin oranges
    and juice

Frosting:
1 (20-ounce) can crushed pineapple
    and juice
1 (3.4-ounce) package instant
    coconut cream pudding
1 teaspoon vanilla
1 (9-ounce) container Cool Whip

Cake:
Preheat oven to 350 degrees. Flour and grease three 8- inch or 9- inch round cake pans. Combine cake mix, eggs, oil, and Mandarin oranges. Mix well. Pour into prepared round cake pans. Layers will be thin. Bake at 350 degrees for 15 minutes.

Frosting:
Combine pineapple and juice with the pudding mix. Stir until mixture begins to thicken. Add vanilla and stir again. Fold in whipped topping. Spread frosting on each layer as you stack cake. Any remaining frosting can be distributed on the top layer.

Makes 8-10 servings

Pear Tart

3 large ripe pears, peeled and cut
    into ½-inch slices
½ cup apricot jam
½ cup Vemouth or white wine
6 macaroon cookies, crushed
1 tablespoon butter, melted

Preheat oven to 350 degrees. Arrange pear slices in a single layer in the bottom of a flat 8 x 8-inch baking dish. Coat pears with jam. Sprinkle macaroon cookies over the pears. Pour wine and butter over this mixture. Bake at 350 degrees for 20 to 25 minutes.

Makes 4 servings

Desserts

Peanut Butter Sheet Cake

Cake:
2 cups flour
1 teaspoon baking soda
2 cups sugar
½ teaspoon salt
½ cup oil
¾ cup butter (1½ cubes)
½ cup peanut butter
1 cup water
2 eggs, beaten
1 teaspoon vanilla
½ cup buttermilk

Icing:
½ cup evaporated milk
1 cup sugar
1 tablespoon butter
½ cup extra crunchy peanut butter
½ cup miniature marshmallows
1 teaspoon vanilla

Cake:
Preheat oven to 350 degrees. In a 2-quart bowl, mix together flour, sugar, soda and salt. Set aside.

In a saucepan, bring oil, butter, peanut butter and water to a boil. Pour over dry ingredients and mix. Add eggs, vanilla and buttermilk. Blend well. Pour batter into a greased and floured 11 x 15 x 1-inch sheet cake pan.

Bake at 350 degrees for 15 to18 minutes.

Icing:
While cake bakes, combine evaporated milk, sugar and butter in a saucepan. Bring to a boil and cook for 2 minutes. Remove from heat and add peanut butter and marshmallows. Stir until melted. Stir in the vanilla.

Pour warm icing over the warm cake and spread to cover evenly.

Makes 16-20 servings

Desserts

Prune-Spice Cake

½ cup butter (1 cube)
1 cup brown sugar, packed
2 eggs, unbeaten
1¾ cups flour
1 teaspoon baking soda
¼ teaspoon salt
⅛ teaspoon cloves
½ teaspoon nutmeg
1 teaspoon cinnamon
⅔ cup buttermilk
2 tablespoons molasses
1 cup cooked prunes, pitted,
    chopped and well drained
½ cup walnuts, chopped (optional)

Preheat oven to 350 degrees. Cream butter and sugar thoroughly. Beat in eggs. Sift together flour, baking soda, salt, and spices. Mix alternately with buttermilk and molasses, stirring smoothly after each addition. Stir in chopped prunes and walnuts.

Grease and flour a 11 x 8 x 2-inch pan. Pour mixture into prepared pan. Bake at 350 degrees for 25 to 35 minutes or until cake tests done in the center.

Serve with whipped topping or sprinkle cold cake with powdered sugar.

Makes 12 servings

Rhubarb Crumble Cake

½ cup plus 3 tablespoons butter,
    divided
2½ cups sugar, divided
2 eggs, well beaten
3¼ cups flour, divided
4 teaspoons baking powder
1 cup milk
1 teaspoon vanilla
4 cups rhubarb, cut into ½-inch
    pieces
1 (3-ounce) package strawberry
    Jello

Makes 12-15 servings

Preheat oven to 375 degrees. Cream ½ cup butter with 1½ cups sugar. Add beaten eggs. Blend 3 cups flour and baking powder together. Add butter mixture to the flour mixture alternately with milk. Mix well. Add vanilla. Spread thick batter into a greased 9 x 13-inch pan.

Mix cut rhubarb pieces with ½ cup sugar and strawberry Jello. Place the coated rhubarb pieces over the cake batter layer.

Mix 3 tablespoons butter, ½ cup sugar and ¼ cup flour until it is crumbly. Distribute the crumbly mixture evenly over the rhubarb layer.

Bake at 375 degrees for 35 to 40 minutes or until center is firm.

Thanksgiving Day Cheesecake

1 cup dried cranberries
2 cups graham cracker crumbs
½ cup unsalted butter (1 cube),
    melted and cooled
1¼ cups plus 2 tablespoons sugar,
    divided
4 (8-ounce) packages cream cheese,
    room temperature
½ cup frozen orange juice
    concentrate, undiluted
1 tablespoon orange zest, grated
2 tablespoons orange-flavored
    liqueur
5 eggs
2 cups sour cream

Makes 8 servings

Cover dried cranberries with water (or additional liqueur) and slowly bring to a simmer. Cook until plump (4 to 5 minutes). Cool. Drain liquid from the cranberries.

Preheat oven to 350 degrees.

Mix graham cracker crumbs and ¼ cup sugar. Stir in butter. Press into the bottom and about 2 inches up the sides of a 10-inch spring form pan. Bake at 350 degrees for 10 minutes or until golden. Set crust on a rack to cool.

Mix cream cheese and 1 cup sugar until smooth. Add undiluted orange juice, orange zest and liqueur. Combine until well blended. Beat in eggs one at a time. Fold in drained cranberries. Spoon mixture onto the cooled crust. Place the spring form pan on a cookie sheet and bake at 350 degrees until just set--the center will shake a bit when you jiggle the pan.

Remove from the oven and set on a rack. Stir together the sour cream and the last 2 tablespoons of sugar. Pour over the cheesecake as evenly as possible. Return to the oven and bake 8 to 10 minutes or until the topping is set. Transfer to a rack. Cool completely. Cover and refrigerate overnight.

Slice and serve with whipped cream or fruit sorbet.

Best made the day before you plan to serve.

Desserts

Three Layer German Chocolate Cake

Cake:
4 ounces German sweet chocolate
½ cup boiling water
1 cup butter (2 cubes)
2 cups sugar
4 egg yolks
4 egg whites, stiffly beaten
1 teaspoon vanilla
2½ cups flour
1 teaspoon baking soda
½ teaspoon salt
1 cup buttermilk

Coconut Pecan Frosting:
1 cup evaporated milk
1 cup sugar
3 egg yolks
½ cup butter (1 cube)
1 teaspoon vanilla
1⅓ cups coconut
1 cup pecans, chopped

Cake:
Preheat oven to 350 degrees. Melt chocolate in boiling water, stirring occasionally. Cream butter and sugar until fluffy, add egg yolks, vanilla, and melted chocolate. Combine flour, soda and salt. Add dry ingredients alternately with buttermilk to chocolate mixture. Gently fold in egg whites with just a few strokes.

Pour into three 9-inch cake pans, lined on the bottom with wax paper. Bake at 350 degrees for 30 to 35 minutes. Frost with Coconut Pecan Frosting, leaving sides unfrosted.

Frosting:
Combine evaporated milk, sugar, egg yolks, butter and vanilla in a saucepan. Cook over medium heat, stirring constantly, about 12 minutes. When mixture thickens, remove from heat. Gently stir in coconut and pecans. Cool until spreadable.

Makes 8 servings

Theatre	Orchestra Pit Capacity
Keller	70 musicians
Newmark	35
Winningstad	18
Schnitzer	15

Desserts

Sour Cream Pound Cake

1 cup butter (2 cubes)
3 cups sugar
6 eggs, separated
3 cups flour
⅛ teaspoon salt
¼ teaspoon baking soda
1 teaspoon vanilla
1 cup sour cream

Makes 2 loaves

Preheat oven to 350 degrees. Grease and flour two standard loaf pans.

Cream butter and sugar. Add 1 egg yolk to creamed mixture at a time until all 6 are included. Beat well after each addition. Combine flour, salt, baking soda, and add alternately with sour cream to butter mixture.

In a separate bowl, beat egg whites until soft peaks form. Fold egg whites into butter mixture. Add vanilla. Divide batter into equal amounts for each prepared loaf pan. Bake at 350 degrees for 1 hour and 25 minutes. Cool. Dust with powdered sugar.

Carl Selin

The Newmark's Ghost Light (New Theatre Building) The square footage of the stage is almost equal to that of the orchestra seating area.

Historically, a ghost light has a two-fold purpose for the theater. One is to keep the stage illuminated at a low cost for the comings and goings of theater personnel when no performances are scheduled. Secondly, it is considered good luck to always have the stage illuminated to keep the spirits of poor actors away from your production. Of course, the other theory is to keep the light on so the good spirits find their way to your venue.

Desserts

Chocolate Slims

2 (1-ounce) squares baking
    chocolate
½ cup butter (1 cube)
½ cup flour
1 cup sugar
¼ teaspoon salt
2 eggs, beaten
1 teaspoon vanilla
1 cup nuts, chopped
powdered sugar

Preheat oven to 400 degrees. Grease a cookie sheet.

In medium saucepan, melt chocolate with butter over low heat. Add flour, sugar and salt to chocolate mixture. Blend well. Stir in eggs and vanilla. Add nuts.

Spread on prepared cookie sheet. Bake at 400 degrees for 10 to 12 minutes. After removing from the oven, sift powdered sugar over the surface. Cut into triangles while still warm.

Quick and easy. Kids love these.

Makes 3 dozen

Cranberry Surprise Cookies

1½ cups butter (3 cubes)
1½ cups sugar
2 eggs
2 teaspoons vanilla
3 cups flour
1 cup cornmeal
2 teaspoons baking powder
½ teaspoon salt
1½ cups sweetened dried
    cranberries
sugar for rolling

Preheat oven to 350 degrees.

In a large bowl, cream together butter and sugar until fluffy. Add the eggs and vanilla.

In a separate bowl, mix the flour, cornmeal, baking powder and salt. Add to butter mixture and mix well. Stir in cranberries.

Form balls about the size of a small walnut, then roll in sugar. Place on a baking sheet and flatten. Bake at 350 degrees for 12 minutes, or until lightly browned.

This recipe won First Prize at the New York State Fair.

Makes 5 dozen

Desserts

Jean's Bars

Crust:
½ cup butter (1 cube)
1 cup flour
¼ cup sugar

Filling:
1 cup graham cracker crumbs
½ cup chocolate chips
½ cup nuts, chopped
1 teaspoon baking powder
¼ teaspoon salt
1 (14-ounce) can sweetened
   condensed milk

Topping:
1½ cups powdered sugar
½ cup butter (1 cube), softened
1 teaspoon vanilla

Crust:
Preheat oven to 350 degrees. In a small bowl, cut butter into flour and sugar until crumbly. Press this mixture into the bottom of an ungreased 9 x 13-inch pan. Bake at 350 degrees for 10 minutes. Cool for 10 minutes.

Filling:
In a large bowl, combine graham cracker crumbs, chocolate chips, nuts, baking powder, salt and sweetened condensed milk. Mix well then spread over partially baked crust. Return to oven and bake 15 to 20 minutes, or until golden brown. Cool completely.

Topping:
In a small bowl, mix the powdered sugar, butter and vanilla. Spread over baked bars. Cut into rectangles.

Makes 36 bars

Molasses Crinkles

¾ cup butter
1 cup brown sugar, packed
1 egg
¼ cup molasses
2¼ cups flour
2 teaspoons baking soda
½ teaspoon cloves
¼ teaspoon salt
1 teaspoon cinnamon
1 teaspoon ginger
sugar for dipping

Makes 4 dozen

Mix butter, brown sugar, egg and molasses thoroughly. Set aside. Measure flour by dip-level-pour method. Blend all dry ingredients together. Gradually add the dry mixture to molasses mixture. Stir until blended. Chill dough for at least 1 hour.

When ready to bake, preheat oven to 375 degrees. Roll dough into round balls the size of large walnuts. Dip the top of each ball in sugar. Place sugared side up, 3 inches apart on a greased baking sheet. Sprinkle each ball with two or three drops of water. Bake in 375 degree oven for 10 to 12 minutes.

Molasses Softies

1 cup butter
1⅓ cups sugar
1 egg
⅓ cup molasses
3 tablespoons dark corn syrup
2 tablespoons milk
4 cups flour
2 teaspoons baking soda
2 teaspoons cinnamon
1½ teaspoons ginger
1½ teaspoons ground cloves
sugar for rolling

Preheat oven to 350 degrees. In a large bowl, beat butter, sugar and egg until light and fluffy. Beat in molasses, corn syrup and milk until well blended. Add flour, baking soda, cinnamon, ginger and cloves, beating until well blended. Shape dough into 1-½ inch balls. Roll balls in sugar. Place 3 inches apart on an ungreased cookie sheet.

Bake at 350 degrees for 12 to 14 minutes. Cool for 1 minute before removing from cookie sheet.

Makes 3 dozen

Nut Goodie Bars

12 ounces chocolate chips
12 ounces butterscotch chips
1 (18-ounce) jar peanut butter
1 (16-ounce) jar dry-roasted peanuts
1 cup butter
¼ cup regular vanilla pudding mix (dry from box)
2 pounds powdered sugar
½ cup milk
1 teaspoon maple flavoring

Makes 30 bars

In a double boiler or saucepan, melt together chocolate and butterscotch chips with peanut butter. Spread half of mixture in a jellyroll pan. Refrigerate. Add peanuts to remaining mixture. In another saucepan, combine butter, dry pudding mix and milk. Boil for 1 minute. Remove from heat and add powdered sugar, cup by cup, stirring well after each addition. Add maple flavoring and mix well.

Spread powdered sugar mixture over chilled chocolate peanut butter mixture. Refrigerate for 10-15 minutes. Spread chocolate/ peanut butter mixture on top. (Warming this mixture while in a double boiler or over hot water makes spreading easier.)

Keep in refrigerator. It can be cut into small pieces and frozen.

Desserts

Pecan Pralines

6 ounces evaporated milk
1 pound brown sugar
1½ cups chopped pecans

Makes 2-3 dozen

Using a microwaveable bowl, mix ingredients then cook 12 to 15 minutes on high. Stir every 2 to 3 minutes until it reaches the soft ball stage. Remove. Cool by stirring often--until it thickens. Drop by spoonfuls onto waxed paper or foil. Let it cool completely.

Do not Double. Make each batch separately.

Peanut Butter Oaties

¾ cup butter
1 cup peanut butter
1½ cups brown sugar
2 tablespoons water
1 egg
1 teaspoon vanilla
1½ cups flour
1 teaspoon cinnamon
½ teaspoon baking soda
2 cups raisins
3 cups rolled oats, raw, uncooked

Makes 24-30 squares

Preheat oven to 350 degrees. Cream butter, peanut butter and brown sugar until light and fluffy. Add water, egg, vanilla and beat well. Stir in flour, cinnamon, baking soda. Stir in oats and raisins.

Spread on a cookie sheet. Bake at 350 degrees for 20 to 25 minutes (soft) or 25 to 30 minutes (crispier). Cut into squares to serve.

Substituting 2 cups of chocolate chips for the 2 cups of raisins yields a pleasant surprise.

Desserts

Zesty Lemon Bars

1 cup plus 1 tablespoon flour, divided
½ cup powdered sugar
½ teaspoon salt
6 tablespoons cold butter, cut in pieces
2 large eggs
2 egg whites
⅔ cup sugar
1 tablespoon grated lemon rind
½ cup fresh lemon juice
3 tablespoons milk

Preheat oven to 350 degrees. Prepare 8-inch square baking dish with non-stick spray. Combine 1 cup flour with powdered sugar and salt in a food processor. Add the butter and pulse until mixture forms crumbs. Press this mixture firmly with your fingers into the bottom of the baking dish. Bake at 350 degrees for 16 to 18 minutes.

While the crust bakes, whisk the eggs, egg whites, sugar, lemon rind, lemon juice, milk and 1 tablespoon flour in a bowl until smooth. Pour mixture over warm crust and bake about 15 minutes. Test with a clean knife or toothpick in the center to ensure it has set. Cool completely in the pan on a rack. Cut into bars.

Makes 24 bars

Pear Flan

3 fresh pears, peeled, cored and sliced ⅛-inch thick
1 tablespoon Cognac (optional)
powered sugar

Batter:
¼ cup unsalted butter, melted and cooled
¾ cup milk
3 eggs
⅓ cup sugar
⅓ cup flour
¼ teaspoon salt
2 teaspoons vanilla extract

Preheat oven to 350 degrees. Butter 9-inch flan dish. Arrange pear slices in the dish.

Mix batter ingredients in blender and pour over pears.

Bake 40 to 45 minutes. Cool and drizzle Cognac over the top of the flan while still warm. Sprinkle with powdered sugar.

Use peaches, apples or berries, depending on personal taste and seasonal fruits.

Makes 8-10 servings

Desserts

7-Up Cake

1½ cups butter (3 cubes), softened
3 cups sugar
5 eggs
3 cups flour
2 tablespoons lemon extract
¾ cup 7-Up

Makes 12 servings

Preheat oven to 325 degrees.

Cream butter and sugar until fluffy. Add eggs, one at a time, beating well. Fold in the flour. Add lemon extract and 7-Up.

Pour batter into well-greased and floured jumbo bundt pan. Bake at 325 degrees for 1 to 1¼ hours. Cool in pan for 10 to 15 minutes. Loosen edges with a knife and turn out onto a rack and cool completely.

A family favorite since 1972. Freezes well.

"Philly" Velvet Cream

1½ cups chocolate wafer cookies, finely chopped
⅓ cup butter, melted
1 (8-ounce) package cream cheese, softened
½ cup sugar, divided
1 teaspoon vanilla
2 egg yolks, beaten
1 (6-ounce) package semisweet chocolate chips, melted and slightly cooled
2 egg whites
1 cup whipping cream, whipped
¾ cup pecans, chopped

Makes 8 servings

Preheat oven to 325 degrees.

Combine butter and chocolate wafer cookies. Press this mixture on the bottom of a 9-inch spring form pan. Bake at 325 degrees for 10 minutes. Remove and cool.

Combine the cream cheese, ¼ cup sugar and vanilla. Mix until well blended. Stir in egg yolks and chocolate chips.

In a separate mixing bowl, beat egg whites until soft peaks are formed. Gradually add ¼ cup sugar.

Fold egg whites into chocolate mixture. Fold in whipped cream and add pecans. Pour mixture over cooled cookie crust. Freeze until very firm.

Desserts

Blueberry Sorbet

1 cup sugar
½ cup light corn syrup
1 cup water
1 quart fresh blueberries
¼ cup lemon juice

In a small saucepan, combine sugar, corn syrup, and water. Stir over low heat until sugar is dissolved. Set aside.

In a food processor, purée blueberries. Strain, if desired. In a medium bowl, combine puréed blueberries, lemon juice and syrup mixture. Cool to room temperature. Pour into ice cream freezer and freeze.

Makes 6 cups

Crunchy Ice Cream Bars

2½ cups corn flakes
1 cup brown sugar
½ cup butter (1 cube)
½ cup walnuts, chopped
1 (8-ounce) bag coconut
½ gallon vanilla ice cream

Makes 6 servings

Grease a 9 x 13-inch pan. Set ice cream aside to soften. Preheat oven to 250 degrees.

In a mixing bowl, combine cereal, sugar, nuts, butter and coconut. Place on cookie sheet and toast for 10 minutes, or until golden brown. Take half the mixture out of the pan and set it aside. Press the remaining half of the mixture into the bottom of the prepared pan to create the bottom crust.

Slice ice cream into thick chunks and lay on top of the bottom crust until the whole pan is covered. Top with remaining mixture, spread to cover as a top crust.

Chill for 30 minutes, or until solid. Slice and serve.

Rectangular containers of ice cream work best.

Desserts

Maraschino Cherry Dessert

30 vanilla wafer cookies, finely
    chopped
½ cup butter (1 cube)
1 cup powdered sugar
2 eggs, separated
1 teaspoon vanilla
1 cup whipping cream
½ cup walnuts, chopped
½ cup maraschino cherries,
    chopped

Place vanilla wafers in the bottom of an ungreased 8-inch square cake pan. Save a few vanilla wafer crumbs to sprinkle on top. Cream butter and powdered sugar; add egg yolks and vanilla. In a separate bowl beat egg whites until stiff and add them to egg yolk mixture. Spread this mixture over wafer layer.

Whip the whipping cream until stiff. Fold in the walnuts and cherries. Spread over the egg yolk mixture. Freeze. Thaw slightly before serving. Decorate with the extra vanilla wafers.

Makes 9 servings

Eclair Cake

Cake:
1 cup water
½ cup butter (1 cube)
1 cup flour
4 eggs

Frosting:
4 cups milk
1 (8-ounce) package cream cheese,
    cut into pieces
2 (3.4-ounce) packages instant
    vanilla pudding
1 (8-ounce) container Cool Whip
chocolate syrup, for drizzling

Cake:
Preheat oven to 400 degrees. In a medium saucepan, bring water and butter to a boil. Add flour, all at once, and stir to form a ball. Remove from the heat and cool slightly. Add the eggs, one at a time, into the butter mixture. Mix well, then spread on a 11 x 15-inch cookie sheet. Bake at 400 degrees for 25 minutes.

Frosting:
In mixing bowl, place cream cheese and milk. Add pudding mix and beat according to pudding directions. Spread this mixture over the cooled crust. Refrigerate for 15 minutes. Just before serving, spread Cool Whip over the cake and drizzle with chocolate syrup.

Must keep refrigerated!

Makes 16-20 servings

Desserts

Baked Fruit Cocktail

1 cup sugar
1 (15-ounce) can fruit cocktail,
   drained
1 cup flour
1 teaspoon salt
1 teaspoon baking soda
1 cup brown sugar
nuts, chopped

Preheat oven to 325 degrees.

In mixing bowl, combine fruit cocktail, sugar, flour, salt and baking soda. Spread into an 8-inch square cake pan and cover with brown sugar and nuts to taste. Bake at 325 degrees for 50 to 60 minutes.

A simple but surprisingly tasty dessert.

Makes 9 servings

Bourbon Balls

1 (12-ounce) box vanilla wafers,
   crushed
1 cup powdered sugar
½ cup cocoa
1 cup pecans, finely chopped
½ cup bourbon
3 tablespoons corn syrup
powdered sugar for rolling

In a mixing bowl, combine wafer crumbs, sugar, cocoa and pecans. Add bourbon and corn syrup, and mix.

After thoroughly mixing, roll into ½ to 1-inch balls. Roll each ball in powdered sugar. Place balls in covered container and refrigerate to let flavors combine.

May substitute bourbon with rum, if desired.

Makes 40 balls

Desserts

In the fall of 1997, the PCPA obtained the electronic reader board for the Broadway side of the New Theatre Building. A grant from the Rose E. Tucker Foundation, in conjunction with the Friends of the PCPA, made the acquisition possible.

Danish Pancake Balls (Aebleskiver)

4 large eggs, separated
1 cup flour
1 cup buttermilk
⅛ teaspoon salt
¼ teaspoon ground cardamom
vegetable oil for frying

Makes 14-20 balls

Beat egg whites until soft peaks are formed. Set aside. In a large bowl, combine egg yolks, flour, buttermilk, salt and cardamom and mix well. Gently fold in egg whites.

Heat aebleskiver pan to medium-high heat. Put ½ to 1 teaspoon oil in each cup. When oil is smoking hot, put about 1 tablespoon of batter in each cup. The batter will puff into a ball. When small holes begin to appear on the surface of the ball, gently turn each ball every 30 seconds to evenly brown each ball. After 4 to 5 minutes, they should be done in the center. Remove balls from the pan and serve immediately or place in oven-proof bowl lined with a clean kitchen towel or napkin and keep warm in a low oven.

These are delicious served with powdered sugar and lemon juice or jam, jelly or applesauce. A serving of three pieces with powdered sugar and jam makes a unique dessert for each guest. You can also add a bit of crème fraîche (see page 197), whipped cream or double Devonshire cream. This recipe can be doubled. Aebleskiver pans are available in Scandinavian shops and in finer cooking stores.

Macaroon Nut Frosting

1 (7-ounce) package flaked coconut
1 cup walnuts or nuts of your
    choice, chopped
½ cup light corn syrup
½ teaspoon vanilla

Mix coconut, walnuts, corn syrup, and vanilla. Spread this mixture on a freshly baked sheet cake or loaf cake just removed from the oven.

Broil 5 to 7 minutes until golden brown. Watch very carefully.

Desserts

Marshmallow Fudge

2 cups sugar
¼ cup evaporated milk
1 cup semisweet chocolate chips
½ cup butter (1 cube), cut into
    pieces
16-18 marshmallows
1 teaspoon vanilla
½ cup nuts, chopped

Butter sides of 2 or 3 quart saucepan. Combine sugar and evaporated milk in saucepan. Bring this mixture to a full boil. Boil until soft ball (236 degrees) is reached. Cook for 4 minutes, stirring continuously. Remove from heat. Add chocolate chips, remaining butter, marshmallows, vanilla and nuts to hot mixture. Mix until chocolate chips and marshmallows are completely melted. Pour into a buttered 9 x 9-inch pan. Cool until firm and cut into squares.

Makes 1 pound

Old Fashioned Peanut Brittle

2 cups sugar
1 cup water
1 cup white Karo syrup
2 cups raw Spanish peanuts
1 tablespoon butter
1 teaspoon baking soda

Makes about 1 pound

In saucepan, combine sugar, Karo syrup and water. Stir until the sugar is dissolved. Cook to 236 degrees (soft ball) without any additional stirring (this takes awhile). Add nuts and fold them under the surface. Continue cooking to 295 degrees (hard crack) stirring slightly to prevent the peanuts from burning.

Remove from the heat and stir in baking soda and butter. Pour onto two large, buttered cookie sheets and spread as thin as possible (a wooden spatula works well). As soon as the brittle cools enough to touch and begins to set, loosen it and begin to stretch it with your hands (it will still be hot, so be careful). As soon as the edges begin to set, start breaking the brittle into pieces. Let cool completely and store in an airtight container.

Perfect holiday gift for family and friends. Use a candy thermometer for best results.

Desserts

Pavlova

4 egg whites
1¼ cups sugar
¼ teaspoon salt
3 tablespoons cold water
1 tablespoon cornstarch
1 teaspoon vanilla
1 teaspoon vinegar
1 cup whipping cream, whipped
kiwi fruit, strawberries or other
    fresh fruit, sliced

Makes 6 servings

Tradition says that when this dessert was first presented to guests at a fine hotel in Australia, one of them exclaimed, "It's as light as Anna Pavlova!" Pavlova was the world-famous Russian ballet dancer, who was touring in the area at the time.

Preheat oven to 350 degrees. Prepare an 8-inch spring form pan by cutting a circle of wax paper to fit bottom. Cut a strip of wax paper long enough to line sides of pan and about 2 inches wider than depth of pan. Line pan and grease paper well. Dip hand into cold water and shake over prepared pan. In large bowl of electric mixer, beat egg whites until soft peaks form. Add sugar and salt and continue beating until sugar is thoroughly incorporated. Add water and beat well. Beat in cornstarch. Add vanilla and vinegar and beat until whites are glossy and stiff peaks form when beater is lifted. Turn meringue into pan and spread evenly over bottom with spatula. Top should be fairly even.

Bake at 350 degrees for 15 minutes. Check pavlova to see if it has begun to rise. If so, turn oven off and let pavlova sit for 1 hour if oven retains heat, reduce heat to 175 degrees after first 15 minutes and bake for 1 hour longer. If pavlova hasn't risen, bake another 10 to 15 minutes at 250 degrees and then turn the oven off for 1 hour. When cool remove from pan. Top with whipped cream and fresh fruit.

Peanut Clusters

2 cups sugar
¾ cup evaporated milk
¼ cup butter
1 cup semisweet chocolate chips
½ (10½-ounce) bag miniature
    marshmallows
1 pound salted peanuts

Cook the sugar, milk, and butter to the soft ball stage (236 degrees), about 5 minutes or less. Stir so it doesn't stick. Remove from heat. Add chocolate chips and marshmallows, stirring until blended. Add peanuts. Drop by teaspoon onto waxed paper. Allow to cool.

Makes 2-3 dozen pieces

Desserts

Pineapple Bake

½ cup butter (1 cube), softened
2 cups sugar
8 eggs
2 (20-ounce) cans crushed
    pineapple, drained
3 tablespoons lemon juice
10 slices day-old white bread, cubed

Makes 12 servings

Preheat oven to 325 degrees. In a large mixing bowl, cream butter and sugar. Add eggs, one at a time, beating well after each addition. Stir in the well-drained pineapple and lemon juice. Fold in the bread cubes. Pour into greased 9 x 13-inch baking dish.

Bake, uncovered, at 325 degrees for 35 to 40 minutes or until set. Serve warm.

Great as a side dish for baked ham or roast chicken, too!

White Chocolate Macadamia Nut Biscotti

½ cup butter (1 cube), softened
¾ cup sugar
3 tablespoons zest of orange
2 eggs
1 teaspoon vanilla
2 tablespoons Amaretto or almond
    extract
2 cups plus 2 tablespoons flour
1 teaspoon baking powder
¼ teaspoon salt (optional)
⅔ cup macadamia nuts, cut into
    small pieces
⅔ cup white chocolate chips

Makes 48 servings

Preheat oven to 325 degrees. Cream butter, sugar, and orange zest until fluffy. Beat in eggs, Amaretto and vanilla. Add flour, baking powder and salt. Mix until well blended and smooth. Fold in nuts and chips and blend well.

On a floured board, divide dough into two logs. Pat until firm and 12 inches in length. Place on a greased cookie sheet 2 inches apart. Bake on middle rack of oven for about 25 minutes, or until lightly brown and firm. Remove from oven and cool for 10 minutes. Carefully place each log on a cutting board and cut diagonally at a 45 degree angle, about ½-inch thick. (Use a sharp serrated knife.)

Place each individual slice on a baking sheet. Place baking sheet back in the oven for about 8 minutes or until slightly toasted and dry. Let cool and store in a tightly covered container.

Desserts

Blueberry Pie

½ cup mashed blueberries
1 cup sugar
½ cup water
3 tablespoons cornstarch
3 tablespoons lemon juice
4 cups blueberries
1 baked 9-inch pie shell
whipped cream

In a saucepan, place mashed blueberries, sugar, water, corn starch and lemon juice, and cook until clear and thick. Cool.

When sauce has cooled, put in a large bowl. Add fresh blueberries and stir until well mixed. Put in baked pie crust and refrigerate. Serve with whipped cream.

Makes 6-8 servings

Buttermilk Pie

½ cup butter (1 cube), softened
1¼ cups sugar
3 eggs, well beaten
3 tablespoons flour
1 cup buttermilk
dash vanilla extract
dash lemon extract
1 unbaked 9-inch pie shell

Preheat oven to 350 degrees.

In mixing bowl, cream butter and sugar. Add eggs and flour, and mix well. Add buttermilk and extracts (to taste). Pour into unbaked pie shell and bake at 350 degrees for 45 to 60 minutes.

Makes 6-8 servings

Theatre	Dressing Room Capacity
Keller	250 performers
Schnitzer	90
Newmark	32
Winningstad	23

Desserts

Easy Lemon Pie

4 eggs
1½ cups sugar
1-2 lemons
2 tablespoons butter, melted
1 teaspoon vanilla
1 unbaked (9-inch) pie shell

Preheat oven to 350 degrees. Slice the lemon including the skin into four sections. Place the lemon sections, sugar, eggs, butter and vanilla into a food processor. Blend well.

Pour into an unbaked pie shell. Bake at 350 degrees for 45 minutes. Add your favorite topping.

The number of lemons used in this recipe depends on flavor desired.

Makes 6-8 servings

Peaches and Cream Pie

1 10-inch pie crust, unbaked
¾ cup flour
½ teaspoon baking powder
¼ teaspoon salt
1 (3.4-ounce) package vanilla
   pudding mix (not instant)
3 tablespoons salad oil
½ cup milk
2-4 cups peaches, sliced
1 (8-ounce) package cream cheese
3 tablespoons peach nectar
1 cup sugar
1 teaspoon vanilla
cinnamon for sprinkling

Preheat oven to 350 degrees. Blend flour, baking powder, salt, pudding mix, salad oil and milk and spread into unbaked pie shell.

Place peaches on the pudding layer. Cover thoroughly. Blend cream cheese, peach nectar, sugar and vanilla and pour over the top of the peaches. Generously sprinkle with cinnamon.

Bake at 350 degrees for 45 minutes.

This pie usually runs over the edge so bake on a cookie sheet.

Fresh peaches are best but canned may be used.

Makes 6-8 servings

Desserts

Pumpkin Chiffon Pie

1¼-1½ cups cooked pumpkin
3 eggs, separated
½ cup milk
½ cup canned milk
1 cup sugar
½ teaspoon ginger
½ teaspoon cinnamon
¼ teaspoon salt
¼ teaspoon nutmeg
1 unbaked pie shell

Preheat oven to 450 degrees. Beat all ingredients together except egg whites. In a separate bowl, beat egg whites until stiff. Fold the egg whites into the pumpkin mixture. Pour mixture into unbaked pie shell.

Bake at 450 degrees for 15 minutes. Turn heat down to 350 degrees and continue to bake for 30 minutes more. The pie is done when a knife inserted in the center comes out clean.

Serve warm or cold--with or without whipped topping.

Makes 8 servings

Sour Cream Lemon Pie

Filling:
1 cup sugar
3 tablespoons cornstarch
dash of salt
1 cup milk
3 egg yolks, slightly beaten
4 tablespoons butter
¼ cup fresh lemon juice
1 teaspoon lemon peel
1 cup sour cream

Meringue:
3 egg whites
¼ teaspoon cream of tartar
½ teaspoon vanilla
6 tablespoons sugar

1 unbaked pie shell

Preheat oven to 350 degrees. In medium saucepan, combine sugar, cornstarch and salt, making sure blended well. Slowly stir in milk. Bring to boiling point, stirring constantly. The mixture should be thickened. Gradually blend the slightly beaten egg yolks (approximately 1 tablespoon at a time) into the milk mixture. Cook and stir for 2 minutes. Remove from heat. Add butter, lemon juice and lemon peel. Cover and cool. When cool, fold in sour cream. Put into unbaked pie shell.

Meringue:
Beat egg whites to form soft peaks. Add sugar, 1 tablespoon at a time, beating to peaks. Add cream of tartar and vanilla. Beat to firm peaks. Place meringue on top of lemon mixture in the pie shell. Bake at 350 degrees for 12 minutes or until meringue is golden brown.

Makes 8 servings

Desserts

Baked Devil's Float

1 cup flour
¾ cup sugar
½ teaspoon baking soda
2 teaspoons baking powder
½ tablespoon cocoa
½ cup milk
2 tablespoons butter
1 teaspoon vanilla

Pudding:
½ cup sugar
½ cup brown sugar
5 tablespoons cocoa
1¼ cups hot water

Makes 9 servings

Preheat oven to 350 degrees. Grease an 8 x 8-inch baking dish.

In mixing bowl, sift dry ingredients. In saucepan, warm milk and butter, then add to dry ingredients, mixing well. Add vanilla and pour into prepared baking dish.

Pudding:
In mixing bowl, combine all pudding ingredients. Pour over batter and bake at 350 degrees for 40 minutes.

When finished baking, the cake will be on top and the pudding will be on the bottom.

Banana-Caramel Bread Pudding

4 cups sturdy white bread cubes
2 bananas, peeled and sliced
1 cup semisweet chocolate chips
½ cup pecan halves
½ cup prepared caramel sauce
3 cups milk
3 large eggs
1 (3-ounce) package cream cheese, softened
½ teaspoon cinnamon

Makes 9 servings

Preheat oven to 325 degrees. Butter a 9-inch square baking pan.

Arrange bread cubes evenly in prepared pan. Arrange banana slices over the bread cubes, then sprinkle chocolate chips and nuts. Drizzle caramel sauce evenly over the top.

In a blender, whirl milk, eggs, cream cheese, and cinnamon until smooth. Pour over bread cubes. Let stand at room temperature for 15 minutes. Bake at 325 degrees for 50 to 60 minutes, or until the top is set. Let stand for 10 minutes.

Serve warm.

Desserts

Chocolate Pots de Crème

1 cup heavy cream
¾ cup whole milk
12 ounces semisweet chocolate,
    finely chopped
6 egg yolks
1 tablespoon Kahlua
whipped cream, as garnish

Makes 9 servings

In a 2½-quart saucepan, heat cream and milk over medium heat. Bring milks to a boil. While milk is cooking, melt chocolate over 1-inch of water in a double boiler over medium high heat. Whisk egg yolks into melted chocolate. Slowly pour boiling milk into chocolate/egg mixture, whisking constantly. Bring temperature to 160 degrees for about 3 to 4 minutes.

Remove from heat and transfer to a stainless steel bowl. Add Kahlua. Cool in an ice water bath, whisking constantly to 90 degrees (4 to 5 minutes). Divide between 8 custard cups. Cover with plastic film and refrigerate for 2 to 3 hours, or until well set.

To serve, garnish with whipped cream. Keeps for up to two days.

Grapefruit Snow Pudding

1 envelope unflavored gelatin
¼ cup cold water
¼ cup hot water
½ cup sugar
¼ teaspoon salt
¾ cup fresh grapefruit juice and
    pulp
¼ cup orange juice
1 tablespoon lemon juice
2 egg whites, stiffly beaten

In mixing bowl, soften gelatin in cold water. Add hot water and stir until dissolved. Add sugar, salt, fruit juices and pulp. Mix thoroughly and cool.

When gelatin begins to thicken, beat until frothy and fold in egg whites. Pour into one Jello mold or into individual molds. Refrigerate until serving time.

Makes 4 servings

Leftover Coffee Cake Bread Pudding

8 ounces left over coffee cake or
    stale French bread, torn and
    crumbled
3 eggs
⅓-¾ cup sugar depending on the
    amount of sweetness in the left
    over bread
3 cups milk
2 teaspoons vanilla
1 teaspoon fresh nutmeg, grated
½ cup raisins

Makes 8-10 servings

Preheat the oven to 350 degrees. Lightly grease a 9 x 13-inch glass baking dish. Place bread in a large bowl. Combine eggs, sugar, milk, vanilla, nutmeg, and raisins. Blend well and pour over bread. Let stand until egg mixture is well absorbed.

Place baking dish in larger pan. Pour enough hot water into larger pan so it rises to mid-point of baking dish. Bake uncovered at 350 degrees until the top is lightly browned (about 45 minutes to 1 hour) or until knife comes out clean. Serve while still warm.

Serve with Warm Berry Sauce - see recipe below

Warm Berry Sauce

2 cups fresh or frozen raspberries
2 cups fresh strawberries
⅓ cup sugar
⅓ cup orange juice, freshly
    squeezed if possible
3 tablespoons lemon juice

Combine the berries, sugar, orange and lemon juice in a saucepan. Cook over medium heat, stirring continuously, until the fruit begins to break up, about 5 minutes.

Purée quickly in a food processor or blender and return to the saucepan to keep it warm until ready to serve. Garnish with fresh berries.

Great served on pancakes, waffles or over ice cream.

Makes about 2 cups

Desserts

Holiday Steamed Pudding

¼ cup butter
¼ cup brown sugar
½ cup sugar plus some for pan
    preparation
3 tablespoons orange marmalade
1 cup milk
1¼ cups flour
¼ teaspoon cinnamon
1 teaspoon baking soda
1 teaspoon vanilla
½ teaspoon salt
½ cup light raisins
whipped cream

Makes 6 servings

Grease a steam pudding pan really well and sprinkle with sugar. Combine butter, brown sugar and sugar. Add the marmalade, milk, flour, cinnamon, baking soda, vanilla, salt and light raisins. Pour mixture into prepared pan.

Cover pan with foil and pan lid. Set pan on a trivet (or canning jar rings) in large steamer container. Fill container with enough water to measure 1½ inches up the side of the pudding pan. Cover steamer and boil gently for 2 hours. Remove pudding pan from the water and cool for 10 minutes before removing lid and foil.

Serve with a dollop of whipped cream.

Carl Selin

*Heather Hall decked out for the holidays
(New Theatre Building)*

The New Theatre Building was designed with the theme of "theater within a theater". Patrons begin to experience the theater as soon as they walk into the rotunda. Imagine the lobby area as a stage with three tiers of cherry wood-paneled balcony seats. Each niche is a comfortable seating area to "see and be seen".

Desserts

CONVERSIONS FOR CHEFS

3 teaspoons (tsp.) = 1 tablespoon (tbsp.)
4 tablespoons = ¼ cup
5⅓ tablespoons = ⅓ cup
8 tablespoons = ½ cup
16 tablespoons = 1 cup or 8 ounces
1 cup = 8 fluid ounces (oz.)
1 pound = 16 ounces (oz.)
1 quart = 4 cups

1 square chocolate = 3 tablespoons cocoa + 1 tablespoon butter
1 tablespoon cornstarch (for thickening) = 2 tablespoons flour
1 cup buttermilk = 1 cup yogurt
1 cup milk = ½ cup evaporated milk + ½ cup water
1 cup sour milk = 1 cup milk + 1 tablespoon lemon juice or vinegar
1 cup cake or pastry flour = 1 cup all-purpose less 2 tablespoons
1 teaspoon baking powder = ¼ tsp. baking soda + ½ tsp. cream of tartar
1 cup sugar = 1 cup honey (use ¼ cup less liquid in recipe)
1 cup brown sugar = 1 cup granulated sugar
1 cup oil =½ pound butter or margarine
1 tablespoon prepared mustard = 1 teaspoon dry mustard
1 clove garlic = ⅛ teaspoon garlic powder

1 slice bread = ½ cup crumbs
14 graham cracker squares = 1 cup crumbs
18 chocolate wafers = 1 cup crumbs
22 vanilla wafers = 1 cup crumbs

Macaroni: 1 cup uncooked = 2 ½ cups cooked
Noodles: 1 cup uncooked = 1 cup cooked
Spaghetti: 8 oz. uncooked = 4 cups cooked
Rice: 1 cup uncooked = 3 cups cooked

CHEESE: 4 ounces = 1 cup shredded 1 pound = 4 cups shredded
BUTTER: 1 cube = 1 stick = ½ cup = 8 tablespoons   4 sticks = 2 cups = 1 pound
1 teaspoon dried herbs = 1 tablespoon fresh
1 pound granulated sugar = 2 cups granulated sugar

Desserts

List of Contributors

The PCPA Cookbook Committee wishes to thank those who submitted the recipes in this book

Patricia Alexandre
Sally Allenby
Kathy André
Anonymous
Rosie Apodaca
Jeannie Baker
Patrice Baker
Sharon Baker
Jenna Barnett
Norma Barney
Terri Barton
Rachel Baus
Louise Beauchamp
Karen Black
Erwin Boge
Betty Brace
Fred Brace
Jan Braman
Sonia Bryant
Betty Burke
Pam Cach
Katie Cassatt
Roz Collins
Sharon Comstock
Joy Conger
Joanne Cook
Lis Cooper
Peggy Corgan
Deb Coss-Fricke
Charlotte Cridland
Cally Davenport
Julie Davies
Sharon Dawson
Emily Diehm
Janet Donnelly
Darlene Downey
Faith Durkheimer
Joe Durr
Barbara Edgren
Ella Edmison

Jean Edmison
Deanne Erickson
Sharon Fantz
Dennis Frantz
Barb Fritz
Carol Fuller
Gary Fuqua
Alice Furey
Mercy Galicia
Patricia Gayley
Linda Gilbert
Kathy Graham
Ella Green
Connie Guist
Bea Hager
Carole Hallen
Leah Hammer
Jane Henderson
Joanne Henkel
Joanne Higgins
Don Hinrichs
Janet Hinrichs
Pat Hodel
Barbara Hodgson
Bozena Hollaway
Elizabeth Horn
Leslie Houston
Elvira Hudson
Elizabeth Huenick
Margie Humphreys
Margi Jenks
Virginia Keefer
Ray Kimlinger
Shirley Kimlinger
Kathrine Klein
Anna Kornfeld
Bev Koutny
Amy Krings
Rebecca Landau
Jane Lebsack

Sharon Lindersmith
Bev Llewellyn
Sandra Lockwood
Jan Loewen
Inga Lothian
Gwen Luhta
Elaine Lycan
Catherine Marcina
Yvonne Martin
Anne Matson
Nancy Matthews
Alice McCarthy
Barbara McCormick
Beverly McCormick
Jo McGeorge
Anne McGinnis
Sally McLaughlin
Karen McWhorter
Anna Mehrer
Terry Mischke
Marge Morgan
P.J. Morgan
Beth Morris
Albert Morris
Lucy Morris
Mary Negravel
Marg Nelson
Caye Nollette
Jeanne Nordtvedt
Nita Perlas
Joleen Phillips
Shirley Piel
Amy Plumb
Irene Pugh
Bennie Ramirez
Bob Rawson
Jesse Reding
Susan Robblee
Bernice Robins
Rebecca Robinson

Forrest Romig
Karen Rottink
Maryann Roulier
Linda Rutledge
Barbara Ryan-Baxter
Carrie Saito
Chip Saturn
Carl Selin
Kathleen Shattuck
Judy Siemssen
Ed Sienkiewicz
Barbara Simons
Selma Smith
Charlann Snider
LeNeva Spires
Mary Springer
Camille Stark
Scott Stephens
Bev Sterling
Jane Swan
Cayman Thomas
Rosy Twedt
Audrey Underhahl
Annette Utz
Barbara Utz
Susan Verheyleweghen
Sue Vonderheit
Dottie Waddell
Maggie Walter
Fern Waltz
Barbara Wetzel
Monica Wheeler
Eleanor Wiese
Pauline Williams
Robyn Williams
Evelyn Wilson
Rose Winters
Bob Witham

Volunteer Recognition Night, June 30, 2004
(Arlene Schnitzer Concert Hall)

The PCPA Volunteers - Our Recipe for Success!

Some Final Words of Thanks

It is hard to believe that this major collaborative effort was just a mere, wispy idea 12 short months ago. Yet, here it is - our completed cookbook! The Cookbook Committee would like to thank the following people for making this fund-raising project a reality. Without their help and special talents, we would never have had this wonderful outcome.

First, like any good theatrical production, we needed a financial "angel". In our case, we had a very special person who believed in what we wanted to do. Because of the generous gift received, we were able to create a very stylish book and include many upgraded features. We are very grateful for the financial support of our benefactor, who prefers to remain anonymous.

We are so excited about our restaurant contributors. We are honored to have the recipes for their signature dishes within our book. These establishments support the performing arts in many different ways. These restaurants will always be our favorites because of their community spirit as well as their wonderful food.

Next, we want to say thank you to all the PCPA volunteers who helped make this book possible. They collected family favorite recipes that were tried and true. They suggested names for the title. They kept us going through the tough spots with their interest and enthusiasm. They reached into their pockets to prepay orders for a book that was only a concept. We are proud to be part of an organization with a volunteer corps as willing to pitch in and help as ours.

Thank you Indexplorations for doing such a wonderful job on the index.

We owe a special thank you to Cayman Thomas for his talent of finding the right software at the right time.

Thank you Margie Norton for removing the mystique from the entire printing process. Without your guidance, we would still be going through the trial and error method of exploring the possibilities.

We wish to acknowledge that Carl Selin went far beyond the call of duty. For the many man-hours he spent hunched over a PC on our account, we are grateful. He is our hero!

Margie Humphreys deserves a standing ovation! As the Volunteer Coordinator for PCPA, she is always tireless in her efforts to see that everything is done in the proper manner. None of us would be able to function without her direct support. We wish to thank her for having faith in us and trusting that the end result would be worthy of bearing the PCPA name.

The PCPA Cookbook Committee

Index

Index

Index

Index

Index

Index

Index

Index

Index

Portland Cooks for the Performing Arts

PCPA
1111 SW Broadway
Portland, OR 97205-2999

Additional copies available through the PCPA website
visit **www.pcpa.com**

Index